FREE PUBLIC REASON

FREE PUBLIC REASON
Making It Up As We Go

FRED D'AGOSTINO

New York   Oxford
OXFORD UNIVERSITY PRESS
1996

Oxford University Press

Oxford   New York
Athens   Auckland   Bangkok   Bombay
Calcutta   Cape Town   Dar es Salaam   Delhi
Florence   Hong Kong   Istanbul   Karachi
Kuala Lumpur   Madras   Madrid   Melbourne
Mexico City   Nairobi   Paris   Singapore
Taipei   Tokyo   Toronto

and associated companies in
Berlin   Ibadan

Published by Oxford University Press, Inc.
198 Madison Avenue, New York, New York 10016

Oxford is a registered trademark of Oxford University Press

Library of Congress Cataloging-in-Publication Data

D'Agostino, Fred.
Free public reason : making it up as we go / Fred D'Agostino.
p.   cm.
Includes bibliographical references (p.   ) and index.
ISBN 0-19-509761-0
1. Political science—Philosophy.   2. Justification (Theory of knowledge)
3. Reason.   I. Title.
JA71.D26   1996
320'.01—dc20   95-6838

1 3 5 7 9 8 6 4 2
Printed in the United States of America
on acid-free paper.

This book is dedicated to
Ellen Parks, Kay Warren, Sally Robertson,
Maureen Sheehan, Stephanie Lawson, and Cathy Waters

Preface

The essence of the liberal ideal . . . is its commitment to a form of power which is 'horizontal' and reciprocal rather than 'vertical' and managerial . . .

STEPHEN MACEDO, Liberal Virtues

The contents of this book were puzzled out and then written down during and immediately after a two-year spell as Associate Dean of Arts at the University of New England. During this time, many changes to university administration were implemented. Foremost among these was the substitution of the 'new managerialism' for age-old democratic principles and practices. The notion of 'line management' displaced collegiality. Deans of faculties, for instance, were now meant to be conduits between higher level 'bosses' and lower level 'workers', transmitting commands from above to below and 'feedback' from below to above. Obviously, this understanding of university administration is totally at odds with the recommendations made here for the administration of public political life. In the academic world, 'traditional' communities of interpreters, like those described in Chapter 9, are now increasingly replaced by highly stratified societies of self-styled experts on the one hand and under-resourced under-laborers on the other.

I mention these circumstances for two reasons. First, they are worthy of comment in their own right. It cannot be guaranteed, if present trends are consolidated, that the university will long survive as an embodiment of democracy. Second, though, is an autobiographical possibility — that my thinking about the question of public justification has been influenced by these developments and by my (largely ineffectual) involvement in resistance to them. It is, of course, notoriously difficult, and in any event probably unprofitable, to inquire too closely into the secret springs of even such limited creativity as may be manifest on the pages that follow. I nevertheless probably have this much to be thankful for. My experiences in dealing with and opposing the 'new managerialism' convinced me more than ever of the inestimable value of our democratic institutions and thus invigorated the reflections reported here.

One comment on the text. As readers are sure to notice, I have used a great many quotations. I hope this will not be disturbing or undermine the reader's confidence in my own powers of thought, limited as these may be. I have used a great many quotations as an expression, stylistically, of a substantive point I am very concerned to make — that all thought is a collective enterprise and profits from being recognized as such — or, as Benjamin Barber puts it (*The Conquest of Politics,* p. 210), "the individual is foolish, the multitude wise." Of course, an individual has had to compile the wisdom he sees in the multitude whose work has influenced his. It therefore cannot be guaranteed that the wisdom has survived its encounter with his foolishness. I hope that some of it has.

Armidale, New South Wales   F. D.
June 1995

Acknowledgments

My greatest intellectual debts of a kind admitting personal acknowledgment are to Jerry Gaus. Without his interest, advice, and support, I would never have embarked on the project whose (interim) results are reported here. Thanks especially for an early look at his manuscript *Justificatory Liberalism* (Oxford University Press, forthcoming) and for several days' intense dissection of an earlier version of *this* work in Wellington, New Zealand, in late August 1993.

Thanks also to my friends and colleagues Robert Elliot, Steffie Lawson, Jeff Malpas, Janice Reilly, and Cathy Waters. In particular, Steffie first interested me in democratic theory, and Janice and Cathy in feminist theory. I've learned a lot about the matters discussed here from working with postgraduate students in the last few years, particularly Steve Loveday, Josie Wild, and David Woodberry. Thanks to them and to Peter Forrest, the head of my department, for permitting me to inflict my interests on this generation of Honors students. Thanks to Philip Pettit and Michael Smith for their encouragement and support, and to Bob Goodin for some very trenchant comments on an earlier essay of mine treating the same general matters covered here. He made me realize that a more systematic presentation and a more critical one was possible. Thanks to Loren Lomasky for pointing me to the work of Bruce Ackerman; this was crucial in the development of my own thinking. Thanks especially to Graham Maddox for his friendship and interest, his support during my tenure as Associate Dean of the Faculty of Arts, and the chance to read his manuscript *Religion and the Rise of Democracy* (Routledge, forthcoming). Thanks too to the anonymous reader for the Press, whose generosity and acuity in commenting on an earlier version of the work sustained and heartened me. Thanks also to the Study Leave Committee of the University of New England for a generous grant of one year's leave in 1993, during which time this work was written.

Some of the material presented here was presented at a seminar at the Australian National University in December 1990, at a mini-conference on contemporary political theory at Monash University in May 1993, and at a conference on non-formal foundations of reason at Newcastle University in August 1993. My thanks to organizers and participants on these occasions.

Thanks, finally, to the editorial staff at Oxford University Press.

Contents

FREE PUBLIC REASON

Let every man be fully persuaded in his own mind.

ROMANS, 14:5

The reason, alone, of the public ought to control and regulate the government.

The Federalist, No. 49

For practical purposes . . . in a well-governed democratic society under reasonably favorable conditions, the free public use of our reason in questions of political and social justice would seem to be absolute.

JOHN RAWLS, *Political Liberalism*

[T]he public and free use of autonomous reason will be the best guarantee of obedience, on condition, however, that the political principle that must be obeyed itself be in conformity with universal reason.

MICHEL FOUCAULT, "WHAT IS ENLIGHTENMENT?"

1

Introduction

1. Précis

"[O]ur exercise of political power is fully proper only when it is exercised in accordance with a constitution the essentials of which all citizens as free and equal may reasonably be expected to endorse in the light of principles and ideals acceptable to their common human reason. *This is the liberal principle of legitimacy.*"[1] I try to show in this book how we can best deploy this idea of public justification, a key idea in recent, broadly 'liberal' political theorizing about normative political claims. I proceed in three parts.

In Part I, "Construction," I try to spell out what is involved in the idea of public justification. In particular, I identify a number of different conceptions of this concept and a number of desiderata that would have to be satisfied by any conception of that concept adequate to play the role of that concept. I group these desiderata into two families, which I call realistic and moralistic, and try to show how the various conceptions of the concept of public justification express or embody these desiderata.

In Part II, "Deconstruction," I argue, first, that there is prima facie incompatibility between the two families of desiderata. If one family is chosen for realization in a particular approach, then the other will, apparently, necessarily be slighted. I suggest that this marks, at least prima facie, the essential contestability of the concept of public justification and so its political, rather than its meta- or pre-political status. Second, I also consider a number of ways in which we might seek to overcome the prima facie incompatibility that we have identified — ways made familiar, though at a different level of concern, by such theorists as Bruce Ackerman, S. L. Hurley, David Gauthier, Gerald Gaus, and others. I argue that none of these techniques of reconciliation is adequate to the task, and, therefore, that the prima facie incompatibility between realistic and moralistic requirements is apparently sustained. There are, seemingly different, indeed competing conceptions of public justification that reason, in a certain sense, is incompetent to distinguish. There can therefore be no unequivocal answer to questions about the legitimacy of regimes. (I call this the problem of public justification.) The liberal approach to the problem of political legitimacy is therefore, in turn, doomed inevitably to failure.

In Part III, "Reconstruction," I try to show how the failure to solve this problem is an artifact of the formalistic, analytical orientation that is common to the techniques of reconciliation most favored in this regard. I then argue that this project can nevertheless be carried forward, though not necessarily 'completed', in a two-stage, but probably never-ending process of constitutional interpretation, based on some ideas of Ronald Dworkin and Thomas Kuhn. This part of the argument confirms the political character of the project of public justification and shows that, while there are limits to political theorizing (of a certain kind), these limits need not impede, and anyway suggest the necessity of, a certain kind of political practice, embedded in a certain kind of polity and collectivistic in a profound sense.

This is an essay in political theory. It is both theory, in one sense but not another, and political, and not just in being about politics: it is also a part of politics. William Connolly says: "To examine and accept, or to examine and revise, the prevailing terms of political discourse is not a prelude to politics but a dimension of politics itself."[2] This essay, then, is theory not in a sense that pre-empts political judgment, but in a sense that clarifies the prospects and, indeed, establishes the need for it. I will therefore try to show, as Benjamin Barber puts it, that "political judgment is not the application of abstract, independent standards to political actuality . . . [but rather] the forging of common actuality in the absence of abstract, independent standards."[3] Indeed, I will try to describe a community (of interpreters) in which "the forging of common actuality" might perhaps occur — if, indeed, it can occur anywhere.

Along the way, I also aim to make a contribution to the development of a pluralistic account of value. I will argue, especially in Part II, that there are multiple desiderata for conceptions of public justification and no obvious technique for reconciling the competing demands they make. This demonstration is of meta-level pluralism, however, rather than, as is more customary, of pluralism at the level of first-order values. Still, the demonstration, if successful, complements and strengthens already familiar arguments. Furthermore, if the concept of public justification is itself subject to pluralistic incommensurability, then it cannot be recruited to play its role in reconciling first-order pluralistic incommensurability — not, at least, in the ways that might normally be hoped.

One final point. This is an essay in what James Fishkin, following John Rawls, calls 'ideal theory', which "pursues the question whether a solution to the legitimacy problem is possible at all, given favorable conditions."[4] I agree with Fishkin that "[u]nresolvable dilemmas or troubling indeterminacies would not be surprising under situations of tragic conflict or extreme scarcity,"[5] and I have as little interest as he does in pursuing these matters. What I aim to show, as he does, is that, at least prima facie, such dilemmas arise even in so-called favorable conditions.

2.   Retrospective

The inspiration for this book is the work, during the 1950s, of the sociologist Robert Merton, the philosophers Karl Popper and Michael Polanyi, and the popularizer

Jacob Bronowski.[6] These theorists developed the fundamental analogy, between democratic politics and the practices of scientists, on which much of this work is based. Their idea was that the scientist and the democratic citizen-politician share many values, foremost among them those of tolerance, mutual respect, and self-criticism, and that it is their commitment to these values, and to the institutions that support and are supported by them, to which they owe the success of their otherwise distinct enterprises. There is a lot to be said for this basic idea, but it failed to spawn productive reflections about the nature either of science or of democracy. The ground of the analogy was, I believe, too 'thin' to sustain extended reflection. While I propose exploiting and developing this analogy, I attempt to do so on a different basis. In particular, I look to an idea recently touted as being of fundamental significance — the idea of *public justification.*

Simplifying considerably, I believe the idea of public justification is relevant to problems of legitimacy or validity. In the political context, we may say that a system of social arrangements is legitimate for a particular community if each member of that community finds the system a reasonable one. In the epistemic context, we might say, by extension, that claims of fact are legitimate for a community if each member of that community finds, in relevant circumstances, that these claims are reasonable ones to make.

Aside from its intrinsic interest, the idea of public justification also offers the best hope for achieving some adequate understanding of the concept of *objectivity.* Crudely, claims are objective if and only if they can be publicly justified. As Rawls says, "[A] conception of objectivity must establish a public framework of thought sufficient for the concept of judgment to apply and for conclusions to be reached on the basis of reasons and evidence after discussion and due reflection."[7] Indeed, this analysis of objectivity enables us to overcome, or at least avoid, metaphysical and epistemological difficulties that we will encounter if we embrace an account of objectivity based on the notion of 'access' to some independent realm of objects that our claims are held to be 'about'.[8] We might call my preferred conception a 'political' conception of objectivity.[9] Richard Rorty puts well the points I would like to make:

> Those who wish to ground solidarity in objectivity — call them "realists" — have to construe truth as correspondence to reality. So they must construct a metaphysics which has room for a special relation between beliefs and objects which will differentiate true from false beliefs. . . . By contrast, those who wish to reduce objectivity to solidarity — call them "pragmatists" — do not require either a metaphysics or an epistemology. . . . For pragmatists, the desire for objectivity is not the desire to escape the limitations of one's community, but simply the desire for as much intersubjective agreement as possible, the desire to extend the reference of "us" as far as we can.[10]

For 'pragmatists', the idea of objectivity is to be 'cashed out' by the idea of public justification.[11]

Most important in relation to public justification is the prospect that we might use this idea to redeem older speculations about the relation between scientific and democratic practices.[12] Certainly, the alleged analogies between science and democracy *were* a preoccupation of the theorists whom I have already mentioned. H. B. Mayo might speak for all of them when he says that "science and democracy are natural bedfellows . . . [in that they] share many of the same moral values . . . impartiality, persistence, honesty, tentativeness, integrity. . . ."[13] Indeed, these ideas probably pre-date their embodiment in these particular forms. According to Onora O'Neill, the analogies were already recognized by Kant: "Reason and justice are two aspects to the solution of the problems that arise when an uncoordinated plurality of agents is to share a possible world."[14] Indeed, Jean-François Lyotard gives a much earlier provenance, suggesting that "[t]he question of the legitimacy of science has been indissociably linked to that of the legitimation of the legislator since the time of Plato."[15]

Whatever the antiquity of this view, the concept of public justification is the one that is best adapted to establishing it on a sound footing. My analysis of politics should therefore be transferable to the epistemic domain; I believe, with Steve Fuller, that "the philosophy of science is nothing other than the application of political philosophy" to the scientific community.[16]

One final comment would be in order about the relation of democracy to science. The idea of 'direction of fit' can be recruited to clarify the distinction between these twin projects of public justification.[17] In the case of science, the direction of fit is 'our beliefs must fit the world', whereas in the case of democracy, the direction of fit is 'our world must fit our beliefs (about how it should be)'. While 'publicity' is required in both cases, this is for different reasons. In the case of science, we require publicity, as a measure of fitting, because the world itself is public, whereas, in the case of democracy, we require publicity in order to ensure the fittingness of our social world to all our various interests and concerns.

3. Prospective

The idea of *public justification* has recently been identified as a fundamental, indeed perhaps, as the fundamental basis for much contemporary but especially avowedly liberal political theorizing.[18]

According to Gerald Gaus, "Liberals insist that moral and political principles are justified if and only if each member of the community has reason to embrace them. Liberals thus stress *public justification*. . . ."[19] Or again according to Gaus, "This idea of public justification is at the heart of contractual liberalism."[20] Jeremy Waldron agrees: "[L]iberals are committed to . . . a requirement that all aspects of the social order should either be made acceptable or be capable of being made acceptable to every last individual."[21] Thomas Nagel likewise claims that "[t]he task of discovering the conditions of [political] legitimacy is traditionally conceived as that of finding a way to justify a political system to everyone who is required to live under it."[22]

On another front, it is, according to Seyla Benhabib, the "central insight of communicative or discourse ethics" that "[o]nly those norms and normative institutional arrangements are valid . . . which individuals can or would freely consent to. . . ."[23] Writing from the point of view of democratic socialism, Joshua Cohen concurs, mentioning "the intuitive ideal of a form of social order in which the justification of the terms of association proceeds through public argument among equal citizens."[24]

Also recently much emphasized by many ethical and political theorists is one or another kind of evaluative pluralism, a doctrine that emphasizes, in particular, the incommensurability of certain values, principles, or aims that figure in moral, indeed even in purely prudential reasoning.

As William Galston says, "Modern liberal-democratic societies are character-ized by an irreversible pluralism, that is, by conflicting and incommensurable con-ceptions of the human good. . . ."[25] In these circumstances, according to Steven Lukes, "there is no single currency or scale on which conflicting values can be mea-sured, and . . . where a conflict occurs no rationally compelling appeal can be made to some value that will resolve it."[26]

Because of evaluative pluralism, "[t]here will be cases," says Susan Wolf, "in which there are good reasons for one position and good reasons for an incompatible position and no further overarching principle and perspective from which these can be put into any further objective balance."[27] Indeed, even Rawls, who had earlier rejected pluralism,[28] now acknowledges that "we make many of our most important judgments subject to conditions which render it extremely unlikely that conscien-tious and fully reasonable persons, even after free discussion, can exercise their powers of reason so that all arrive at the same conclusion."[29] (Rawls's pluralism, deriving from his analysis of the "burdens of reason,"[30] is a *weak* or epistemological doctrine,[31] whereas the pluralism of such theorists as Isaiah Berlin and Stuart Hampshire is a *strong* or ontological doctrine.[32])

It is my aim to provide an account of the project of public justification that is plural-istic in orientation. By this I mean, in particular, that I hope to show that the idea of public justification may itself be subject to a kind of indeterminacy that is derived from the incommensurability of some of the values in terms of which this idea is defined. The concept of public justification, which is meant to be 'foundational' for liberal political theorizing, is itself an essentially contestable concept in the sense of W. B. Gallie and so perhaps cannot provide an uncontroversial basis for resolving controversy at other, 'lower' levels of ethico-political discourse. In the next chapter, I lay out some of the apparatus, by now quite familiar, that I will need to develop this suggestion. Before doing so, it will be handy, to prevent misunderstanding, to record four provisos.

First, John Kekes claims to have established the incompatibility of liberalism and pluralism, and thus to have reduced to absurdity the project of articulating a lib-eral approach to justification in a pluralistic setting. But his argument depends on a fundamental error in identifying the logical form of the pluralist doctrine. It depends, crucially, on the claim that "pluralism excludes overriding commitment to *any* value,"[33] which means, I take it, that for arbitrary pairs of values, neither always overrides the other in cases of conflict between them. In this case, distinctively lib-eral values would always be vulnerable to being overridden by other kinds of val-ues, and a coherent liberalism would be undermined. But a much more sensible interpretation of the pluralist doctrine implies only that, for some pairs of values, neither always overrides the other.[34] Of course, it is consistent with this account that at least some distinctively liberal values might always override other kinds of values. And, in this case, there is no reason why the pluralist cannot also be a liberal (or vice versa). Furthermore, this interpretation of pluralism is arguably supported by much current usage, on which, see Wolf's "there will be cases," not 'in every case'. See also Lukes's brisk statement: "To believe in incommensurability [and hence pluralism in my sense] is not to hold that all or even most value conflicts or even moral conflicts are of this sort; only that some are and that they are non-trivial."[35]

Second, at least in Parts I and II, I shall ignore, even by implication, the possibility, in effect canvassed by F. A. Hayek, that the whole project of public justification is altogether misconceived, reflecting, as on most accounts it undeniably does, what he calls 'constructivist' assumptions — namely, "that human institutions will serve human purposes only if they have been deliberately designed for these purposes."[36] Such an approach is one that Hayek rejects as beyond the powers of human beings; he proposes, instead, an understanding of legitimacy based on the usual device of the 'methodological conservative' — the idea of evolution.[37] I will eventually take up these concerns in section 30, where I consider the prospects for a 'traditionalist' alternative to the project of public justification, and in section 41, where I show that my approach does not embody the 'constructivist' assumptions that Hayek deprecates.

Third, the idea of public justification that I have in mind differs a bit from Rawls's idea. As I understand it, public justification is justification of the norms and practices by which our behavior is regulated. Rawls seems to have in mind a different notion, however. He is looking, I think, for a way to use these norms and practices to justify concrete claims on social resources. He says, for instance, that "[o]ur society is not well-ordered: the public conception of justice and its understanding of freedom and equality are in dispute . . . and a basis of public justification is still to be achieved."[38] The idea here seems plainly to be that public justification involves appealing to accepted principles in order to ground lower level claims. On the now more common understanding, the project is that of grounding the principles, not the lower level claims. Obviously, there is nothing untoward about the notion Rawls has in mind, but the current understanding is of a deeper notion; it is, in any event, the one I have in mind.

Fourth, when I say that I want to consider the concept of public justification in a pluralistic setting, this might, but should not be taken to, mean what many other writers would indeed mean were they to say some such thing — that I want to consider how public justification might be possible of some system of social arrangements, despite the fact that individuals entertain a variety of incompatible and possibly incommensurable conceptions of the good.[39] It is certainly some such project that Rawls has in mind.[40] Again, there is nothing untoward or confused about the project Rawls and others have in mind. But it is not my project. I am not particularly worried about the fact that *input* to a project of public justification might be pluralistic in character. What I am worried about is the fact that the 'machinery' that that input is input for is itself subject to pluralistic indeterminacy. It is illusory to think that there is some determinate conception of the good to which we could appeal in developing an account of legitimacy.[41] In a similar way, it may be illusory to think that there is some determinate conception of justification that we could appeal to for that purpose. There are a plurality of conceptions of the good and a plurality of conceptions of public justification. The first point is now widely acknowledged; the second is the subject of this book.

I will be concerned, then, with what I call the problem of public justification, which arises as follows. Without a determinately best conception of the concept of public justification, the question of the legitimacy of a given regime for a given community may continue to be contested and thus will not be answered to the satisfaction of all those concerned with it. If there are competing conceptions, and if one implies that a regime is legitimate for a community, whereas the other implies that the regime is not legitimate for the community, then we have no way of settling the question of the regime's legitimacy for the community until we discover or invent a way of settling the prior question, "Which of the competing conceptions is the better (preferably, best) conception of public justification?" I will be concerned with the conditions under which this question does not, and those under which it might, have an adequate answer. That is my project in this book.

One final preliminary point. Some might wonder whether the rather elaborate procedure sketched in the preceding paragraph is really called for if the 'problem of public justification' is to be solved. Surely, there is a more direct and straightforward alternative, applicable even given a plurality of different conceptions of this concept. Find that system of social arrangements that is 'dominant' in the sense that whatever one's conception of public justification, that system is better, according to *that* conception, than other systems.[42] In this case, no choice is necessary between different conceptions because that choice is irrelevant to the identification of the best regime — which is, after all, what the 'problem' really is. Why do I not proceed in the way implied by these observations? Why do I not examine ('ground plans' for) regimes in search of a dominant regime rather than examining conceptions of justification in search of a demonstrably best conception?

My formal answer to this question is given in sections 23–27, but enough can be said now to give worried readers a motive to continue. There are grounds for thinking that there is no 'dominant' regime and therefore no such 'direct' solution as is envisaged. The most obvious point is that prominent theorists of public justification typically propose both a conception and a (kind of) regime that they take to be warranted by that conception. But in this case there can be no dominant regime because the regimes proposed differ from theorist to theorist, and therefore from conception to conception. For instance, Rawls identifies a conception involving original position argumentation framed by reflective equilibrium with the public culture of 'our' society. He tries to show that a particular kind of regime, subject to his two principles of justice, is endorsed or required by this conception. John Harsanyi, on the other hand, formulates a conception using the ideas of impartiality and utility-maximization, and he tries to show that this conception demands a regime in which average utility is maximized. (For further discussion of these conceptions, see Chapter 4.) Clearly, the 'optimal' regimes allegedly demanded by these different conceptions are themselves different. Assuming that the 'derivations' are valid of these regimes from the conceptions in which they are embedded, there is no 'dominant' regime in the sense necessary to avoid the arduous indirect labors I have set myself. Which regime is 'optimal' depends on which conception is preferred. To determine the *publicly* 'optimal' regime, it will be necessary to determine the public conception of public justification.

This does not mean that all of my argumentation will be directed, *heuristically,* to the discovery of a public conception, rather than a 'dominant' regime. Indeed, a great deal of the material that follows, especially in Chapters 6 and 8, is concerned, prima facie and for expository purposes, with the problem of identifying a 'dominant' regime. Still, whatever the proper 'heuristic' mode of presentation, the difficulty in solving this problem is grounded, fundamentally, in the difficulties associated with identifying a public conception of public justification. And that is my real problem, however I might approach it.

My question, in what follows, is that of Publius; it is, as he put it, that of deciding

> the important question whether societies . . . are really capable or not of establishing good government from reflection and choice, or whether they are forever destined to depend for their political constitutions on accident and force.[43]

Notes

1. John Rawls, *Political Liberalism,* p. 137, emphasis added.
2. *The Terms of Political Discourse,* p. 3.
3. *The Conquest of Politics,* p. 209.
4. *The Dialogue of Justice,* p. 118.
5. *The Dialogue of Justice,* p. 49.
6. See Merton, "Science and Democratic Social Structure"; Popper, "Public Opinion and Liberal Principles"; Polanyi, "The Republic of Science"; and Bronowski, *Science and Human Values.*
7. *Political Liberalism,* p. 110.
8. Cf. Arthur Fine, "Unnatural Attitudes," p. 150: "For realism, science is ab*out* something; something out there, 'external' and (largely) independent of us."
9. Cf. Rawls, *Political Liberalism,* p. 114: "Political constructivism doesn't use this idea of truth, adding that to assert or to deny a doctrine of this kind goes beyond the bounds of a political conception of justice framed so far as possible to be acceptable to all reasonable comprehensive doctrines." Rawls is referring, of course, to an idea of truth in relation to moral claims, but a reasonable and 'political' conception of objectivity would have to prescind from any 'realistic' idea of truth in other, perhaps purely 'theoretical' domains. This idea is controversial in those domains as well.
10. *Objectivity, Relativism, and Truth,* pp. 22–23. Cf. *Philosophy and the Mirror of Nature,* pp. 333–34.
11. Some care is needed here. Insofar as procedures of public justification aim at identifying 'the facts', these procedures perhaps ought not to be construed as procedures of 'construction' (as might be perfectly appropriate in other, non-factual contexts). As Rawls says, *Political Liberalism,* p. 122, "The idea of constructing facts seems incoherent." On the other hand, perhaps this is too strong; certainly there are 'postmodernist' theorists of science who would endorse exactly this allegedly incoherent claim. What may be more appropriate, to identify the significance of public justification, is the use of a vocabulary neutral between 'realism' and 'constructivism'.

12. In saying this I register my disagreement with Bernard Williams's notion that science and ethico-political theorizing are constituted on fundamentally different bases. I have no interesting opinion about his claim that, in any case of "convergence of ethical outlook . . . it will not be correct to think it has come about because convergence has been guided by how things actually are," at least if this is interpreted as involving some ontological commitment. But I am much less sanguine than he seems to be about the prospect that "convergence in the sciences might be explained in that way if it does happen." Cf. *Ethics and the Limits of Philosophy,* p. 136 and ch. 8 passim.

Much depends on how one is to understand the perhaps sloppy phrase "guided by how things actually are." There are, to use a distinction of Rorty's, representational and purely causal readings of this notion. Cf. *Objectivity, Relativism, and Truth,* p. 97.

On the representational reading, "how things actually are" can be interpreted intensionally, and the convergence of scientists on some theoretical account can be understood as grounded in the semantic similarity of that account to some privileged representation of "how things actually are." I reject this reading; there are no such privileged representations unless they are the representations, as some early modern scientists thought, in 'the mind of God'.

On the purely causal reading, "how things really are" influences though it certainly does not in any important sense 'guide' our inquiries because the things interact causally with various devices that we have invented to help us discover answers to the questions we use these devices to put to these things. In this case, convergence, should there be any, is undeniably the product of at least two factors: causal relations between things and devices, and the interpretation of the devices by the community of scientists. Scientists converge in judgments about things, on this account, at least partly, and in many cases largely, because they have achieved consensus in interpreting the devices that they use to interrogate the world. Of course, on this account there is little difference between scientific theorizing and ethico-political theorizing. In both cases, convergence is largely dependent on some prior consensus about the appropriateness of using certain devices — in my terms, the devices associated with the project of public justification.

13. *An Introduction to Democratic Theory,* p. 232.

14. *Constructions of Reason,* p. 16.

15. *The Postmodern Condition,* p. 8.

16. *Social Epistemology,* p. 6. Cf. John Ziman, *Reliable Knowledge,* pp. 3, 56.

17. On 'direction of fit', cf. Mark Platts, *Ways of Meaning,* pp. 256–57 and, originally, G. E. M. Anscombe, *Intention,* sec. 2.

18. Robert Nozick even identifies this idea as a "candidate for a fundamental self-subsuming principle of morality" and thus for some sort of foundational status for all ethical theorizing. Cf. *Philosophical Explanations,* pp. 541–42.

19. Gaus, "Public Justification and Democratic Adjudication," p. 251.

20. *Value and Justification,* p. 456.

21. "Theoretical Foundations of Liberalism," p. 128.

22. *Equality and Partiality,* p. 3.

23. *Situating the Self,* p. 24.

24. "The Economic Basis of Deliberative Democracy," p. 30.

25. "Pluralism and Social Unity," p. 711.

26. *Moral Conflict and Politics,* p. 12.

27. "Two Levels of Pluralism," p. 788.

28. Cf. *A Theory of Justice,* sec. 7.

29. "The Domain of the Political and Overlapping Consensus," p. 238.

30. Cf. "The Domain of the Political and Overlapping Consensus," sec. II.

31. Cf. "The Domain of the Political and Overlapping Consensus," p. 237, n. 7; "The

Idea of an Overlapping Consensus," p. 4, n. 6; and *Political Liberalism,* p. 57, n. 10: "[A] political conception tries to avoid, so far as possible, disputed philosophical theses and to give an account . . . that rests on plain facts open to all."

32. For Berlin's views, cf. *Four Essays on Liberty,* p. li: "[S]ince some values may conflict intrinsically, the very notion that a pattern must in principle be discoverable in which they are all rendered harmonious is founded on a false a priori view of what the world is like." For Hampshire's, cf. *Morality and Conflict,* pp. 20–21: "The virtues and vices are plural . . . [because] the ways of life men aspire to and admire and wish to enjoy are normally a balance between, and combination of, disparate elements; and this is so, partly because human beings are not so constructed that they have just one overriding concern or end, one overriding interest, or even a few overriding desires and interests. They find themselves trying to reconcile, or to assign priorities to, widely different and diverging and changing concerns and interests, both within the single life of an individual and within a single society."

33. "The Incompatibility of Liberalism and Pluralism," p. 148. Cf. George Crowder, "Pluralism and Liberalism," p. 304.

34. Cf. Berys Gaut, "Moral Pluralism," p. 37, n. 1: "Note that the claim is not that there are no circumstances where one can say that one principle should rank above the other."

35. *Moral Conflict and Politics,* p. 12.

36. *Law, Legislation and Liberty,* vol. 1, p. 8.

37. It is important, I believe, to distinguish methodological and substantive conservatism. The methodological conservative is skeptical or pessimistic about the powers of human reason and rather optimistic (it seems to me) about the beneficence of cultural evolution. She says that what justifies some arrangement of social relations is not some propositionally embodied theory of its legitimacy but, instead, the fact of its historical survival in the face of competition from alternative forms. The substantive conservative is, perhaps, one who stresses the relative importance of order in comparison to either liberty or substantive equality. Hayek is a substantive liberal even though he is undeniably a methodological conservative. Fishkin also differentiates methodological and substantive versions of liberalism. Cf. *The Dialogue of Justice,* p. 45: "One approach would classify normative theories or ideologies as 'liberal' in terms of what they prescribe, while another approach would classify them in terms of how they prescribe it. The first approach relies on the substantive prescriptions resulting from a theory, while the second relies on the kinds of arguments employed by a theory to support its substantive prescriptions."

38. "Kantian Constructivism in Moral Theory," p. 519.

39. Cf. Stephen Macedo, *Liberal Virtues,* p. 203: "The liberal project is to find regulative political principles for people who disagree . . . about ends, goals, and the good life. . . ." According to Nagel (*The View from Nowhere,* p. 188), public justification "would have to be something . . . which acknowledges the plurality of values and reasons arising within all those perspectives."

40. *Political Liberalism,* p. xix.

41. Cf. Rawls, "Justice as Fairness," p. 249: "[A] teleological political conception is out of the question: public agreement on the requisite conception of the good cannot be obtained."

42. Cf. John Dryzek, *Discursive Democracy,* p. 66: "If any model can represent but one perspective of a complex situation, then a legitimate variety of perspectives is inevitable. To cope with this variety, . . . [o]ne could seek interventions that are robust across different perspectives. . . ."

43. *The Federalist,* #1, emphasis added, quoted by Bruce Ackerman, *We the People,* p. 205.

I

CONSTRUCTION

This is why debates about the structure of public reason play a central role in the ongoing philosophical enterprise. It is only when citizens can come to terms about the appropriate models of public argument . . . that they can proceed to the business of social justice.

BRUCE ACKERMAN, "POLITICAL LIBERALISMS"

2

Some Apparatus

I want to discuss the family of ideas *about* ideas that is constituted by the notions concept, conception, ideal, and public conception.[1] I also want to consider pluralism and essential contestability. We will then have an understanding of the vocabulary that is needed to state the main interim thesis of this book—namely, that *in view of the incommensurability of some of the values that constitute its ideal, the concept of public justification is apparently an essentially contestable concept,* much like the first-order normative concepts that Gallie, Lukes, and Connolly have analyzed.[2]

4. Ideas about Ideas

The concept/conception distinction is already found in Rawls's *A Theory of Justice,* and Rawls acknowledges its proximate source in the work of H. L. A. Hart.[3] Basically, a concept of X offers some vague and partial specification of the nature of X—a specification sufficiently vague, in fact, to command widespread assent. According to Rawls, the concept is "specified by the role which . . . [its] different . . . conceptions have in common,"[4] or, perhaps, "the concept is the meaning of a term."[5] But since the concept, according to Hart,[6] "is by itself incomplete . . . [and so] cannot afford any determinate guide to conduct," for example, in routinely distinguishing Xs from non-Xs, it must be supplemented to give a conception that is specific enough to provide a basis, without extensive supervision, for the relatively reliable and socially reproducible application of the concept to concrete phenomena. As Rawls says, "a particular conception includes . . . the principles needed to apply" the concept,[7] so that those who accept a particular conception of X can say, in a variety of cases, whether or not a is an X. In the case of ethico-political concepts, we can expect that, while there may be widespread agreement at the level of concepts, there is likely to be very little or anyway much less agreement at the level of conceptions, at the level, in other words, where concepts are 'articulated' to phenomena: "People can agree on the meaning of the concept . . . and still be at odds. . . ."[8] Dworkin says:

> The contrast between concept and conception is . . . a contrast between levels of
> abstraction. . . . At the first level agreement collects around discrete ideas that are

15

uncontroversially employed in all interpretations; at the second level the controversy latent in this abstraction is identified and taken up.[9]

Whereas all or most will agree that justice requires, at the level of concepts, that no
arbitrary distinctions be made in the distribution of burdens and benefits (or, as Hart
puts it, that like cases be treated alike),[10] there will be much disagreement, at the
level of conceptions, about which distinctions *are* arbitrary with respect to the distribution of some given burden or benefit (alternatively, which cases are like and
which unlike). Since it is at the level of conceptions that an idea is articulated to
concrete phenomena, there will be much disagreement about what kinds of behavior
or practices are just or unjust.

Since concepts are too vaguely and incompletely specified to provide, in themselves, a basis for determinate behavior — for example, for a determinate categoriza-
tion of a as an X or of ϕing as Xish — we may need, where there are a plurality of
interpretations or conceptions of X and where the concept of X plays some important role in the coordination or regulation of social behavior, to discover or construct
a public conception of X. This is a specification of the nature of X that, like the concept, commands widespread assent, but that also, like the various conceptions, is
specified completely and determinately enough to permit its application to concrete
phenomena in a socially reproducible and reliable way.

Because a public conception of X is both widely accepted and determinate
enough to be reliably articulated to the phenomena, we can appeal to it in order to
induce agreement in the face of prior disagreement. Since the public conception of
X is determinate, then, for every question about the status of a with respect to X, this
conception gives a determinate answer. Furthermore, since the public conception is
widely accepted, if A and B disagree about whether a is an X, they can settle their
disagreement by appealing to that conception, for they both accept it and therefore
can be expected to accept its (determinate) implications for specific cases. In the
case of the concept of justice, the applicability of a public conception to concrete
cases is secured, where it can be, by the demand that such a conception "must
impose an ordering on conflicting claims," and the widespread assent commanded
by such a conception is secured because its principles "would be agreed to in an initial situation of equality."[11] As Rawls says, "a well-ordered society is . . . regulated
by its public conception of justice" which "is to be publicly recognized as a final
court of appeal for the ordering of conflicting claims."[12]

How do we discover or construct a public conception of X in the face of a plurality
of competing conceptions of this concept? We do so, briefly, by identifying the conception that best satisfies the desiderata implicit in the ideal of X. We make this identification, in turn, by determining which conception is best fit to play the role of X in the circumstances of X. For instance, that conception of justice is the public conception which
is best fit to play the role of justice in adjudicating competing claims in the circumstances of justice, for example, in the case of moderate scarcity and limited sympathy.

Under the heading of "constructive interpretation," Dworkin provides a useful
characterization of the procedure that is relevant here. As he says, "[C]onstructive
interpretation is a matter of imposing purpose on an object or practice in order to
make of it the best possible example of the form or genre to which it is taken to

belong."[13] Certainly, this is Rawls's procedure, though it is not his language. As already indicated, the public conception of justice is that conception which is most fit to play the role of justice (identified, in part, by the "formal constraints of the concept of right") in the circumstances of justice. And which conception that is is determined by interpreters — in Rawls's case, the parties to the so-called original position — who try to discover which conception is indeed best fit to play this role. As Rawls says, "[T]he question of justification is settled, as far as it can be, by showing that there is one *interpretation* of the initial situation which best expresses the conditions that are widely thought reasonable to impose on the choice of principles. . . ."[14] Reasoning on the basis of that interpretation, we derive a public conception of justice and so establish a basis for social coordination and cooperation.

5. Pluralism

There is an important link between the pluralism of such theorists as Berlin and the contestability theses of such theorists as Gallie. To develop this point, let me first say something about pluralism.

The key points are the following.

1. In many cases, there are a number of different evaluative dimensions, $\delta_1 \ldots \delta_n$ with respect to which alternatives might be ranked.

2. In many such cases, there is no guarantee that variation along one of these dimensions will track and/or be tracked by variations along others.[15] It is possible for X to both δ_1-superior and δ_2-inferior to Y.

In relation to points (1) and (2), Rawls says that pluralistic (in his vocabulary, 'intuitionistic') theories "consist of a plurality of principles which may conflict to give contrary directives in particular types of cases."[16]

3. In many such cases, there is no canonical weighting of the different dimensions that is enjoined by reason itself or, in other words, that every individual must employ or fail in rationality.[17] There is, in this case, no way of synthesizing or aggregating X's δ_1-superiority with its δ_2-inferiority with respect to Y to yield some overall ranking of X and Y that all rational individuals must accept. As Hampshire says, "[T]here is no morally acceptable and overriding criterion . . . to be appealed to, and no constant method of resolving conflicts."[18] Stanley Benn insists that, in such cases, "one cannot look for a resolution of conflicts . . . by a quasi-arithmetical offsetting of gains and losses that would be compelling for all rational appraisers. . . ."[19]

4. In many such cases, any given individual may nevertheless be able to arrive at some reasonable judgment about how these dimensions are to be weighted and so about what to choose, prefer, or do in a certain situation of value conflict. For instance, because she weights δ_1 more heavily than δ_2, A might be able to decide that, as far as she is concerned, X is better, overall, than Y. As Kekes says, "[I]t does not follow, and it is not true, that incommensurable possibilities must always or even frequently produce conflicts in individual lives."[20]

5. Finally, in many such cases, individuals who reach different conclusions about the overall relative merits of alternatives may recognize the reasonableness of

each other's decisions. Whereas *A* prefers *X* to *Y* and *B* prefers *Y* to *X*, each may recognize that, in the absence of some canonical weighting of the different dimensions, the preference of the other is a perfectly reasonable one and, indeed, may be rationally unassailable. As Gallie says, "[A] certain piece of evidence or argument put forward by one side in an apparently endless dispute can be recognized to have genuine logical force, even by those whom it entirely fails to win over or convert to the side in question."[21] David Wong concurs: "Though the relative emphases and priorities held by others are not ones that are adopted in one's own ethic, one understands how these others arrived at the choices made. . . ."[22]

These claims define evaluative pluralism. They are nicely summarized by Hampshire:

> The virtues and vices are plural . . . [because] the ways of life men aspire to and admire and wish to enjoy are normally a balance between, and combination of, disparate elements; and this is so, partly because human beings are not so constructed that they have just one overriding concern or end, one overriding interest, or even a few overriding desires and interests. They find themselves trying to reconcile, or to assign priorities to, widely different and diverging and changing concerns and interests, both within the single life of an individual and within a single society. . . . They also admire, and pursue, virtues which could not be combined, without abridgement, in any imaginable world.[23]

Pluralism in this sense is grounded, I believe, in a fact about the human situation that is itself both deeper and more general. We unavoidably approach the world, our lives, and our fellows from some particular perspective, defined, in part, by our temperament, our character, our historical situation, our aptitudes, our interests, and so on. The situation or point of view of any one person differs, at least de facto and arguably necessarily, from that of every other. What any one person understands about and how she evaluates the situation she encounters will therefore differ from the interpretations and evaluations of that situation which others might endorse. Since no person can (really) simultaneously occupy more than one of these perspectives, and since the 'whole truth' about matters at issue cannot really be grasped from any one of them, any particular person's interpretations and evaluations are necessarily incomplete. Since no person is permanently rooted in some given perspective, every person learns about other perspectives as she lives and perhaps comes to have sympathy for these perspectives and their occupants.

Some will still question the viability, indeed the coherence, of such a pluralistic outlook. Surely it is tantamount to, indeed perhaps provides a basis for, a form of relativism that many philosophers find anathema.[24] This charge cannot be sustained.

Suppose that *A*, weighting δ_1-superiority more heavily than δ_2-superiority, prefers *X* and that *B*, who assigns the opposite weights, prefers *Y*. Are we now forced to say that there are, as the relativist would have it, *two* right answers to the question "Which of *X* and *Y* is better?" — namely, that *X* is better than *Y* is right for *A*, and that *Y* is better than *X* is right for *B*. We are not. There is a pluralistic alternative to the relativistic proliferation of (sometimes 'incompatible') right answers to questions of preference, choice, and decision. According to the pluralist, "for each and every one of us, the question of what is right in some cases lacks a unique and determinate answer. Rightness, on this view, is not relative to anything, it is not a matter of perspective. It is just indeterminate."[25] There are, in other words, not two, but *no* right answers to questions that arise with respect to incommensurable alternatives; there are, as Thomas Hill puts it, "moral gaps."[26]

Have we jumped out of the relativist frying pan into the irrationalist fire? It may seem that we have. If there is no reason for thinking that X is better than Y, then what do we say of the individual who actually chooses one of these alternatives? Doesn't she act without any reason for doing so? And isn't this irrationalism? I do not think so.

First, each of A and B presumably has or comes to have something like a motive for choosing as she does. Both Hampshire and Benn mention that the agent's character will play an important role in determining her decision. As Benn says, "Each person is supplied by his upbringing in a complex cultural environment with a variety of principles and ideals, and in putting together a consistent character as he faces innovation and diversity of experience, he may well be able to impose on it an order which constitutes the person he is."[27]

Second, it is one thing to say that reason can not determine a socially valid decision in these cases and altogether a different thing to say that reason has nothing to do with individuals' (various) decisions. Indeed, A can say that he chose X on account of its δ_1-superiority to Y, and B can say that she chose Y on account of its δ_2-superiority to X. And certainly *both* X's δ_1-superiority and Y's δ_2-superiority would be reasons, *ceteris paribus,* for preferring, respectively, X to Y and Y to X. As Loren Lomasky reminds us, in these kinds of cases, "[a] choice whichever way it goes will have reason behind it. . . ."[28]

Third, it is wrong to identify irrationalism with underdetermination. As Michael Slote points out, "It is not . . . a general condition of rationality that in choosing between two options one has a reason to choose one of those options rather than the other — otherwise, we would sometimes really be in the position of Buridan's ass." He continues: "When two equally (or incommensurably) good or self-beneficial options present themselves, it need not be irrational to choose one of them, even though one has no reason to prefer it to the other."[29] So while it would be a mistake to identify incommensurability with indifference *tout court,*[30] there is nevertheless at least this resemblance: it cannot be irrational simply to *choose* among alternatives that reason is incompetent to distinguish in terms that command universal assent.

The pluralist is neither a relativist nor an irrationalist. The pluralist doctrine is anyway a compelling one, especially in relation to the phenomenology of choice. As Hampshire says, "Unavoidable conflict of principles, and not a harmony of purposes, is the stuff of morality as we ordinarily experience it. . . ."[31] Or, as Rawls puts it, "This pluralism is . . . the natural outcome of the activities of human reason under enduring free institutions."[32] It must therefore be taken into account, indeed built into any adequately conceived project of public justification. Certainly, I will do so.

6.   Essential Contestability and the Problem of Public Justification

Taking up Hampshire's point, I claim that contestability of concepts is clearly the stuff of ethico-political reflection as we ordinarily experience it. As Dworkin says,

"[T]here will be inevitable controversy, even among contemporaries, over the exact dimensions of the practice they all interpret. . . ."[33] What does this mean? Why is it so?

What it means is that key ethico-political concepts will be articulated, as conceptions, in a variety of different ways that reason may be unable to rank unequivocally.[34]

Why is this so? This is so because such concepts are symbolic loci for expressing the evaluative pluralism that I have described.[35] In the case of an essentially contested concept X, there is a plurality of different conditions for its application to concrete phenomena, $C_1 \ldots C_n$.[36] Perhaps we expect that a paradigm X will satisfy each and every one of these conditions. These conditions may in turn reflect different modes of evaluation, so that, for example, some object or event does satisfy the condition C_i only if it ranks highly (enough) with respect to some evaluative dimension δ_i.

Of course, if this and other values are themselves incompatible in the way already analyzed, so that, for example, δ_1-superiority is likely to be linked, empirically, with δ_2-inferiority, then it follows that, in many cases, no object, among those being considered in relation to X, will satisfy *all* the conditions for the application of this concept. If δ_i-acceptability is linked with C_i-satisfaction and if δ_1-superiority is linked with δ_2-inferiority, then any object that satisfies C_1 ipso facto fails to satisfy C_2, and vice versa. But in this case, the application of the concept to objects is likely to be contested. If A applies X to a on account of its satisfying C_1, then, necessarily, he ignores or downplays the fact that a ipso facto does not satisfy C_2, a condition for the application of X that B, on the contrary, may choose to emphasize.

And if because of δ_1/δ_2 *incommensurability*, there is "no further overarching principle and perspective from which these [values] can be put into any further objective balance,"[37] it follows immediately that there is no rational basis for deciding which one of the two is right in the ways in which she applies the concept X to concrete phenomena.[38] Without some canonical method for 'trading off' δ_1-superiority against δ_2-superiority, we have the same kind of 'moral gap' in relation to the concept X that we have already exhibited in relation to judgments of overall value.

On account of their character — or, perhaps, their position in society — some individuals may of course consistently apply the concept to concrete phenomena, but there will be other people who, on account of their differing characters or social positions, will apply this concept, again consistently, but in consistently different ways. As Gallie says, "The scales are tipped for him . . . by his recognition of a value which, given his particular marginal appraisive situation, is conclusive for him, although it is merely impressive or surprising or worth noticing for others."[39] And there will be, in cases of incommensurability, no consideration that any such group could appeal to that ought to be telling with all rational individuals and that could provide a basis for the uniform application of this concept by all of them. A concept's usage is essentially, and not merely accidentally contest*able*, and not merely contest*ed*. Agreement about the proper use of such a concept may nevertheless be essential for the coordination or regulation of important social activities. In this case, a public conception will be required.

In fact, this is just the situation that we face in relation to the concept of public justification. Whether or not some social institution is legitimate and therefore should be honored or, perhaps, overturned, depends, in the framework I am considering, on whether or not that institution can be publicly justified. Whether or not the institution can be publicly justified depends, in turn, on whether or not there is some (determinate) procedure for the public justification of social arrangements that does or does not provide a basis for the justification of that institution. Whether or not there is such a procedure — and therefore a determinate answer to our original question — depends, finally, on whether there is some uniquely best (available) conception of public justification. And there is such a conception only if there is no incommensurability with respect to the various evaluative dimensions that lie behind the various conditions a method must satisfy in order to constitute a method of public justification. In fact, I will try to show that there are a number of incompatible and arguably incommensurable evaluative dimensions implicated in our understanding of public justification and thus, arguably, that there is no public conception of this concept.

To be sure, it would follow from such a demonstration that there may be no determinate answer whether or not some arbitrary social institution is in fact legitimate.[40] In the absence of a determinately best conception of public justification, there are only the various essentially contestable conceptions of this concept. According to one conception, that institution is legitimate. But according to another conception, that institution is not legitimate. And since there is no way of establishing which of these conceptions is the better one, there is no way of establishing whether or not the institution is legitimate. The concept of public justification thus could not play the role that liberal theorists have wanted it to play in these circumstances.

Notes

1. Cf. Rawls, *Political Liberalism*, p. 14, n. 15: "I use 'ideas' as the more general term and as covering both concepts and conceptions."

2. Cf. Gallie, "Essentially Contested Concepts"; Lukes, *Power: A Radical View;* and Connolly, *The Terms of Political Discourse.*

3. *A Theory of Justice*, p. 5. Cf. Hart, *The Concept of Law,* pp. 155–59.

4. *A Theory of Justice*, p. 5.

5. *Political Liberalism*, p. 14, n. 15.

6. *The Concept of Law*, p. 155.

7. *Political Liberalism*, p. 14, n. 15.

8. Rawls, *Political Liberalism*, p. 14, n. 15.

9. *Law's Empire*, pp. 70–71.

10. Rawls, *A Theory of Justice*, p. 5 and Hart, *The Concept of Law,* p. 155.

11. Rawls, *A Theory of Justice*, pp. 133–34, 21.

12. *A Theory of Justice*, pp. 454, 135.

13. *Law's Empire*, p. 52.

14. *A Theory of Justice*, p. 121, emphasis added.

15. As Gaus points out, this kind of failure of 'tracking' is the source of the economist's notion of 'opportunity costs'. Cf. *Value and Justification*, pp. 221–22: "[G]iven the states of affairs that are actually realizable . . . , promoting, protecting, or instantiating one thing a person values has severe opportunity costs in terms of promoting other valued things."

16. *A Theory of Justice*, p. 34.

17. This claim is rejected by Galston. See *Liberal Purposes*, p. 173: "It may well prove possible to arrive at shared judgments about the relative weights to be attached to increments of two or more goods that cannot be reduced to a single substantive value. As Griffin has argued, pluralism does not imply incommensurability." Perhaps not, but it will be the burden of much of the argumentation in Chapters 6 and 7 that commensuration is not easily managed in relation to the problem at issue here.

18. *Morality and Conflict*, p. 165.

19. *A Theory of Freedom*, p. 16.

20. *Moral Tradition and Individuality*, p. 160.

21. "Essentially Contested Concepts," p. 190.

22. "Coping with Moral Conflict and Ambiguity," p. 779.

23. *Morality and Conflict*, pp. 20–21.

24. Galston does so on more or less ethical grounds. He says (*Liberal Purposes*, p. 90): "Full skepticism about the good leads not to tolerance, not to liberal neutrality, but to an unconstrained struggle in which force, not reason, is the final arbiter."

25. Wolf, "Two Levels of Pluralism," p. 789.

26. "Kantian Pluralism," p. 755.

27. *A Theory of Freedom*, p. 18. Cf. Hampshire, *Morality and Conflict*, pp. 41–42.

28. *Persons, Rights, and the Moral Community*, p. 236.

29. *Beyond Optimizing*, p. 21.

30. Cf. Joseph Raz, *The Morality of Freedom*, p. 334: "Incomparability does not ensure equality of merit and demerit. It does not mean indifference. It marks the inability of reason to guide our action."

31. *Morality and Conflict*, p. 116.

32. *Political Liberalism*, p. xxiv.

33. *Law's Empire*, p. 67.

34. Cf. Andrew Mason, "On Explaining Political Disagreement," pp. 85–86.

35. As Gallie says ("Essentially Contested Concepts," p. 171), such a concept is "*appraisive* in the sense that it signifies or accredits some kind of valued achievement." Cf. Connolly, *The Terms of Political Discourse*, p. 10.

36. As Connolly says (*The Terms of Political Discourse*, p. 10): "[T]he practice described is *internally complex* in that its characterization involves reference to several dimensions." Cf. Gallie, "Essentially Contested Concepts," p. 171.

37. Wolf, "Two Levels of Pluralism," p. 788. Cf. Gallie, "Essentially Contested Concepts," pp. 171–72: "[P]rior to experimentation there is nothing absurd or contradictory in any one of a number of possible rival descriptions of its total worth, one such description setting its component features in one order of importance, a second setting them in a second order, and so on."

38. Cf. John Gray, "On the Contestability of Social and Political Concepts," p. 332: "According to Gallie's account, essentially contested concepts are such that their criteria of correct application are multiple, evaluative, and in no settled relation of priority to one another."

39. "Essentially Contested Concepts," p. 191.

40. Even in this situation, there might be a determinate answer to the question of what regime is legitimate if, for instance, there is a regime that is 'dominant' in the sense that, whatever conception of public justification is adopted, that regime is legitimate according to that conception. I have already suggested (sec. 3) and will later try to show (secs. 23–26) that no such 'dominant' regime can be identified by any of the usual methods for establishing dominance.

3

The Idea of Public Justification

The problem of public justification is that of determining whether or not a given regime is legitimate and therefore worthy of our loyalty or, instead, illegitimate and therefore, presumably, to be transformed or resisted if possible. This problem arises and may be difficult to solve because it may not be possible to identify a public conception of public justification. In order to pose this problem clearly, I am going to consider this concept and some of its dimensions. I will then identify some different conceptions of this concept and show how they are ranged along the various dimensions I have identified. Before doing so, I will consider some preliminary matters. (Critical analysis begins in Chapter 6.)

7. The Circumstances of, Conditions for, and Limits on Politics

It will be important, in what follows, to keep in mind that the problem of public justification arises only in certain circumstances, which I call the circumstances of politics. These circumstances are, in fact, much more general and abstract than those that constitute the circumstances of justice whose significance Rawls has stressed. According to Rawls, we find ourselves in the circumstances of justice when we find ourselves in a situation of moderate scarcity, involving cohabitation with and dependence on mutually disinterested individuals approximately equal to us in their capacity for and vulnerability to predation.[1] On my account, we find ourselves in the circumstances of politics when we find that we disagree with one another (a) about how our lives together are to be conducted[2] and (b) in the absence of straightforward 'empirical' techniques for the resolution of our disagreement.[3] As Barber says:

> [A] political point takes the form: "What shall we do when something has to be done that will affect us all and we wish to be reasonable, yet we disagree on means and ends and are without independent grounds by which we might arbitrate our differences?"[4]

If we need to agree on some course of action in order to avoid avoidable burdens or to attain attainable benefits, then, if we antecedently *dis*agree, we face the circumstances of politics. As Stephen Macedo puts it, "Politics is the final recourse for people who cannot agree."[5]

Absent what Barber calls "independent grounds" for resolving our disagreement, we will have to resort, in such a situation, to specifically political processes. As Barber says, "Where reason claims to speak, politics is silent"; "Politics is what men do when metaphysics fails."[6] But whereas Barber seems to want to confine political disputation to situations in which we have "interests in opposition [that] can be adjudicated only by such political means as bargaining and exchange,"[7] I want to contemplate a somewhat broader range of possibilities. In particular, I do not preclude, as Barber seems to, that our disagreement might turn out to be one about which 'reason', suitably interrogated, is not ultimately 'silent' — one that might be susceptible to treatment by broadly 'empirical' techniques.

All that I require for the dispute to be political is that *existing* empirical techniques of the *usual* kind are incompetent to settle the matter without *residual* controversy.[8] In other words, I want to accept the possibility that the disagreement may be 'factual', rather than grounded in a 'mere' conflict of 'interests' or irreducible preferences, but that it may nevertheless be intractable in the short term, perhaps because of what Rawls calls the "burdens of judgment."[9] For instance, how the budget should be divided or taxation imposed is clearly a political question in a sense in which the question of how the seeds might be sown (usually) is not. In the latter case, we have well-understood, widely accepted, and antecedently available techniques for answering the question. Use of these techniques typically results in the formation of a new consensus or the strengthening of an existing one. In the former case, no such techniques are likely to be available antecedently, though we may develop them in the course of exploring this kind of issue.

In any event, the pertinence of these matters to my main theme is straightforward. Any solution to the problem of public justification is ipso facto a telling response to the challenge posed by the circumstances of politics. If we need to make some decision bearing on matters of mutual concern, we will be glad if there is some determinate account of public justifiability to which we can appeal. Showing that one or another substantive response to our situation is in fact publicly justifiable *does* constitute an effective solution of the problem.

On my account, the circumstances of politics are those features of situations that make politics necessary. I believe that it is useful to distinguish what other theorists, particularly Rawls, have not distinguished.[10] I say that the conditions for politics are what makes politics likely, when it's necessary, to succeed, for example, in resolving disagreement.

And what are the conditions for politics? Recognition of the Rawlsian "burdens of judgment" and, encompassing this, a commitment to the requirements of "reasonableness." Let me take these points in turn.

What are the "burdens of judgment"? Crudely, they are those infirmities or limitations of human judgment that are grounded in the fact of our "finitary predicament,"[11] as well as in an irreducible pluralism of values — factors that prevent us from reaching consensus on disputed issues within relevant constraints of time and other resources.[12] As Rawls says, "[M]any of our most important judgments are made under conditions when it is not to be expected that conscientious persons with full powers of reason, even after free discussion, will all arrive at the same conclusion."[13] David Held provides a useful summary:

> Diversity in capacities and faculties, fallibility in reasoning and judgement, zeal for
> a quick opinion, attachment to different leaders, as well as a desire for a vast range
> of different objects — all constitute 'insuperable obstacles' to uniformity in the
> interpretation of priorities and interests.[14]

Of course, the *fact* of the burdens of judgment is among the circumstances of politics — that we are infirm in this sense makes politics necessary. On account of these burdens, no 'empirical techniques' are likely to be available that could be employed to compose the disagreement with which we are faced. The point to be emphasized here is that *recognition* of this fact is among the conditions for politics. If we acknowledge that issues may not admit of resolution, we may accept the reasonableness of the fact of disagreement and, with it, the reasonableness of those who disagree and, in turn, the reasonableness of nevertheless attempting to find a resolution that all can accept. "[R]easonable persons will think it unreasonable to use political power, should they possess it, to repress comprehensive views that are not unreasonable, though different from their own."[15] Macedo concurs: "People disagree for a variety of reasons which do not impugn their reasonableness or undermine their claim to respect. Public justification offers a way of accepting the infirmities of reasonable citizens."[16]

To be sure, without recognition of these burdens, it is not clear that we *could* resolve disagreements that arise in the circumstances of politics. Individuals who refuse to recognize the reasonableness of others are unlikely to employ political processes to settle disagreements. If they were to, they would do so merely as a modus vivendi and not on any principled grounds. For one thing, it is not reasonable to search for a settlement with them. Their reasonableness, which is denied, is a precondition of engaging in such a search.

And what does reasonableness consist in? In a disposition to search for social arrangements whose demands and prerogatives can be justified to all who will be affected by them. Indeed, Thomas Scanlon sees this as fundamental to the moral perspective. As he says, "[T]he source of motivation that is directly triggered by the belief that an action is wrong is the desire to be able to justify one's actions to others on grounds they could not reasonably reject."[17] Rawls fills out this characterization:

> People are reasonable in one basic respect when, among equals say, they are ready
> to propose principles and standards as fair terms of cooperation and to abide by
> them willingly, given the assurance that others will likewise do so. Those norms
> they view as reasonable for everyone to accept and therefore as justifiable for them;
> and they are ready to discuss the fair terms that others propose.[18]

Again, being reasonable is clearly a condition for politics generally and for public justification specifically. People who are not prepared to listen to others, or people who expect others to abide by arrangements that they are not themselves prepared to abide by, clearly cannot come to any uncoerced agreement about the terms of their relations with one another. The achievement of a publicly justified system of social arrangements is possible, then, only on the assumption that all parties are reasonable in something like this sense. (If this assumption seems 'generous', it is not. Remember too that this is an essay in 'ideal' theory, and my question is "Can public justification be achieved *if* people *are* 'reasonable'?" That it could not if they are not is [almost] obvious.)

The circumstances of politics are those features of our world that make political activity necessary — that is, disagreement and mutual dependence. The conditions for politics are those features of our personalities that make political activity feasible — that is, reasonableness and recognition of the burdens of judgment. The limits on politics are therefore encountered whenever we find ourselves in the circumstances without the conditions being realized.[19] If we disagreed with one another in a state of mutual dependence but did not think of one another as reasonable, we would need to but would not be able to resolve our disagreement politically. Because of our mutual dependence, we would need to find some way of resolving our disagreement. On account of our 'unreasonableness', we could not do so politically (or, a fortiori, 'empirically') but only, perhaps, by exercising force or engaging in fraud. Here we run up against the limits on politics, the point at which political disputation is futile or fatuous.

Indeed, it will be the burden of much subsequent discussion that there may be non-trivial limits on politics; that is, that there may be questions we would like to settle politically that we cannot settle in that way — because we cannot identify a uniquely best conception of public justification.

8. The Rationale for and Realm of Public Justification

There are many different stories about why it is important that we provide public justification.

First, there is the idea that the requirements of public justification effectively express our moral personality. According to Rawls, the machinery of public justification that he favors — original position argumentation — embodies and is chosen so that it will embody conditions that "represent the freedom and equality of moral persons as understood in such a society" as ours.[20]

Second, the requirements of public justification are sometimes tied to a related notion, that of autonomy or, in other words, to "each person's claim to moral independence."[21] Nagel characterizes the liberal "search for legitimacy" as "an attempt to realize some of the values of voluntary participation, in a system of institutions that is unavoidably compulsory." As he says, "To show [people] that they all have sufficient reason to accept [such a system] . . . is as close as we can come to making this involuntary condition voluntary."[22] According to Jeffrey Reiman, only the public justification of existing or imagined social structures answers the demand that we defeat the 'suspicion of subjugation' that naturally arises between people with differential power. He says: "Since relations of subjugation are imposed on people against their wills, we can find nonsubjugating relations by asking what it would be reasonable for people willingly to accept."[23]

Third, the requirements of public justification may express "a distinctively moral motive, namely the desire to behave in accordance with principles that can be defended to oneself and others in an impartial way."[24] As Macedo says, "The commitment to public justification reflects a desire to regard certain kinds of reasons as authoritative in politics: moral reasons that can be openly presented to others, critically defended, and widely shared by reasonable people."[25] On this account, the project of public justification is one that is intimately associated with the idea of impartiality: "To say that a principle could not reasonably be rejected by anyone covered by it is . . . a way of saying that it meets the test of impartiality."[26]

Fourth, we find the notion, associated nowadays with Jürgen Habermas, but not by any means exclusive to him, that the requirements of public justification might have some transcendental grounding.[27]

Fifth, the requirements of public justification may express the ideal of the 'rule of law'. As Macedo says, "[T]o have a government of laws rather than of men is to have government based on reasons that all ought to be able to accept."[28] The idea is, presumably, that where government is not publicly justified, it is based, at best, on 'reasons' that only some can accept. In this case, it is not these reasons but, instead, the fact that they are the reasons of particular individuals that would legitimate, if anything did. But then legitimacy would be person-, not reason-oriented. The regime would be the rule *of* persons (who didn't have these reasons) *by* persons (who did), not the rule of law.

Finally, we have the idea that public justification is necessary for broadly prudential reasons. Unless social arrangements are reasonable for all, it is possible that none will enjoy their benefits. Benn says, for instance, that "it is important that we be able to justify ourselves" to others because "we require the[ir] cooperation" in achieving our own aims.[29] David Gauthier and James Buchanan are also prominent representatives of this school of thinking.[30] Indeed, even Rawls sometimes seems to suggest such an approach. He says, for instance, that the appropriate test for principles of justice is that they would be agreed to by persons concerned "to win for themselves the highest index of primary social goods."[31]

In fact, these approaches can be divided into two main families: those that ground the justificatory project in already explicitly moral ideas and demands—the appeal to our "free and equal moral personality" is representative in this regard; and those that ground this project in ideas and demands that are not themselves explicitly moral—representative in this regard is the appeal to "the interest of rational maximizers in securing the effective cooperation of others." We have moralistic and realistic rationales for the project of public justification.[32]

Indeed, these two families may themselves reflect an even deeper idea, one tapped, perhaps, by Habermas; namely, that the requirements of public justification are just, either way, the requirements of rationality. As Gauthier and Brian Barry remind us, there are, after all, two distinct conceptions of rationality that mirror the two main families I have identified. We have, in Barry's terms, "the equation of rationality with the effective pursuit of self-interest" contrasted with the rationality of caring "about what can be defended impartially."[33] In Gauthier's terms, we have a "*maximizing* conception of rationality," according to which "the rational person . . . seeks the greatest satisfaction of her own interests" contrasted with a "*universal-*

istic conception of rationality," according to which "the rational person seeks to satisfy all interests."[34] Indeed, Rawls distinguishes 'the reasonable' and 'the rational' in much the same terms, tracing the distinction to Kant's between pure and empirical practical reason.[35]

Why do we pursue the project of public justification? We do so in order to satisfy the demands of rationality, whether, by these demands, we understand those of a maximizing, self-interested conception or, instead, those of an impartial, universalizing conception.

So much for the rationale for public justification. What about the *realm* of public justification?

Especially in its unanimity requirement, the concept of public justification is clearly highly idealized and thus cannot have any application, even to a first approximation, except in some very restricted setting. The prospects for even a first approximation to the demands of public justification are better for fundamentals than they are for the regulatory minutiae that are nevertheless an essential part of institutional life. For instance, it is much more likely that individuals will collectively endorse some purely procedural arrangements for the conduct of their affairs than substantive arrangements about whose merits they might, quite reasonably, differ.[36] Indeed, they might be able to agree on procedures for deciding these more substantive matters even if they could not agree (at least unanimously) about the issues themselves.[37] As Kurt Baier says, "[A]lthough there seems to be no consensus on a conception of justice, there is a consensus on something else, namely, on the procedures for making and interpreting law and, where that agreement is insufficiently deep to end disagreement, on the selection of persons whose adjudication is accepted as authoritative."[38]

In fact, we can adapt a Rawlsian idea to develop this point—that of the basic structure of society.[39] Our ideas about the so-called basic structure of society are somewhat different, however, since Rawls is concerned with the problem of justice, and I am concerned with the problem of justification. Where Rawls quite properly emphasizes institutional arrangements that are likely to affect an individual's life prospects,[40] I emphasize those arrangements that are implicated in enforceable social decision making.[41]

The basic *political* structure is embodied in the fundamental procedures and principles that determine how substantive decisions are made about generally enforced social arrangements: the qualifications for voting, the system of representation, the requirements for the passage of legislation, constitutional restrictions on the powers of the legislature, and so on.[42] What in the United States is known as the constitutional basis for government—this is the politically basic structure of society.

Four points are relevant.

First, questions about the basic political structure most realistically constitute the realm of public justification. This is so because it seems more likely that the requirements of public justification might be met, at least to a first approximation, in this domain than elsewhere in the political system as a whole. Certainly, if they cannot be met here, they will be unattainable elsewhere. Notice, furthermore, that any agreement on such constitutional fundamentals is more likely to be justified 'transparently' than agreements that might be reached on other kinds of issues. Rawls says:

> Whether the constitutional essentials covering the basic freedoms are satisfied is more or less visible on the face of constitutional arrangements and how these can be seen to work in practice. But whether the aims of the principles covering social and economic inequalities are realized is far more difficult to ascertain. . . . Thus, although questions of both kinds are to be discussed in terms of political values, we can expect more agreement about whether the principles for the basic rights and liberties are realized than about whether the principles for social and economic justice are realized.[43]

Second, it seems more necessary in this domain than in others that these requirements be met at least to a first approximation. Without agreement even on how to settle disagreements and determine generally enforceable principles, there are limited prospects for a collective life based on anything other than force and fraud. As Rawls says, "There is the greatest urgency for citizens to reach practical agreement about the constitutional essentials."[44]

Third, a constitutional consensus of the kind envisaged may be the most that we should reasonably hope for; a more detailed and substantive consensus might be stifling. This is a point pressed by Baier.[45] In view of the argument in section 41, it is one that I enthusiastically endorse.

Finally, public justification may be 'transitive' when basic constitutional arrangements have been publicly justified. Even if it is unrealistic to seek public justification for substantive regulations, some measure of indirect public support is conferred on them if these regulations were decided on and implemented in accordance with procedures and principles that *were* publicly justified. As Rawls says, "[S]o long as there is firm agreement on the constitutional essentials . . . , willing political and social cooperation between free and equal citizens can normally be maintained."[46]

(This is my answer to Rawls's claim that "a purely political and procedural constitutional consensus will prove too narrow," particularly in failing to settle "basic matters of justice."[47] Rawls seems to think that there will be conflict about these matters unless they are determined at what is the 'pre-constitutional' stage of original position argumentation. I am content to let them be settled 'legislatively' by whatever means are adopted at the stage of the constitutional convention for the settlement of such disputes. They 'earn' their legitimacy 'transitively', in the manner described. Frankly, I do not understand Rawls's claim that "unless a democratic people is sufficiently unified and cohesive, it will not enact the legislation necessary to cover . . . basic matters of justice," particularly in view of his belief that these matters *can* be settled by original position argumentation. If these kinds of issues could be settled by original position argumentation, then my preferred approach really ought to work perfectly well. To suppose that it would not seems equivalent, within a Rawlsian framework, to supposing that stability could not be achieved. On Rawls's account, what is not stably justified via original position argumentation is not genuinely justified via such a technique.[48])

The appropriate realm of public justification is basic constitutional arrangements, especially those that are relevant to basic political institutions and practices.[49]

In trying to clarify the requirements of public justification, I am therefore seeking clarification of the requirements for a constitutional convention, whose delegates can be thought of as trying to achieve public justification for the constitution they are charged with framing.[50] The notion of public justification is intended to provide a standard by which the results of the deliberations of such delegates are to be judged. We can reasonably ask, of any constitutional device that might be proposed, whether this device can achieve public justification at least to a first approximation. This is the role of that concept.

9. The Concept and Some Dimensions of Public Justification

The concept of public justification is best expressed in this way: *No regime is legitimate unless it is reasonable from every point of view.* In fact, this concept is multiply ambiguous, and whereas all theorists committed to the project might be willing to endorse it, "there will be inevitable controversy, even among contemporaries, over the exact dimensions of the practice they all interpret. . . ."[51] In what follows, I propose to identify some of these dimensions. More specific conceptions of the concept can then be arrayed, and some taxonomic order introduced into the welter of competing interpretations. (See Chapter 4.)

First of all, we have a distinction between those conceptions that stress a consensus between relevant individuals and those conceptions that stress a convergence from diverse points of view. If both A and B share a reason R that makes a regime reasonable for them, then the justification of that regime is grounded in their consensus with respect to R. If A has a reason R_A that makes the regime reasonable for him, *and* B has a reason R_B that makes the regime reasonable for her, then the justification of that regime is based on convergence on it from separate points of view.[52] Nagel says:

> Defences of political legitimacy are of two kinds: those which discover a possible convergence of rational support for certain institutions from the separate motivational standpoints of distinct individuals; and those which seek a common standpoint that everyone can occupy, which guarantees agreement on what is acceptable.[53]

It may be useful to distinguish two types of convergence. When we appeal to R_A and R_B to justify a regime, what we appeal to is sometimes merely indexically characterized and is sometimes, instead, substantively characterized. If we appeal to A to accept some particular regime on the grounds that his preferences will thereby be satisfied, our reference to his preferences is purely indexical. What we are saying is that his preferences, whatever they might be, will be satisfied if he accepts that regime. We are not appealing substantively to him, claiming that his preferences, namely, for apples over oranges or for security over liberty, will be satisfied if he accepts it.[54]

Second, we have a distinction between those conceptions that require, positively, that it be reasonable to accept a regime and those conceptions that require, negatively, that it not be reasonable to reject a regime. Scanlon gives the canonical formulation of the negative, reasonable rejectability requirement: "An act is wrong if its performance under the circumstances would be disallowed by any system of rules for the regulation of behavior which no one could reasonably reject as a basis for informed, unforced general agreement."[55] (What makes a conception of public justification a negative conception is not that the substance of what is justified is negative, as for instance in Popper's so-called negative utilitarianism.[56] It is, rather, that the criterion for justification is a negative one: "No one could reasonably reject" whatever the norms might be, and they do so quite independently of *their* 'logical form'.) Nicholas Rescher's distinction is closely related to Scanlon's — namely, between "[c]onsensus-seeking societies [that] aim to *maximize* the number of people who approve of what is being done . . . [and] acquiescence-seeking societies [that] seek to *minimize* the number of people who disapprove very strongly of what is being done."[57]

Third, we have a distinction between those conceptions that, volitionally, stress desire-satisfaction and those conceptions that, cognitionally, stress belief-induced commitment as a basis for judging the reasonableness of regimes.[58] Such a distinction is implicit in Gaus's remarks about the particular form of contractual argumentation that he prefers. "Principles are accepted by all not because they advance everyone's values, but because everyone shares the convictions that the principles articulate."[59]

A regime might seem reasonable from every point of view because it fits the desires of relevant individuals. For instance, Gauthier's regime is alleged to fit the desire of each individual that her preference-satisfaction be maximized. It 'fits' that desire in the sense that it constitutes a situation in which that desire can be realized. On the other hand, Rawls's regime might be alleged to fit the beliefs that individuals have about the kind of regime that is a reasonable one for them. It 'fits' those beliefs in the sense that it constitutes a situation about which those beliefs would be true.[60]

(That a regime is one in which A can reasonably expect his desires to be satisfied gives A, *ceteris paribus,* both a reason and a motive for conforming his behavior to its requirements.[61] But how can the fact that a regime fits beliefs that A might have be thought to motivate such conformity? Benn and Gaus offer some help here. According to their theory of practical rationality, someone who has a certain belief may be committed, because she has that belief, to act in certain ways.[62] For instance, someone who believes that she is A's friend is committed, by the fact that she has this belief, to act in a way appropriate to their friendship, and so, for instance, if friendship requires φing in Σ, she is committed to φing in Σ.[63] In the case at hand, someone who believes that she is Rational and Reasonable may be committed, by these beliefs, to acting in certain ways — for example, to limiting her Rational pursuit of her own interests in accordance with the demand, implicit in her belief that she is Reasonable, that she justify herself to others, or be prepared to, in certain kinds of situations. And this may give her a motive as well as a reason to conform to certain requirements.[64])

Fourth, we have a distinction between those conceptions that insist that a regime must be directly reasonable from the point(s) of view of *A* and *B* themselves and those conceptions that insist, on the contrary, that a regime must be indirectly reasonable — reasonable, that is, from the point(s) of view of surrogate(s) for *A* and *B*.[65] Michael Davis says: "Contract theory seems to have two strains. One strain relies on hypothetical consent; the other, on actual consent."[66] Also relevant is Nagel's distinction between an "actual unanimity among persons with the motives they happen to have" and "a unanimity which could be achieved among persons in many respects as they are, provided they were also reasonable and committed within reason to modifying their claims, requirements, and motives in a direction which makes a common framework of justification possible."[67] In each case, we have a contrast between what A and *B would* accept based on their actual beliefs and desires, and what they *could* accept if their beliefs and desires were filtered or supplemented in some way — for example, by the requirements of Rationality and Reasonableness.

Perhaps further refinement is called for of what may be a too-crude distinction between direct and indirect modes. Certainly, Nagel's requirement for indirect justification is not very substantive. It is more nearly procedural than the requirements that others seem to have had in mind. What Nagel seems to require of the surrogates for *A* and *B* is not that they have some particular system of substantive first-order beliefs and desires but, instead, that they have some *second-order attitude* toward the actual beliefs and desires of *A* and *B*. Benhabib, on the other hand, seems to be envisaging a situation in which some determinate system of substantively identified attitudes and attributes is substituted for the actual characteristics of the relevant individuals.[68] (Certainly, many feminists distrust indirect modes of justification. According to Elizabeth Grosz, the logic of indirect justification "consists in neutralizing and eliminating differences, in reducing them to a common measure which accords with socially privileged (masculine) attributes."[69])

Fifth, we have the distinction between justifications whose results, economically, represent a compromise between individuals' interests and justifications that result, politically, from a consideration of the various issues at stake and that represent the common good.[70] This distinction is implicit, for instance, in Nagel's observation that "[e]ven though he might be able to think of alternative arrangements more advantageous to him, still on balance, taking everyone's point of view into account together with his own, no one living under such a system will have grounds for objection. . . ."[71]

Sixth, we can see a distinction in a question asked long ago by A. D. Lindsay: "Is democracy a means of bringing it about that the people shall consent to what the government proposes to do, or that the government shall do what the people want?"[72] Is the test, with respect to *A* and *B,* that, as they are or would be now, *A* and *B* would find the regime a reasonable one? This is a prior reading of the requirement of public justification. Or is the test, instead, that *A* and *B* would find the regime a reasonable one, as they would be were they to live in it? This is a posterior reading of the requirement. Of some contemporary relevance here is Cohen's insistence that "the pluralistic consensus test does not itself command a search for *de facto* points of agreement at all." He continues:

The test is this: Consider a proposed conception of justice in operation, and then consider whether the principles, ideals, and terms of argument that figure in it provide moral reasons within the views that could be expected to arise among those who live in a society governed by it.[73]

Finally, we have a distinction between a process that involves interaction between the parties — an interactive reading — and a process that involves no such interaction — a non-interactive reading.[74] Chandran Kukathas and Philip Pettit put it this way:

In Gauthier's picture, the parties are involved in a process of economic negotiation with one another. . . . [But] Rawls's own conception of the contract is non-interactive. He sees the parties as deciding what to choose without the necessity of negotiating with one another.[75]

There are, then, at least these dimensions of variation among conceptions of public justification:

consensual	versus	convergent
positive	versus	negative
volitional	versus	cognitional
direct	versus	indirect
economic	versus	political
prior	versus	posterior
interactive	versus	non-interactive

Notes

1. Cf. *A Theory of Justice,* sec. 22.

2. Cf. Mayo, *An Introduction to Democratic Theory,* p. 67: "Political systems are devised because there is conflict and disagreement." Cf. Don Herzog, *Without Foundations,* p. 18: "Disagreement and doubt thus create the demand for justification." Cf. also Ackerman, "Why Dialogue?" p. 9: "Despite their ongoing disagreements, all groups find themselves on the same planet, in potential conflict over the planet's scarce resources. Hence the problem of liberal politics: How are the different groups to resolve their problem of coexistence in a reasonable way?" Finally, cf. Hillel Steiner, *An Essay on Rights,* p. 188 on the "native habitat" of the idea of justice — namely, "adversarial circumstances."

3. Cf. Ackerman, "Why Dialogue?" p. 10: Politics "recognizes that, for the moment at least, neither [party to the dispute] is going to win the moral argument to the other's satisfaction, and proceeds to consider the way they might live together despite their ongoing disagreement." Cf. also Chantal Mouffe, *The Return of the Political,* p. 4: "Once we accept the necessity of the political and the impossibility of a world without antagonism, what needs to be envisaged is how it is possible under these conditions to create and maintain a pluralistic democratic order."

4. *The Conquest of Politics,* p. 206.

5. *Liberal Virtues,* p. 53.

6. *The Conquest of Politics,* pp. 205, 209.

7. *The Conquest of Politics,* p. 208.

8. As will emerge, I take the possibility of actual assent, in certain circumstances, a great deal more seriously than some other theorists concerned with public justification. Cf. Gaus, *Justificatory Liberalism,* sec. 1.1. But this should not, and I think does not, affect my characterization of the circumstances of politics. Whereas I might have the achievement of agreement in mind as a response to the fact of disagreement, other, less 'pragmatic' theorists might have some mode of legitimation that does not necessarily involve such an achievement.

9. Cf. *Political Liberalism,* ch. 2, sec. 2.

10. That Rawls fails to distinguish explicitly what makes justice necessary from what makes it possible is obvious in *A Theory of Justice,* p. 126: "The circumstances of justice may be described as the normal conditions under which human cooperation is both possible and necessary." That Rawls nevertheless does implicitly distinguish what I call circumstances from what I call conditions is clear in "The Domain of the Political and Overlapping Consensus," p. 245: "History tells of a plurality of not unreasonable comprehensive doctrines. That these comprehensive doctrines are divergent makes an overlapping consensus necessary. That they are not unreasonable makes it possible." I have adapted some observations of Susan Mendus to develop the circumstances/conditions distinction. Cf. her *Toleration and the Limits of Liberalism,* p. 87.

11. Christopher Cherniak, *Minimal Rationality,* p. 8.

12. That human beings are subject to such a 'finitary predicament' seems to be disputed by Roberto Unger. Galston reports (*Liberal Purposes,* p. 57) that "[f]or Unger, the essence of human personality is that it is 'infinite' . . . [having] the capacity to transcend all contexts: traits of character, moral rules, political institutions, cognitive structures, and so forth."

13. *Political Liberalism,* p. 58. Cf. Galston, *Liberal Purposes,* p. 27.

14. *Models of Democracy,* p. 62.

15. Rawls, *Political Liberalism,* p. 60.

16. *Liberal Virtues,* pp. 47–48.

17. "Contractualism and Utilitarianism," p. 116.

18. *Political Liberalism,* p. 49.

19. My idea of the limits on politics must be distinguished from Rawls's idea of "The Limits of Public Reason" (*Political Liberalism,* ch. 6, sec. 8), by which he seems to mean substantive limits on what kinds of considerations can properly be introduced into political disputations aiming at public justification. Cf. p. 247: "I have often referred to these limits. To this point they would appear to mean that, on fundamental political matters, reasons given explicitly in terms of comprehensive doctrines are never to be introduced into public reason."

20. "Kantian Constructivism in Moral Theory," p. 520.

21. Ackerman, "What Is Neutral about Neutrality?" p. 388.

22. *Equality and Partiality,* p. 36.

23. *Justice and Modern Moral Philosophy,* p. 36.

24. Brian Barry, *Theories of Justice,* p. 272.

25. "The Politics of Justification," p. 281.

26. Barry, *Theories of Justice,* p. 372.

27. Cf. Kenneth Baynes, *The Normative Grounds of Social Criticism,* p. 5: "For Kant, the 'principle of publicity' is introduced as a principle of practical reason that possesses a transcendental status. It functions primarily as a criterion or standard for assessing the legislation and public policies of the political sovereign." Cf. also David Ingram, "The Limits and Possibilities of Communicative Ethics for Democratic Theory," pp. 307–8.

28. *Liberal Virtues,* p. 191.

29. *A Theory of Freedom,* p. 2.

30. For Gauthier, cf. *Morals by Agreement,* pp. 145–46; for Buchanan and Gordon Tullock, cf. Michael Lessnoff, *Social Contract,* p. 125.

31. *A Theory of Justice,* pp. 175, 144.

32. Cf. Rawls, "Kantian Constructivism in Moral Theory," p. 528: "Fair terms of coop-eration articulate an idea of reciprocity and mutuality: all who cooperate must benefit, or share in common burdens. . . . This element in social cooperation I call the Reasonable. The other element corresponds to the Rational: it expresses a conception of each participant's rational advantage, what, as individuals, they are trying to advance." Of course, the distinc-tion may be slightly artificial. Rawls seems to think so. He says (*Political Liberalism,* p. 17, n. 18): "Barry thinks justice as fairness hovers uneasily between impartiality [the moralistic rationale] and mutual advantage [the realistic rationale], where Gibbard thinks it perches . . . on reciprocity. I think Gibbard is right about this."

33. *Theories of Justice,* p. 285.

34. *Morals by Agreement,* p. 7.

35. Cf. *Political Liberalism,* pp. 48–49, n. 1.

36. Cf. Hampshire, *Innocence and Experience,* p. 108: "Substantial conceptions of jus-tice and fairness . . . are derived from particular conceptions of the good . . . and convergence on universal agreement is not to be expected. Universal agreement can be expected, in the name of rationality, only on the methods of fair argument which will arbitrate between the different answers to these questions, where an answer is needed for public purposes and social arrangements."

37. Cf. Fishkin, *The Dialogue of Justice,* p. 127: "A related point which prevents the the-ory's requirements from becoming utopian is that whatever consensus is achieved need be only procedural. It may be consensus merely specifying agreement on how to disagree. . . ."

38. "Justice and the Aims of Political Philosophy," p. 775.

39. Cf. *A Theory of Justice,* sec. 2.

40. Cf. *A Theory of Justice,* p. 7: "Taken together as one scheme, the major institutions define men's rights and duties and influence their life-prospects, what they can expect to be and how well they can hope to do."

41. Rawls explicitly recognizes, and implicitly rejects, this strategy in a discussion of Baier's views. He says (*Political Liberalism,* p. 149): "[A]s Baier has suggested, a less deep consensus on the principles and rules of a workable political constitution may be sufficient for less demanding purposes and far easier to obtain. . . . So rather than supposing that con-sensus reaches down to a political conception covering principles for the whole of the basic structure, a consensus may cover only certain fundamental procedural political principles for the constitution."

42. Cf. Iris Marion Young, *Justice and the Politics of Difference,* p. 33: "[J]ustice names the perspectives, principles, and procedures for evaluating institutional norms and rules."

43. *Political Liberalism,* pp. 229–30.

44. *Political Liberalism,* p. 227.

45. "Justice and the Aims of Political Philosophy," p. 779.

46. *Political Liberalism,* p. 230.

47. *Political Liberalism,* p. 166.

48. Cf. *Political Liberalism,* ch. 4, sec. 2.

49. Of course, restriction to such a setting might not be necessary and is not necessary if certain very implausible claims are true. These claims might be called 'thick essentialism' and 'Socratism'. (On 'Socratism', cf. Rorty, *Objectivity, Relativism, and Truth,* p. 188, who characterizes it as the doctrine "that our essence is rational and that argument can eventually penetrate it.") According to essentialism, all human beings share certain essential characteris-tics, largely in the form of dispositions to think, feel, and act in particular ways in particular circumstances. According to thick essentialism, people share a great deal more than is usually thought. What they share, at least essentially, is more than enough, when this essence is real-

ized (as it will be if Socratism is true), to provide a basis, in these shared beliefs, desires, and dispositions, for the public justification of quite specific substantive arrangements and not merely an abstract system of procedural institutions.

50. Cf. Rawls, *A Theory of Justice,* pp. 197, 196, where he entertains the supposition that, with "the veil of ignorance . . . partially lifted," the parties to the original position "move to a constitutional convention . . . [where] they are to decide upon the justice of political forms and choose a constitution."

51. Dworkin, *Law's Empire,* p. 67.

52. Cf. the following. Raz, "Facing Diversity," p. 21: "Starting from different standpoints, all end up endorsing the same principles." Rawls, "The Idea of an Overlapping Consensus," p. 9: "Since different premises may lead to the same conclusions, we simply suppose that the essential elements of the political conception . . . are theorems, as it were, at which the comprehensive doctrines in the consensus intersect or converge." Rawls, "Justice as Fairness," p. 247: "We might say that they recognize its concepts, principles, and virtues as theorems, at it were, at which their several views coincide." Nagel, *Equality and Partiality,* p. 38: "Legitimacy is the result of a convergence from different perspectives on a single arrangement. . . ." Dryzek, *Discursive Democracy,* pp. 16–17: "[C]onsensus on what is desirable . . . is possible in the absence of a shared commitment to the ultimate reasons why it is desirable."

53. "Moral Conflict and Political Legitimacy," p. 218.

54. Cf. Nagel, "Moral Conflict and Political Legitimacy," p. 218: "A convergence theory may begin from motives that differ widely from person to person, or it may begin from a single type of motive, like self-interest, which differs from person to person only because it is self-referential."

55. "Contractualism and Utilitarianism," p. 110. Cf. Nagel, *Equality and Partiality,* p. 38: "Legitimacy is the result of a convergence from different perspectives on a single arrangement as satisfying the condition of nonrejectability for each of them."

56. Cf. *The Open Society and Its Enemies,* vol. 1, pp. 158–59.

57. *Pluralism,* p. 189.

58. This distinction is not quite the same distinction as Michael Sandel's. Referring to Rawls's notion of original position argumentation, he says (*Liberalism and the Limits of Justice,* p. 121): "Once we imagine the parties to the original position seeking principles of justice, we can similarly conceive two possible accounts of justification, a voluntarist account in which the parties arrive at the principles through an act of choice or agreement, and a cognitive account in which the parties arrive at the principles through an act of discovery or collective insight."

59. "Public Justification and Democratic Adjudication," p. 255.

60. The notion of 'direction of fit' has been identified as a basis for distinguishing between beliefs and desires as different kinds of reasons that might figure in the justification of ethical and political norms. Cf. Platts, *Ways of Meaning,* pp. 256–57 and David McNaughton, *Moral Vision,* p. 107.

61. Cf. Martin Hollis, *The Cunning of Reason,* p. 75: "'[T]he truth of the sentence [A has reason to φ] implies, very roughly, that A has some motive which will be furthered by his φ-ing.'"

62. Cf. Michael Smith, "The Humean Theory of Motivation," for an account of 'quasi-beliefs' that seem to have both 'directions of fit'.

63. Cf. Benn and Gaus, "Practical Rationality and Commitment."

64. Cf. Rawls, "Kantian Constructivism in Moral Theory," p. 530: "The way the Reasonable is represented in the original position leads to the two principles of justice."

65. Cf. Fishkin, *The Dialogue of Justice,* p. 50: "When the motivation for choosing principles has been altered or filtered in the interests of impartiality, I will classify it as 'refined';

when people choose, or are imagined to choose, with unaltered motivation . . . I will classify those motivations as 'brute.'" Closely related to this distinction is Williams's distinction between R's being a reason that can be given to A to find some particular regime a reasonable regime (the direct reading) and R's being a reason for A to find that regime a reasonable regime that couldn't, however be given to A (the indirect reading). (*Ethics and the Limits of Philosophy,* p. 40. Cf. Hollis, *The Cunning of Reason,* p. 75.)

66. "The Moral Legislature," p. 303.

67. *Equality and Partiality,* pp. 33–34.

68. *Situating the Self,* pp. 152–53.

69. "Philosophy," p. 166.

70. Cf. Chandran Kukathas and Philip Pettit, *Rawls: A Theory of Justice and Its Critics,* p. 32: "The economic way is for each to calculate what best suits his own interests and then to try to get this. . . . The political way is for the parties to put aside their own particular interests and to debate about the arrangement that best answers to such considerations . . . as all can equally countenance as relevant." Cf. Raz, *The Morality of Freedom,* p. 80 and Barry, *Political Argument,* p. 80.

71. *Equality and Partiality,* pp. 33–34. Jon Elster draws a distinction between the 'market' and the 'forum' as models for political activity. Adopting the market model, we are committed to discovering the "optimal compromise between given, and irreducibly opposed, private interests." Adopting the forum model, we are committed, on the contrary, to "engaging in public debate with a view to the emergence of a consensus." ("The Market and the Forum," p. 103.) Also of relevance here is Habermas's distinction between strategic action and communicative action. In the market, stability is achieved strategically because or to the extent that individuals' "egocentric utilities mesh." In the forum, resolution of conflict is achieved via the dialogically mediated formation of consensus. (*Moral Consciousness and Communicative Action,* p. 133.)

72. *The Essentials of Democracy,* p. 29.

73. "Moral Pluralism and Political Consensus," p. 16.

74. Cf. Benhabib, *Situating the Self,* p. 163: "In Kantian moral theory, moral agents are like geometricians in different rooms who, reasoning alone for themselves, all arrive at the same solution to a problem."

75. *Rawls: A Theory of Justice and Its Critics,* pp. 33–34. Cf. Pettit, "Habermas on Truth and Justice," p. 215.

4

Some Conceptions of
Public Justification

It will be helpful, in order to consolidate the largely taxonomic work of the previous chapter, to consider some concrete exemplars of the concept of public justification — some conceptions of this concept. I will therefore first give some brief descriptions of the conceptions of a number of important contemporary theorists and then, in each case, try to locate the conception in terms of the various dimensions that I have just identified. It will transpire that these dimensions are not neutral or inert from an ethico-political point of view. (See sec. 20.) We can therefore expect one of the polar types to have characteristics that differ from those of the other such type and in ways that are significant from the point of view of the project of public justification. The taxonomic work of this chapter will thus provide a basis for discovering, in Chapter 6, how these various conceptions fare with respect to the ideal of public justification.

10. Rawls's Conception

Pride of place must go to Rawls. It is his work that has brought to the fore the idea of public justification. Consider his model of reflective deliberation. On this account, each of the parties to the project of public justification must be shown that she has reason to accept, as a basis for the construction of fair principles of social cooperation, a particular description of an 'initial situation' for the choice of such principles and therefore to accept the principles chosen in that situation. Rawls says:

> [T]he question of justification is settled by working out a problem of deliberation: we have to ascertain which principles it would be rational to adopt given the contractual situation. . . .
>
> But how are we to decide what is the most favored interpretation [of this situation]? I assume, for one thing, that there is a broad measure of agreement that principles of justice should be chosen under certain conditions. To justify a particular description of the initial situation one shows that it incorporates these widely shared assumptions.[1]

Rawls's conception of public justification involves both convergence and consensus. It involves convergence *on* a particular account of fair conditions for the choice of normative principles *from* diverse points of view (in the form of reasonable comprehensive doctrines). As Rawls says, "[P]olitical liberalism looks for a political conception of justice that we hope can gain the support of an overlapping consensus of reasonable religious, philosophical, and moral doctrines. . . ."[2] It involves consensus *about* these conditions and the derivation from them of the particular normative principles that are fit to play the role of justice for the individuals involved.

This conception involves both direct and indirect modes of justification, with a direct appeal to what we ourselves think about the conditions that are fair for the identification of normative principles ("the conditions embodied in the description of this situation are ones that we do in fact accept"[3]) and then, indirectly, the laying out of a situation of choice in which these conditions are embodied and with respect to which the principles themselves are derived or constructed.[4]

This conception involves both economic and political modes of justification, one embedded within the other.[5] On the one hand, individuals reason directly from the various comprehensive ethical doctrines that they accept and thus identify a basis for determining substantive issues that would be fair to all. On the other hand, surrogates for these individuals reason economically about the interests of the individuals they represent, within such a framework of fairness. As Rawls says:

> While the original position as a whole represents both moral powers [for rationality and for reasonableness], . . . the parties as rationally autonomous representatives of persons in society represent only the rational: the parties agree to those principles which they believe are best for those they represent as seen from these persons' conception of the good. . . . The reasonable . . . [on the other hand] is represented by the various restrictions to which the parties are subject in the original position and by the conditions imposed on their agreement.[6]

This conception may well involve both prior and posterior modes of justification. Rawls's test of stability is precisely the question "Would individuals living in a regime regulated by these principles be able to honor them freely and to accept their burdens (and benefits) willingly?" — clearly a posterior test of validity. On the other hand, justification of the framework of fairness involves reliance on the comprehensive doctrines that concrete individuals actually already have.

Again, Rawls's conception has both interactive and non-interactive elements.[7] At the stage when surrogates reason economically on behalf of concrete individuals, the mode of justification involves no interaction between the surrogates. Their superficial plurality is purely heuristic since each will reason just as all the others do. As Rawls says, "[S]ince the differences among the parties are unknown to them, and everyone is equally rational and similarly situated, each is convinced by the same arguments . . . [and] we can view the choice in the original position from the standpoint of one person selected at random."[8] On the other hand, at the stage when concrete individuals lay out the framework of fairness within which their surrogates subsequently deliberate, there is at least some point to their interaction. Presumably only actual conversation and/or disputation will establish a relevant point of convergence among the various comprehensive doctrines that they endorse. Such an understanding is implied by what Rawls says about political controversy.

> There are periods, sometimes long periods, in the history of any society during which certain fundamental questions give rise to sharp and divisive political controversy, and it seems difficult, if not impossible, to find any shared basis of political agreement. . . . One task of political philosophy in a democratic society is to focus on such questions and to examine whether some underlying basis of agreement can be uncovered and a mutually acceptable way of resolving these questions publicly established.[9]

This conception, despite its embedded and embedding elements, seems to be purely volitional, however. The surrogates try to satisfy the desire to maximize the total of social primary goods that the individuals they represent can count on receiving.[10] The framework of fairness within which their deliberations take place is constructed to reflect the desire of concrete individuals that they behave in a reasonable way.[11]

Finally, this conception does seem to be unequivocally a positive one. Both individuals and their surrogates have reason to accept, respectively, (a) the framework of fairness and (b) the normative principles constructed within this framework.

Summing up, we can characterize Rawls's approach as follows

Cs/Cv	+/-	Vol/Cog	Dir/InDir	Ec/Pol	Pr/Post	Int/Non-Int
both (Cv)	+	Vol	both (Dir)	both (Pol)	both	both (Int)

(Where I have indicated, for instance, that Rawls's method is both interactive and non-interactive, my parenthetical emphasis on its interactive character is meant to signal that this characteristic is exhibited by the 'embedding' framework, i.e., the framework that establishes the fundamental character of the method.)

11.   Gauthier's Conception

Gauthier's approach to public justification is best described, in line with his own terminology, in terms of bargaining. According to Gauthier, each member of a community must be shown that there are principles of social interaction whose acceptance facilitates the realization of that individual's (agent-relative) desires. For A, that the satisfaction of his preferences will be facilitated by the joint acceptance of these principles, for B that the satisfaction of her preferences will be facilitated by the joint acceptance of these principles, and so on. Gauthier says:

> Rational persons, faced with the costs of natural or market interaction in the face of externalities, agree to a different, cooperative mode of interaction. They agree to act, not on the basis of individual utility-maximization, but rather on the basis of optimization, where the optimal outcome is determined by the principle of minimax relative concession. In reaching this agreement, of course, each seeks to maximize his own utility.[12]

Gauthier's approach is oriented to attaining convergence rather than relying on some antecedent consensus. He begins "from individuals choosing, each from his own perspective, principles for social interaction — principles which will of course reflect the chooser's concern to maximize his own utility."[13]

Gauthier's approach involves direct rather than indirect modes of justification. He says:

> Each human being is an actor with certain preferences and certain physical and mental capacities which, in the absence of her fellows, she naturally directs to the fulfilment of her preferences. This provides a basis, in no way arbitrary, from which we may examine and assess interaction, introducing such conceptions as bettering and worsening. A principle that abstracted from this basis would not relate to human beings as actors. A principle that did not take this basis as normatively fundamental would not relate impartially to human beings as actors.[14]

Gauthier's approach also involves both prior and posterior modes of justification. Indeed, much of the argument in *Morals by Agreement* is devoted to meeting a challenge, that "the step from hypothetical agreement *ex ante* on a set of social arrangements to *ex post* adherence may no longer seem straightforward."[15] While "[m]oral principles are introduced as the objects of fully voluntary *ex ante* agreement among rational persons," "it may be that the very characteristics of human nature that enter into the grounding of these constraints . . . serve also to undermine the conditions under which compliance with them would be rational." For this reason it is necessary to establish that "[p]eople come to take an interest in their fellows because they recognize their mutual willingness not to take advantage of each other, and to share jointly produced benefits on a shared basis."[16] In other words, individuals living according to principles that would be agreed to by constrained maximizers will come to value constrained maximization for the benefits it makes possible and so will accept these constraints, and thus retrospectively validate the principles that would have been agreed to *ex ante*.

Gauthier's approach involves economic rather than political reasoning. As he says, "[M]orality . . . emerges quite simply from the application of the maximizing conception of rationality to certain structures of interaction." This approach is explicitly contrasted with what is arguably a 'political' conception of rationality, according to which "what makes it rational to satisfy an interest does not depend on whose interest it is. . . ."[17]

Gauthier's approach is interactive rather than non-interactive, depending, as it does, on the bargains, struck according to the principle of minimax relative concession, that relevant individuals enter into. According to Gauthier, "Through bargaining, individuals arrive at a basis for co-operative interaction that enables them to relate costs and benefits. . . ."[18] As Kukathas and Pettit say, "In Gauthier's picture the parties are involved in a process of economic negotiation with one another, each seeking to drive the best bargain they can get."[19]

Gauthier's approach is volitional rather than cognitional. According to Gauthier, "A just society is concerned only to enable each person to realize the greatest amount of her good, on terms acceptable to all."[20]

Gauthier's approach is arguably negative rather than positive. The particular principles of interaction he imagines agents agreeing on seem to be objects of agreement because no one has any reason to reject them. It may be that individuals have positive reason, in the existence of a cooperative surplus,[21] to agree to *some* principles of cooperative interaction. What is not clear is the basis of their joint determination to act on particular principles of cooperative interaction. There is evidence, however, supporting the interpretation offered here — namely, that the parties lack reasons to reject these principles rather than having reasons to accept them. Gauthier says:

> Each person expects that what he gets will be related to what he claims. Each wants to get as much as possible; each therefore claims as much as possible. But in deciding how much is possible, each is constrained by the recognition that he must neither drive others away from the bargaining table, nor be excluded by them. . . . Since one wants to benefit from a share of the cooperative surplus, one has no interest in causing the process of bargaining to fail, as its failure would result in non-co-operation and so no surplus.[22]

The basic idea seems to be that the bargaining equilibrium, and with it the principles agreed to, is the point at which no person has any reason to reject the share she is assigned by these principles.

Summing up, we can characterize Gauthier's approach as follows.

Cs/Cv	+/−	Vol/Cog	Dir/InDir	Ec/Pol	Pr/Post	Int/Non-Int
Cv	−	Vol	Dir	Ec	both	Int

12. Ackerman's Conception

Ackerman's approach to public justification is a conversational one, but it needs to be approached with some care. As with Rawls, there are two justificatory 'layers' in play in Ackerman's model. First, we have 'embedded' *political*-conversational argumentation intended to determine the legitimacy of particular regimes.[23] Second, we also have 'embedding' *philosophical*-conversational argumentation intended to demonstrate the legitimacy of those constraints on political-conversational argumentation that give it its 'bite'. Ackerman says:

> The task of *political* conversation is to make it possible for each citizen to defend his power without declaring himself intrinsically superior to any other citizen. The task of *philosophical* conversation is to make it possible for a person to reason his way to Neutrality without declaring that the path he has chosen is intrinsically better than any other route to liberalism.[24]

The 'embedding' argumentation justifies the style of reasoning employed in the 'embedded' justificatory story.

Given these provisos, the basic idea behind this approach is simple enough. Each of the parties to the project of public justification must be shown that she has beliefs, possibly different beliefs, that preclude her rejection of those principles of Neutral Dialogue that she uses, in turn, to determine the legitimacy of regimes.

Ackerman's approach involves convergence from different starting points rather than antecedent consensus from some common standpoint. He says: "Liberalism does not depend on the truth of any single metaphysical or epistemological system. Instead, liberalism's ultimate justification is to be found in its strategic location in a web of talk that converges upon it from every direction."[25] Indeed, this is true both of the embedding argumentation, as indicated in the passage just quoted,[26] and in the embedded argumentation, in which the liberal principle of dialogical Neutrality constrains but does not uniquely determine the argumentative pathways that can be used in the assessment of concrete institutions and practices. As Ackerman says, "While the constraints of Neutrality are broad, they may nonetheless permit more than one [kind of reason] *R* to break the conversational barrier."[27]

Ackerman's conception of public justification invokes a negative criterion of reasonable rejectability, especially in relation to the 'embedding' and therefore fundamental 'layer' of argumentation. According to Ackerman, justification of Neutral Dialogue proceeds by trying to defeat the reasons people might invoke for rejecting it. He says: "Once you verbalize the reasons you are troubled, perhaps I can show you that they are not as persuasive as you might have thought: *that even within your own view of the world,* you should find ultimately unpersuasive the reasons you can give for your initial disquiet."[28] Indeed, Ackerman sees considerable advantage in such a test. It requires that individuals defeat not some one particular argument for Neutral Dialogue but, in fact, a whole range of partially independent arguments. He says:

> [L]iberalism's ultimate justification is to be found in its strategic location in a web of talk that converges on it from every direction. Each strand is itself sufficient to support a reasoned belief in Neutrality; yet to cut oneself off from a single strand hardly liberates from the web of belief. Instead, you must keep on hacking for a very long time before you can cut your way to freedom.[29]

Ackerman's approach involves an appeal to beliefs rather than desires and is thus cognitional in character. For instance, the beliefs that power corrupts, that critical examination of ethical propositions is a necessary preliminary to their acceptance as a basis for action, that the autonomy of persons is valuable, and that there are reasonable grounds for skepticism about the existence and/or accessibility of any transcendent reality — these beliefs, according to Ackerman, are among the main reasons why individuals will not reject the demands of Neutral Dialogue.[30]

Ackerman's approach is political rather than economic. It is not clear that his arguments satisfy some narrow definition of political argumentation, one that demands that "people should . . . seek to find a basis of agreement that is acceptable from all points of view. . . ."[31] In particular, the multistranded character of the 'embedding' argumentation is advocated precisely because it does not seek to reduce the discussion of matters at issue to some 'lowest common denominator'.[32] The arguments he appeals to nevertheless make no reference to individuals' interests or desires for social primary goods, and thus they are broadly political rather than in any sense economic.

Ackerman's approach is interactive rather than non-interactive. In relation to the 'embedding' argumentation that is intended to establish the legitimacy of Neutral Dialogue, Ackerman says of his own multistranded argument that it is not meant to offer "the last word in the vindication of liberalism." He continues:

> To the contrary, it is the first move in an ongoing dialogue with the reader. The aim is to provoke dialectical engagement and response — if the reader will explain why he finds each of the four arguments unpersuasive, these reactions may provide grist for the further dialogic defense of Neutrality; and on and on so long as the questioner finds further dialogue necessary to resolve his doubts about liberalism.[33]

Arguably, Ackerman's approach involves posterior rather than prior modes of justification. This emerges most clearly in his discussion of 'intuitionism,' by which he refers to techniques that depend on an appeal to our 'intuitive' sense of what is right or wrong, valid or invalid, legitimate or illegitimate. According to Ackerman, "[T]he intuitionist cannot cope with the charge that his very intuitions have been tainted by unjust social structures."[34] And Ackerman recommends, as an antidote, that "no exercise in reflective equilibrium can be complete until the legitimacy of *each and every* intuition is vindicated through dialogue."[35] But in this case, Neutral Dialogue is legitimated if there are strands of argumentation supporting it that survive conversational testing in a regime regulated by it. The test, in other words, is posterior, not prior acceptability.

Ackerman's approach involves direct rather than indirect modes of justification.[36] Addressing both the 'ideal spectator' theorist and the Rawlsian contractarian, he complains that "[t]he root of the problem [with these approaches] is the wrongfulness involved in requiring citizens to affirm the value of any particular exercise in transcendence as a necessary condition for discursive participation."[37] He explicitly contrasts Habermas's indirect appeal to consensus in an ideal speech situation to his own approach, grounded in the attitudes, attributes, and powers of concrete, historically situated individuals. He says of the citizens of a liberal society: "Instead of looking to ultimate conversational victory in some far-distant ideal speech situation, their energies are focused on the formidable task of governing *this* world through a political dialogue that does not require participants to renounce publicly their deepest moral beliefs."[38]

In summary, Ackerman's approach is as follows.

Cs/Cv	+/−	Vol/Cog	Dir/InDir	Ec/Pol	Pr/Post	Int/Non-Int
Cv	−	Cog	Dir	Pol	Post	Int

13. A 'Utilitarian' Conception

Less familiar in the contemporary context, but still of considerable interest, is a broadly 'utilitarian' conception of public justification associated, in particular, with the work of John Harsanyi. (Harsanyi was not explicitly concerned with the problem of public justification, so some reconstruction is involved in my presentation. It is not really his position that is described, but one derived from it.)

By implication, public justification of some particular decision is achieved, on such an account, when there is agreement among utility-maximizing individuals in their evaluations, absent knowledge of their own personal identities, of an additive social welfare function that takes as inputs their subjective assessments of "the consequences of . . . [that] decision on other individuals."[39] To evaluate this function, each individual "must make interpersonal comparisons of utility, which he does through a process of imaginative empathy that involves imaginatively putting himself into the objective and subjective positions of other people."[40] The individual does this on the assumption — which embodies "the thinnest possible veil [of ignorance] consistent with ensuring impartiality"[41] — that "he has an equal probability of being any other [individual] in the society." He will then rank alternative decisions "according to the arithmetic mean of the utility levels that the individual members of society would enjoy" were these decisions implemented.[42] "For there is only one principle that will maximize the expected utility of the person one turns out to be, given that one has an equal chance of being anyone, and that is the principle of maximizing the average utility of all the people concerned."[43] The reasoning, in Rawls's formulation, is obvious:

> He assumes that there is an equal likelihood of his turning out to be anyone, fully endowed with that person's preferences, abilities, and social position. Once again his prospect is highest for that society with the greatest average utility. We can see this in the following way. Let n be the number of persons in society. Let their levels of well-being be $u_1, u_2, \ldots, u_n$. Then the total utility is Σu_i and the average is $\Sigma u_i/n$. Assuming that one has an equal chance of being any person, one's prospect is $1/n \ u_1 + 1/n \ u_2 + \ldots + 1/n \ u_n$ or $\Sigma u_i/n$. The value of the prospect is identical with the average utility.[44]

In practice, since the social welfare function, call it W, "is a subjective W in the mind of an individual," it might seem that "[a] collective W need not exist" and hence that no publicly justified system of social arrangements could in fact be identified. "If individuals differ in their subjective evaluations there will be different Ws for different individuals"[45] and, therefore, divergent characterizations of the system of subjectively justified social arrangements and, therefore, no publicly justified system.

In particular, different individuals engaged in the evaluation of the social welfare function may have different attitudes to risk. Since this function "does not allow for differences in risk aversion among the impartial observers," their evaluations of this function will differ and "unanimous agreement on the social welfare function will not be possible."[46] Ideally, however, such divergence will not arise: "the true extended preference orderings of all persons must coincide."[47] If A and B differently evaluate W on account of A's greater risk-aversion, or B's lesser, then we must suppose that this fact, so far *external* to W, can itself be incorporated in some way *into* W, so that, when A and B evaluate the resultant function W', which includes information about their differences in evaluating W, each will now evaluate W' in the same way.[48] On the assumption that this information *ought* to be included in any adequate social welfare function,[49] unanimity is now ensured and on an ethically sound basis.

Arguably, this 'utilitarian' conception involves an appeal to a common standpoint (a consensus) rather than to convergence from diverse starting points. This is evident in relation to the idea that, when all relevant factors are 'incorporated' into an 'amplified' social welfare function, each individual has the same basis for decision and so draws the same conclusions as every other individual. As Hurley puts it, "since all differentiating features of agents have been extracted from the subjects of extended preference and incorporated into the contents of extended preference, the extended preferences of all subjects must coincide. . . ."[50]

This conception involves an appeal to individuals' positive reasons for acceptance, not to the absence of reasons for rejection. In particular, any given individual will find reasonable that social system in which average utility is maximized. This is so because, in that system, her expected utility is maximized (relative to other systems and on the assumption that she does not know, antecedently, 'who' she is).

This conception involves an appeal to desires, not, at least not primarily, to beliefs. It is the individual's desire to maximize her expected utility that provokes her acceptance of that system in which average utility is maximized. "By choosing [that system] . . . the parties maximize their expected well-being as seen from [the] . . . point of view" defined by Harsanyi's 'veil of ignorance'.[51] To be sure, individuals' beliefs play some role in the implementation of this method, in particular, their beliefs about other individuals' preferences. As Dennis Mueller says, the application of the method depends on "individuals obtaining sufficient information about the positions and psychology of other individuals to allow them to engage in the interpersonal comparisons inherent in the approach."[52] Nevertheless, these beliefs serve only to orient the individual's otherwise indeterminate desire to do as well as she can for herself, subject to the fact that she "does not have knowledge of personal identity."[53]

Arguably, this mode of public justification involves an indirect rather than a direct appeal to the individuals who are party to it. Certainly, actual individuals are not subject to the restrictions on information about personal identity to which Harsanyi's parties are subject and so cannot be counted on to be impartial in the relevant way; "[t]hat one arrangement will be more favorable to me and another more favorable to you should not [but will in reality] make me more likely to support the first and you the second."[54]

This mode of justification employs both economic and political considerations. On the one hand, consider the party evaluating the preferences of all the various individuals whom she might turn out to be. This individual's reasoning is that of the utility-maximizer and so is entirely in the spirit of economic argumentation, where rational self-interest is to the fore. On the other hand, consider the fact that the party's reasoning is subject to the constraint that she does not know 'who' she is, that is, she cannot tell which bundle of burdens and benefits she will receive if some particular social arrangement is implemented. As in the case of the Rawlsian veil, this condition *on* her reasoning represents the demand that she "take everyone's point of view into account along with [her] . . . own."[55] It thus marks the presence of political considerations in the 'embedding' argumentation.

This method involves prior rather than posterior justification. This comes out most clearly in Rawls's characterization, which depends, in turn, on William Vickrey's presentation. Rawls asks us to "[i]magine a situation in which a single rational individual can choose which of several societies to enter."[56] This individual's problem, clearly, is to choose that society in which her expectation of utility is maximized relative to already existing preferences. Her decision problem is not to decide whether the preferences that she would have were she a member of some particular society would be maximally satisfied — the posterior reading. Her problem is, instead, to decide whether the preferences that she now actually has would be maximally satisfied—the prior reading: "the utility functions are evaluated using each individual's own subjective preferences."[57] (Actually, things are a bit more complicated. She's really looking for that society in which 'her' *extended* preferences are maximally satisfied and is doing so in order to ensure the maximal satisfaction of her *particular* preferences. But even in relation to these so-called extended preferences, it is the preferences 'she has' now that count, not the ones 'she would have' were she to be a member of that society.[58])

Finally, the 'utilitarian' method is necessarily non-interactive. If each individual takes up the contemplation of one and the same set of extended preferences and selects that social system in which her prospects are maximized, then she does so non-interactively, given her identity with every other such individual. Interaction between identical beings is otiose; they have nothing to contribute to one another's understanding of their problem.

Summing up, then, we can characterize a 'utilitarian' conception, schematically, as follows.

Cs/Cv	+/−	Vol/Cog	Dir/InDir	Ec/Pol	Pr/Post	Int/Non-Int
Cs	+	Vol	InDir	both	Pr	Non-Int

14. Habermas's Conception

Of special interest, perhaps, is a conception of public justification associated with Jürgen Habermas. Although Habermas in fact draws heavily on the work of many Anglo-American philosophers, especially philosophers of language, his work is sui generis with respect to the broader tradition, in America and Britain, of liberal political theorizing. The work of Rawls, for instance, seems to have influenced Habermas only indirectly, through the appropriation of Rawlsian ideas by Lawrence Kohlberg, whose work Habermas does indeed draw on heavily. It is striking, in light of the very considerable independence of Habermas's ideas from those of other important theorists, how similar his thinking seems to be to theirs. (Striking, but not inexplicably so. Both Habermas and Rawls are 'Kantians'.)

Habermas clearly announces his orientation to a project of public justification:

> [I]f the course of action which needs justification is collective in nature, the members of the collectivity must reach a common decision. They have to try to persuade one another that it is in the interest of each that all shall act as they intend. In the process, one will cite to another the reasons he has for willing that an action be declared socially binding. Each member must be convinced that the proposed norm is equally good for all. . . . Any norm that is put into effect via this route can be called justified because the fact that the decision is reached through a process of argumentation indicates that the norm deserves to be called equally good for all.[59]

The Habermasian conception employs interactive rather than non-interactive modes of reasoning. Habermas says that "the justification of norms and commands requires that a real discourse be carried out and thus cannot occur in a strictly monological form, i.e., in the form of a hypothetical process of argumentation occurring in the individual mind."[60]

The Habermasian conception embodies political rather than economic reasoning.[61] This comes out very clearly when he distinguishes his approach from the otherwise rather similar approach of Ernst Tugendhat: "Tugendhat confounds the conditions necessary for the discursive generation of a rationally motivated consensus with the conditions necessary for negotiating a fair compromise." Rejecting the latter as an adequate explication of the idea of justification, Habermas insists that "[p]articipants in a practical discourse strive to clarify a common interest, whereas in negotiating a compromise they try to strike a balance between conflicting particular interests."[62] Since the common interests alluded to here "are those interests that all participants in a practical discourse could accept with good reasons,"[63] this model is political in the sense of Kukathas and Pettit—namely, "[t]he political way is for the parties to put aside their own particular interests and debate about the arrangement that best answers to such considerations . . . as all can equally countenance as relevant."[64]

Arguably, Habermas's conception involves indirect rather than direct modes of argumentation. On the one hand, while Habermas objects to the Rawlsian procedure of original position argumentation, his target here clearly is its 'monological' rather than its hypothetical character. He says: "Rawls operationalizes the standpoint of impartiality in such a way that every individual can undertake to justify basic norms on his own."[65] On the other hand, Habermas seems to reject reliance on individuals' actual attitudes as a basis for justification:

> A norm has binding character—therein consists its validity claim. But if only empirical motives (such as inclinations, interests, and fear of sanctions) sustain the agreement [to accept the norm], it is impossible to see why a party to the contract should continue to feel bound to the norms when his original motives change. . . . From this reflection, it follows that we cannot explain the validity claim of norms without rationally motivated agreement or at least to the conviction that consensus on a recommended norm could be brought about *with reasons*.[66]

It is not concrete individuals, situated and motivated as they actually are, who decide on the validity of norms. It is, instead, these individuals, situated in a setting "that is removed from contexts of experience and action" and where "all motives except that of the cooperative search for truth are excluded" who decide, consensually, on the validity of disputed norms.[67] As Ronald Beiner says:

> We determine whether judgments are valid, according to Habermas, by asking ourselves what we would rationally agree to in a counterfactual situation of undistorted communication and discourse ideally free of power relations. By projecting ourselves into this ideal space of pure rational dialogue, we win the vantage point for securing the validity of our normative judgments.[68]

Habermas's conception is grounded in the possibility of discovering consensus among participants in justificatory discourse rather than achieving a convergence from diverse points of view. This is already implicit in his rejection of Tugendhat's search for a certain kind of compromise, and it comes out quite clearly in the idea that someone who defends some normative claim is "obligated to show that the interests underlying it are generalizable rather than merely particular,"[69] or in the idea that "proponents and opponents engage in a *competition with arguments* in order to convince one another, that is, in order to reach a consensus,"[70] but perhaps most clearly in the idea that "[i]nsofar as norms express generalizable interests, they are based on a *rational consensus.* . . ."[71]

With respect to the distinction between cognitions and volitions, the status of Habermas's method is somewhat equivocal. On the one hand, he is concerned to establish the cognitive status of normative claims. This comes out clearly in his sustained attempt to show that "normative claims to validity have cognitive meaning and can be treated *like* claims to truth."[72] Furthermore, he seems keen to establish the fundamentally cognitive orientation of his approach to the justification of these claims:

> The cognitive component of norms is, thus, not limited to the propositional content of the normed behavioral expectations. The normative-validity claim is itself cognitive in the sense that it could be discursively redeemed — that is, grounded in consensus of the participants through argumentation.[73]

The idea here seems to be that it is the fact that the normative claim could be "discursively redeemed" that is the 'truth-maker' for that claim. On the other hand, it is clear that lying behind any successful attempt at 'discursive redemption' is the discovery of what Habermas calls "generalizable interests," which are clearly 'desire-like' attitudes. He says, for instance:

> It follows from the aforementioned rules of discourse that a contested norm cannot meet with the consent of the participants in a practical discourse unless (U) holds, that is,
>
> Unless all affected can *freely* accept the consequences and the side effects that the *general* observance of a controversial norm can be expected to have *for the satisfaction of the interests of each individual.*[74]

To speak of the satisfaction of interests, even of "generalizable interests," is to invoke attitudes that are more desire- than belief-like in character. And since we here reach the ultimate substantive basis of justification, it is thus surely right to classify this approach as fundamentally volitional.

Habermas's approach involves a positive appeal to reasons for acceptance rather than a negative appeal to the absence of reasons for rejection. This is already clear and explicit in his characterization of the universalization principle that governs discourse about normative claims: "Unless all affected can freely *accept* the consequences and the side effects that the general observance of a controversial norm can be expected to have *for the satisfaction of the interests of* each individual."[75]

Habermas's approach involves an appeal to individuals' posterior, not their prior, grounds for acceptance. This is already implicit in the idea that it is agreement in an 'ideal speech situation' that constitutes the grounds of validity for normative principles of action. It is by reference to the 'generalizable interests' that *emerge from* the process of discursive criticism that particular normative principles are justified, not to the concrete motives that they *bring into* the argumentative discourse.[76]

Summarizing, we can schematize the Habermasian approach as follows.

Cs/Cv	+/−	Vol/Cog	Dir/InDir	Ec/Pol	Pr/Post	Int/Non-Int
Cs	+	Vol?	InDir?	Pol	Post	Int

15. Gaus's Conception

Gaus's approach provides an informative contrast to other approaches in the broadly liberal tradition. For one thing, Gaus shares Gauthier's insistence on convergence rather than consensus and on compromise as a fundamental element of justification. Like Rawls, however, he rejects the idea that a compromise position should reflect the relative bargaining powers of the individual parties. On Gaus's account, only 'fair' bargains are the objects of publicly justified compromises. Like Rawls, Gaus also insists on the role of non-teleological reasoning in the project of public justification and identifies certain constraints on the teleological pursuit of value with principles that "are accepted by all . . . because everyone shares the convictions that the principles articulate."[77] According to Gaus, public justification is therefore twofold:

> It would seem that an adequate contractualism will employ both types of arguments. . . . Some set of principles can be justified to all on the grounds that (i) they articulate our basic shared intuitions and convictions and (ii) they reasonably advance the values of each.[78]

Gaus's approach involves indirect rather than direct appeals to the motives of concrete, historically situated individuals. He says: "[M]y concern here is to justify moral principles simply in the sense of showing that rational moral agents are committed to them . . . not that all others can be persuaded that they are so committed and will act accordingly."[79] Or, as he says elsewhere, "The aim of public justification is to provide everyone with good reasons for embracing principles and policies, it does not require that everyone actually accepts them."[80]

Gaus's approach is oriented both to convergence from disparate perspectives and to consensus on certain fundamentals. In regard to the first point, which involves 'teleological' reasoning, he says, for instance:

> Let us call such a contractualist justification a constrained teleology: it is teleological insofar as the justification shows that the good (or value) is advanced, but the teleological nature of the argument is constrained because what is of value differs from person to person, and the justification must show that an arrangement advances what is of value from each of these perspectives.[81]

In regard to the second point, he says: "To publicly justify a moral principle deontologically is to show that . . . each person is rationally committed to acknowledging this principle because it is foundational of his evaluational perspective."[82]

On the issue of economic versus political reasoning, Gaus's methodology is harder to characterize in a straightforward way. While he rejects the idea that social arrangements are publicly justified if "they provide each citizen a fair opportunity to advance his interests" and embraces the idea that the "contractual pact . . . articulates *a substantive and moral bargain*," his characterization of the pact is not obviously political in the sense that Kukathas and Pettit have in mind. At least on one reading, I find that Gaus does not call on those who are party to this pact to advance or consider only "such considerations . . . as all can equally countenance as relevant."[83] Indeed, this would be impossible, on Gaus's account. According to Gaus, "[w]e each have different notions of the good" and thus cannot be expected to share (all) the values of our fellows.[84] Instead, he suggests that it is reasonable to require that the pact "be understood as a fair bargain about the division of the fruits of social life . . . or a reasonable compromise that advances the values of everyone . . . ,"[85] even if the values of one will not be shared by others. As Gaus says, "His teleological justification is thus formally constrained by the need to appeal to considerations that are not, from his point of view, values."[86] The idea here seems to be that we need to distinguish those 'compromises' that simply reflect the relative bargaining power of individuals from those that are 'fair' in a moral sense. In this extended sense, Gaus's account is political rather than economic. On his account, the parties to the justificatory project cannot reasonably *seek*, let alone hope to attain, the maximization of their individual interests. He says: "[E]ach will gain (in terms of the promotion of his values), but the extent of gain is constrained by the need to elicit the agreement of others."[87]

Arguably and if so perhaps ironically, Gaus's method is non-interactive rather than interactive. Two points are relevant here. (1) Deontological aspects of Gaus's procedure depend on his analysis of what the non-psychopathic individual is committed to insofar as she has a rational value system—namely, that others are moral agents and that she is too, and so is committed to acting as such.[88] (2) The (constrainedly) teleological aspects of Gaus's procedure involve deriving the "median position result"—namely, that "minimax relative concession will pick out the median point as the rational compromise solution" between ideologically opposed rational (and hence deontologically constrained) individuals,[89] a result that is apparently quite independent of and indeed does not require (or perhaps even permit) any actual negotiation between affected individuals. (See Gaus's insistence that "in a large and diverse society," "no person actually needs to make any calculations," let alone engage in any negotiations, in order to obtain this result.[90])

Gaus's approach involves both cognitional and volitional elements. As already indicated, Gaus recognizes both deontological and constrained teleological reasoning. But the considerations appealed to in deontological argumentation are belief-like in character, whereas those appealed to in constrained teleological argumentation are desire-like in character.

Gaus's approach requires, positively, that individuals have reasons to accept some regime if that regime is to be justified, rather than, as on Ackerman's account (or, originally, Scanlon's), that they lack reasons to reject that regime. He says, for instance, that "moral and political principles are justified if and only if each member of the community has good reason to embrace them,"[91] clearly a positive formulation.

Finally, Gaus's approach seems to involve an appeal to individuals' prior rather than their posterior reasons for embracing some particular system. This is implicit in his discussion of proceduralism. Any procedure for determining which system is to be accepted must itself first "be justified before the outcome has been generated" if it is employed.[92] Even if individuals living in a particular regime do indeed acquiesce in its demands, you cannot reasonably expect them to accept a procedure which would justify that regime if the procedure might assign them roles and shares that they would find unacceptable if their thinking hadn't been 'tainted' by their participation in that regime.

In summary, Gaus's approach can be characterized as follows.

Cs/Cv	+/−	Vol/Cog	Dir/InDir	Ec/Pol	Pr/Post	Int/Non-Int
both	+	both	InDir	Pol	Pr	Non-Int

These views — of Rawls, Gauthier, Ackerman, Harsanyi, Habermas, and Gaus — represent, of course, only some of those associated with the project of public justification. Unconsidered are well-known variants associated with Scanlon[93] or Buchanan and Gordon Tullock[94] — and, no doubt, many others, some perhaps only minor variants (as Charles Larmore's conception may be on Habermas's or perhaps Ackerman's), but others quite different indeed.

In any event, my partial and in some cases rather tentative taxonomizing can perhaps usefully be summed up, again schematically, as shown in Table 4.1

TABLE 4.1.   A Taxonomy of Conceptions of Public Justification

	Cs/Cv	+/−	Vol/Cog	Dir/InDir	Ec/Pol	Pr/Post	Int/Non-Int
Rawls	both (Cv)	+	Vol	both (Dir)	both (Pol)	both	both (Int)
Gauthier	Cv	−	Vol	Dir	Ec	both	Int
Ackerman	Cv	−	Cog	Dir	Pol	Post	Int
Utilitarian	Cs	+	Vol	InDir	both	Pr	Non-Int
Habermas	Cs	+	Vol?	InDir?	Pol	Post	Int
Gaus	both	+	both	InDir	Pol	Pr	Non-Int

This table exhibits some significant variation in the understanding, by various important theorists, of the project of public justification — more than enough variation to prompt a question: *Why are there so many and such diverse interpretations of the idea of public justification?* In the next chapter I will introduce the so-called ideal of public justification and, later, will show, in effect, that none of these particular conceptions does, or could, completely realize this ideal, thus provoking the hypothesis that *there are many different conceptions because each realizes aspects of the ideal that others cannot realize.*

Notes

1. *A Theory of Justice,* pp. 17–18.
2. *Political Liberalism,* p. 10.
3. *A Theory of Justice,* p. 587.

4. As Rawls says, *Political Liberalism,* p. 103: "[A]s a procedural device of representation, is the original position itself constructed? No: it is simply laid out."

5. I thus reject the view of Kukathas and Pettit (*Rawls: A Theory of Justice and Its Critics,* pp. 32–33) that "Rawls's notion of the contract is economic rather than political." While it is true of the 'embedded' reasoning of the parties to the original position that "each [makes] up their minds by reference to their personal interests," this is not true of the 'embedding' reasoning of 'you and me' who do, indeed, "put aside their own particular interests and . . . debate about the arrangement that best answers to such considerations . . . as all can equally countenance as relevant." I also reject Thomas Pogge's account of Rawls's methodology, according to which it crucially involves bargaining of a kind more usually associated with Gauthier's approach. Cf. *Realizing Rawls,* sec. 3. Pogge is right to suggest that there are 'economic' elements in Rawls's approach. But it would be wrong to suggest that the approach is economic wholly and solely. Indeed, if the 'embedding' framework takes precedence, as seems reasonable, Rawls's methodology is fundamentally political, not economic.

6. *Political Liberalism,* p. 305.

7. I again disagree with the taxonomy of Kukathas and Pettit, who ignore the interactive element in Rawlsian justification. Cf. *Rawls: A Theory of Justice and Its Critics,* p. 34: "Rawls's own conception of the contract is non-interactive. He sees the parties as each deciding what to choose without the necessity of negotiating with one another." True, but the individuals the parties represent may well have negotiated or anyway interacted with one another in identifying the favored description of the situation of choice.

8. *A Theory of Justice,* p. 139.

9. "Justice as Fairness," p. 226.

10. Rawls, "Kantian Constructivism in Moral Theory," p. 528.

11. Rawls, *Political Liberalism,* p. 50.

12. *Morals by Agreement,* pp. 145–46.

13. *Morals by Agreement,* pp. 151, 255.

14. *Morals by Agreement,* p. 221.

15. *Morals by Agreement,* p. 12.

16. *Morals by Agreement,* pp. 9, 316, 338.

17. *Morals by Agreement,* pp. 9, 7.

18. *Morals by Agreement,* p. 128.

19. *Rawls: A Theory of Justice and Its Critics,* p. 33.

20. *Morals by Agreement,* p. 341.

21. Cf. *Morals by Agreement,* p. 130.

22. *Morals by Agreement,* pp. 133–34.

23. Ackerman, *Social Justice in the Liberal State,* p. 9.

24. *Social Justice in the Liberal State,* p. 359.

25. *Social Justice in the Liberal State,* p. 361.

26. Cf. also *Social Justice in the Liberal State,* p. 9: "both groups will converge on Z by a process of argument that makes sense to them."

27. *Social Justice in the Liberal State,* p. 14.

28. *Social Justice in the Liberal State,* p. 357.

29. *Social Justice in the Liberal State,* p. 361.

30. Cf. *Social Justice in the Liberal State,* sec. 71 and the summary at p. 369. Cf. sec. 4.

31. Barry, *Theories of Justice,* p. 8.

32. Cf. Ackerman, "Why Dialogue?" p. 14: "I am invited to translate my disagreements into a specially sanitized evaluative framework that promises to purge them of their non-neutral aspect. . . . [But] I refuse to speak a political language that obliges me to falsify my primary moral beliefs. . . ."

33. "What Is Neutral about Neutrality?" pp. 387–88.

34. *Social Justice in the Liberal State,* p. 352.

35. *Social Justice in the Liberal State,* p. 353.

36. I dissent on this point from Fishkin, who says that Ackerman's approach involves a hypothetical situation of choice and 'refined' rather than 'brute' motivation. Cf. *The Dialogue of Justice,* pp. 79–80, esp. p. 80: "The opportunities for contaminating the argument with irrelevant facts are controlled by taking the deliberations to a hypothetical situation. . . ."

37. "Why Dialogue?" p. 16.

38. "Why Dialogue?" p. 19. Cf. *Social Justice in the Liberal State,* sec. 65.

39. Dennis Mueller, *Public Choice,* p. 247.

40. Susan Hurley, *Natural Reasons,* p. 109.

41. Barry, *Theories of Justice,* p. 76.

42. Harsanyi, *Rational Behavior and Bargaining Equilibrium in Games and Social Situations,* p. 51, quoted in Hurley, *Natural Reasons,* p. 109.

43. Barry, *Theories of Justice,* p. 77.

44. *A Theory of Justice,* p. 165.

45. Mueller, *Public Choice,* p. 249.

46. Mueller, *Public Choice,* p. 253.

47. Hurley, *Natural Reasons,* p. 110.

48. Cf. Hurley, *Natural Reasons,* p. 110 and Mueller, *Public Choice,* pp. 252–55.

49. Cf. Mueller, *Public Choice,* p. 250: "Whether social choices should depend on individual attitudes toward risk is a knotty question."

50. *Natural Reasons,* p. 108.

51. Rawls, *A Theory of Justice,* p. 166.

52. *Public Choice,* p. 256.

53. Barry, *Theories of Justice,* p. 77.

54. Barry, *Theories of Justice,* p. 76.

55. Nagel, *Equality and Partiality,* pp. 33–34.

56. *A Theory of Justice,* p. 164.

57. Mueller, *Public Choice,* p. 251.

58. It is not clear 'who' could be the subject of an extended preference in the relevant sense. This is why I put 'she has' and 'she would have' in scare quotes. Hurley herself does not think that we must incorporate into these extended preferences *all* that differentiates individuals. So she does not think, as I do, that nothing will be left behind that could serve as a subject of them. Cf. *Natural Reasons,* pp. 112ff. I can not agree that there is an adequate "theory of human nature" that enables us to 'leave behind', non-arbitrarily, that which is "normal and natural," even if it is not universally shared.

59. *Moral Consciousness and Communicative Action,* p. 71. (Habermas is actually reporting the views of Ernst Tugendhat, views that he rejects. The particular point of conflict between Habermas and Tugendhat, turning on the interpretation of the idea that the norm must be "equally good for all," does not efface the otherwise substantial similarity between their views. Certainly the passage quoted is otherwise a very accurate summary of Habermas's own views.)

60. *Moral Consciousness and Communicative Action,* p. 68.

61. Cf. Kukathas and Pettit, *Rawls: A Theory of Justice and Its Critics,* p. 33.

62. *Moral Consciousness and Communicative Action,* p. 72.

63. Baynes, *The Normative Grounds of Social Criticism,* p. 149.

64. *Rawls: A Theory of Justice and Its Critics,* p. 32.

65. *Moral Consciousness and Communicative Action,* p. 66.

66. *Legitimation Crisis,* pp. 104–5.

67. *Legitimation Crisis,* pp. 107–8.

68. *Political Judgment,* p. 28. Cf. Charles Larmore, *Patterns of Moral Complexity,* p. 56. The contrary interpretation cannot be ruled out. As Baynes says (*The Normative Grounds of Social Criticism,* p. 114), "[T]he transcendent character that belongs to the notion of an ideal speech situation does not rule out the immanence . . . of our discursive practices." Indeed, Habermas is quite clear on this point. He says (*Moral Consciousness and Communicative Action,* p. 103): "It would be utterly pointless to engage in a practical discourse without a horizon provided by the life-world of a specific social group and without real conflicts in a concrete situation in which the actors consider it incumbent upon themselves to reach a consensual means of regulating some controversial social matter." On the other hand, Habermas would seem to reject any purely immanent approach to public justification. He says (*Moral Consciousness and Communicative Action,* p. 108.): "Under the unrelenting moral gaze of the participant in discourse . . . the normative power of the factual has weakened. . . . Under this gaze the store of traditional norms has disintegrated into those norms that can be justified in terms of principles and those that operate only de facto."

69. Stephen White, *The Recent Work of Jürgen Habermas,* p. 75.

70. Habermas, *Moral Consciousness and Communicative Action,* p. 160.

71. Habermas, *Legitimation Crisis,* p. 111.

72. *Moral Consciousness and Communicative Action,* p. 68.

73. *Legitimation Crisis,* p. 105.

74. *Moral Consciousness and Communicative Action,* p. 93; I have added emphasis to the words "for the satisfaction of the interests of."

75. *Moral Consciousness and Communicative Action,* p. 93; I have added emphasis to the word "accept" and to the phrase "for the satisfaction of the interests of." I have suppressed Habermas's original emphasis.

76. *Moral Consciousness and Communicative Action,* pp. 161–62.

77. "Public Justification and Democratic Adjudication," p. 255.

78. "Public Justification and Democratic Adjudication," p. 256.

79. *Value and Justification,* p. 321.

80. "Public Justification and Democratic Adjudication," p. 257.

81. "Public Justification and Democratic Adjudication," p. 254.

82. *Value and Justification,* p. 363.

83. Kukathas and Pettit, *Rawls: A Theory of Justice and Its Critics,* p. 32.

84. "Public Justification and Democratic Adjudication," p. 254.

85. "Public Justification and Democratic Adjudication," p. 252.

86. *Value and Justification,* p. 333.

87. *Value and Justification,* p. 333.

88. Cf. *Value and Justification,* sec. 18.

89. *Value and Justification,* p. 451.

90. *Value and Justification,* p. 449.

91. "Public Justification and Democratic Adjudication," p. 251.

92. *Value and Justification,* p. 355.

93. Cf. "Contractualism and Utilitarianism."

94. Cf. *The Calculus of Consent.*

5

The Ideal of Public Justification

Remember the problem. There are a variety of different conceptions of public justification, ranged along the dimensions identified in section 9. Where there is a plurality of conceptions and where the concept is needed to play some social role, there is need to identify or construct some public conception of that concept which is fit to serve this role.[1] In order to do so, we can usefully consider to what extent each of the available conceptions approximates the ideal of public justification, which is determined, *inter alia,* by functional analysis. Any adequate public conception of X must be fit to play, with respect to the realm of X, the role of X in the circumstances of X. Rawls says: "There are certain formal conditions that it seems reasonable to impose. . . . The propriety of these formal conditions is derived from the task of principles of right in adjusting the claims that persons make on their institutions and one another. If the principles of justice are to play their role . . . these requirements are natural enough."[2] In this chapter, I consider the requirements that are "natural enough" in relation to the project of public justification.

16. Two Families of Desiderata

In fact, we can expect—and indeed will find—that reasonable desiderata for public justification will divide fairly naturally, though not perhaps exclusively, into two main families. This is so because, as Macedo notes, "[a]t its most basic level, public justification has dual aims." On the one hand, "[i]t seeks reflective justification (good reasons)"; on the other hand, "it also seeks reasons that can be widely seen to be good by persons such as they are."[3] There are, then, two primary requirements for any adequate conception of public justification: one is moralistic, reflecting our "desire to act justly . . . to conduct . . . [ourselves] in ways that are capable of being defended impartially";[4] the other is realistic, reflecting the demand that "reasonable individuals . . . be motivated to live by" whatever principles govern a publicly justified regime.[5]

On Nagel's account, these dual aims reflect our own divided nature as actors, and the realistic requirement follows directly from the demand—in Nagel's words, "an ethical and not merely a practical claim"—that "the personal standpoint must be taken into account directly in the justification of any ethical or political system

56

which humans can be expected to live by."[6] Or these two aims may, as Beiner puts it, reflect a duality of standpoints, that of the spectator and that of the agent, that each of us necessarily adopts when we act or contemplate acting.[7] Thinking about matters historically, we see that these 'dual aims' are perhaps precipitates of that "series of disputes . . . [that] run through modern . . . culture, between the demands of reason and . . . universality, on one hand, and the demands of . . . fulfilment . . . or particularity, on the other."[8]

These dual aims also reflect the contrast, already mentioned (sec. 8), between competing conceptions of rationality—on the one hand, 'universalistic' demands that "the rational person satisfy all interests"; on the other hand, 'maximizing' demands that "the rational person . . . seeks the greatest satisfaction of her own interests."[9]

In any event, we must surely be concerned, as Nagel is, about possible incompatibility between moralistic and realistic requirements. "[T]here is a serious question of how they can be jointly realized, and whether they necessarily interfere with one another."[10] Macedo asks: "How can justification go public and remain importantly justificatory?"[11] How, indeed? But that question is a matter, indeed *the* matter, for the next chapter. In this one, I want to introduce these two kinds of requirements.

Some will wonder, of course, whether the realistic desiderata really need to be taken seriously by the moral theorist, who can be imagined prescribing for us *sub specie aeternitatis* and therefore without reference to the problems of implementing whatever is actually justified. Realistic desiderata are all concerned with just such questions of implementation as the hardheaded 'moralist' sees little reason to worry about, except, perhaps, as posing interesting problems of social engineering. In this case, the possibility referred to by Nagel is of much less significance. If realistic desiderata need not be taken account of by moral theory, then their incompatibility with moralistic desiderata is not an 'ethical', but purely a 'practical' problem.

In fact, the reply is clear almost as soon as the proposal itself is formulated. Moral theory is concerned to provide guidance for our conduct in the circumstances in which we find ourselves. While it need not compromise with wickedness and depravity,[12] it must be suitable for presentation to individuals of good will who nevertheless cannot be expected to honor automatically or even indeed to understand all that it might command. As Nagel says, "A theory is utopian in the pejorative sense if it describes a form of collective life that humans, or most humans, could not lead and could not come to be able to lead through any feasible process of social and moral development."[13] That certain proposals that are 'good enough in theory' cannot be implemented in practice is enough to show that they were only apparently, but not really, 'good enough in theory'. As Nagel reminds us, "What is right must be possible. . . ."[14] So-called utopian morality is bad morality, not good morality posing hard problems for the 'social engineer'.[15]

Another point is also pertinent. It is easy to see the moralistic demands as the demands of practical rationality, whereas the realistic requirements simply represent the need to compromise these demands in light of our finitude and fallibility. In this case, it is easy to dismiss the realistic requirements as of little interest to moral theory, though they may, of course, be crucial in relation to moral practice. But any such attitude depends on some *antecedently given* account of the reason/practice distinction, or, in the language of Kant, the distinction between pure practical reason and empirical practical reason.[16] This attitude is therefore especially inappropriate in the present context, and for two reasons.

First, since we are engaged precisely in the project of determining the nature and limits of reason in a practical context, it begs the question to assume that we already know what counts and what does not count as part of this problem.

Second, the underlying ontology is suspect which might support a distinction between theory and practice—and hence a dismissal of realistic requirements. It is precisely this ontology that is under challenge by many pluralists. In a related context, Rorty puts the point very clearly:

> The notion of "absolute validity" does not make sense except on the assumption of a self which divides fairly neatly into the part it shares with the divine and the part it shares with the animals. But if we accept this opposition between reason and passion, or reason and will, we liberals will be begging the question against ourselves. It behooves those of us who agree with Freud and Berlin that we should *not* split persons up into reason and passion to drop, or at least to restrict the use of, the traditional distinction between "rational conviction" and "conviction brought about by causes rather than reasons."[17]

There is no reason for thinking that a distinction between moralistic and realistic desiderata marks that of two *natural kinds,* one subordinate to the other. Indeed, there is reason to suspect that this distinction is simply a *conventional,* and quite possibly superseded, *artifact* of an earlier epoch, persisting into and confounding the understanding of a later one.

17.   The Moralistic Desiderata

Among the 'moralistic' desiderata, the most important are (1) universality, (2) independence, (3) transparency, (4) reflexivity, and (5) determinacy. These requirements reflect the demands of moral reasoning in the context of public political issues.

Universality

According to this requirement, a regime must be reasonable for every member of the community if it is to be justified publicly. All members of the community must be included, none may be excluded if the justification is to be adequate.[18] As Waldron says, "If there is some individual to whom a justification cannot be given, then so far as *he* is concerned the social order had better be replaced by other arrangements, for the *status quo* has made out no claim to *his* allegiance."[19] This requirement is easy to motivate.

The problem of public justification arises only in the circumstances of politics. These are constituted by the facts of antecedent non-agreement and mutual dependence. This problem can be solved, at least in theory, only if the conditions for politics are also satisfied. (See sec. 7.) On the first point, suppose that A and B do not antecedently agree on how they are to behave in relation to each other. With respect to many actions such as φ, *A* wants to and believes himself warranted in φing, whereas *B* wants *A* not to φ and believes herself warranted in wanting *A* to refrain. With respect to the second point, suppose that each of *A* and *B* is in fact reasonable in the Rawlsian sense of wanting, *ceteris paribus,* to be able to justify himself or herself to the other. In this case, no solution to the problem of antecedent disagreement is adequate unless it is 'universal'.

Suppose that some determinate proposal about the status of φing is reasonable for *A* but not for *B*. If the proposal is implemented, then, although *A* is favored, he finds that he cannot justify himself to *B*, and so neither she *nor he* will find that the proposal solves the problem in the appropriate way. (Both want a resolution that each can appeal to in order to justify his or her behavior to the other; that is what being reasonable demands.) The reasoning is symmetrical if the proposal is not implemented. In neither case is the problem solved.

Independence

According to this requirement, the principles of a publicly justified regime must be independent of the possibly biased and ideologically self-serving or self-enslaving attitudes of the members of the community and of the contingencies of their situations that might give some individuals inappropriately greater power than others.[20] If they are not, then, as Michael Sandel says, "there is no assurance that the critical standpoint they provide is any more valid than the conceptions they would regulate."[21]

Remember that we are seeking to justify some regime, not merely to rationalize whatever regime may already happen to exist. In this case, as Reiman points out, "[a] successful justification must refute the suspicion of subjugation" that "characterize[s] any case in which the judgment of one person prevails over the contrary judgment of another simply because it can. . . ."[22] As Michel Foucault puts it, we "run the risk," unless we refute this suspicion, "of letting ourselves be determined by more general structures of which we may well not be conscious, and over which we may have no control."[23] The achievement of independence may therefore require some movement away from actual attitudes and structures. Indeed, this kind of 'distancing' is demanded, as Galston puts it, "not by some exogenous and dispensable metaphysical itch, but by the inner contradictions of daily life."[24] Particularly important, no doubt, are the palpable contradictions between our ideals and the reality we confront, but, as Galston rightly remarks, "[a]cquaintance with other societies [also] forces upon us an awareness of the partiality and cost of our own."[25]

This is a desideratum that Rawls accepts. Considering the possibility that his "conception of justice relies upon the aims of existing individuals," he asks how this doctrine "can determine an Archimedean point from which the basic structure itself can be appraised?" He concludes that, because of the special nature of the motivational assumptions made about the parties to the original position, "justice as fairness is not at the mercy . . . of existing wants and interests . . . [but does set] up an Archimedean point for assessing the social system. . . ."[26]

To be sure, that the Rawlsian machinery did *not* meet this requirement was a common early criticism. "To some extent, a theory which is going to tell us what is right and wrong is being rigged up to match our antecedent judgments of what is right and wrong."[27] It is true that the special assumptions of original position argumentation are, according to Rawls, "ones that we do in fact accept."[28] Do they, then, provide the necessary leverage against ideologically contaminated attitudes and institutions? Or are we trapped in some seamless web of 'total ideology'? As Connolly puts it, "[I]f critical theory points to systematic distortions in participant self-understandings within contemporary society, it must acknowledge standards against which the distortion is measured; but if the distortion is thought to be too systematic, then critical theory must be treated as another symptom of the disease it seeks to diagnose."[29] Clearly, it will be no easy matter to satisfy this desideratum.

Transparency

To justify a regime, the considerations that are held to tell in its favor must be accessible to all members of the community. In particular, if A finds the regime reasonable on account of R_A, then this fact — that he does so — must be accessible to B as well. Of course, B may not have the same reason as A for finding the regime reasonable, nor need she believe that R_A is a reason *for her*, B, to find it reasonable. But she must at least believe that R_A is a reason for A to judge that the regime is a reasonable one. Transparency requires both accessibility and intelligibility. This desideratum demands "open justifications openly arrived at."[30] Nagel gives a canonical formulation:

> Public justification in a context of actual disagreement requires . . . preparedness to submit one's reasons to the criticism of others, and to find that the exercise of a common critical rationality and consideration of evidence that can be shared will reveal that one is mistaken. This means that it must be possible to present to others the basis of your own beliefs, so that once you have done so, they have what you have, and can arrive at a judgment on the same basis.[31]

This desideratum is tied up with an important rationale for public justification — "to regard certain kinds of reasons as authoritative in politics: moral reasons that can be openly presented to others. . . ."[32] And it functions to foster trust between individuals and in their collective institutions and thus to secure stability.[33]

Related to, but in some formulations distinct from, transparency is a desideratum that appears in Rawls's work under the guise of *publicity.* He says, for instance: "By a publicly acceptable basis I mean a basis that includes ideals, principles and standards that all members of society can not only affirm but also mutually recognize before one another."[34] And by this Rawls means, in particular, that the parties to the original position are "to assess conceptions of justice subject to the constraint that . . . [p]rinciples which might work quite well provided they were not publicly acknowledged . . . are to be rejected."[35] Rawls seems to have in mind here the kind of proposal that Henry Sidgwick made — namely, that utilitarianism might serve as an adequate basis for the organization of social arrangements only if it was not known that it was playing this role. The difference between publicity and transparency is a difference of scope. Where the requirement of transparency applies to the *process* of public justification, that of publicity applies to the *products* of this process and to their employment for whatever purposes are relevant. Where I require that the reasoning be accessible to each individual, Rawls requires that the results of reasoning be accessible to each individual.

On the other hand, Rawls has recently emphasized the importance of 'transparency' both of products and of processes of justification. In *Political Liberalism,* he says that "the idea of publicity . . . has three levels" and explicitly adds, to what I have called his views on 'publicity', two further requirements: (1) that "[c]itizens in a well-ordered society roughly agree on" "the general beliefs in the light of which first principles of justice themselves can be accepted" and that they do so because these beliefs "can be supported . . . by publicly shared methods of inquiry and forms of reasoning"; and (2) that "the full justification of the public conception of justice . . . also . . . be . . . publicly known, or better, at least . . . be publicly available."[36] These requirements *do* coincide with those I would impose under the heading 'transparency'.

Reflexivity

If a regime is to be justified, then the apparatus used in its public justification, consisting, say, of standards and evidence, must itself be publicly justifiable. As Benhabib says, it is reasonable to permit participants in justification to "introduce metaconsiderations about the very conditions and constraints under which such dialogue takes place and evaluate their fairness. . . ."[37] And this is reasonable because, if these considerations cannot themselves be tested, at least on demand, then there is necessarily some doubt that the regime is indeed justified. A demonstration of a regime's reasonableness if it is not an adequate basis for establishing the regime's legitimacy based on considerations that, upon examination, some would find unreasonable. At the very least, the standards invoked in defense of the regime must satisfy the requirements that they themselves specify. As O'Neill says, "The principles of reason vindicate their authority by their stamina when applied to themselves."[38]

Not all considerations can be subject to public justification at any one time, and we may have no telling reason at some particular time to question some particular set of standards or some particular component of the evidential corpus. In this case, we would be wise to proceed on the basis of these considerations until we do have some concrete reason to examine them. Indeed, it would be folly, absent such a reason, to subject these considerations to scrutiny. That way lies the regress of justifications which leads, eventually, either to arbitrary stipulation or to skepticism.[39] Harold Brown puts the point well:

> [W]e must resist the impulse, which has become a philosophical reflex since Descartes, to jump directly from the recognition that our starting point can be reconsidered, to the conclusion that it must be reconsidered now. The bare logical possibility that we are wrong . . . is not a sufficient ground for withholding belief . . . we need specific reasons for doubting.[40]

Determinacy

If a regime is to be justified, then we want the regulative principles and practices of that regime to be determinate in their implications, with respect to constitutional fundamentals, for the conduct of individuals. We want them, in Fishkin's terminology, to "*differentiate* among alternatives . . . [rather than] legitimating all (or virtually all) the realistic possibilities . . . [or, on the contrary] ruling out all the realistic possibilities."[41] With respect to every form of conduct φ that might be the object of disagreement within the community, with some members wanting to φ and others wanting there to be no (legitimate) φing, we require that constitutional principles imply some definite judgment about the legitimacy of φing. The principles constituting the regime must imply either that φing is permitted, or that φing is required, or that φing is prohibited.[42] *Ceteris paribus,* one regime is superior from the point of view of public justification if the publicly justified principles of the one are more determinate with respect to constitutional fundamentals.[43]

As Rawls says, "This requirement springs directly from the role of its [publicly justified] principles in adjusting competing demands."[44] The problem of public justification arises only in the circumstances of politics that are constituted, in part, by the fact of antecedent non-agreement. Any 'indeterminate' proposal is inadequate precisely in failing to settle the question that demands an answer in these circumstances.

18.   The Realistic Desiderata

Among the realistic desiderata, the most important are (1) universality, (2) salience, (3 intelligibility, (4) stability, and (5) determinacy. These requirements reflect the demands of practical efficacy in the context of public political issues. Two of these desiderata, universality and determinacy, are also reckoned among the moralistic desiderata that have already been considered. It is appropriate that they appear on both lists. Universality and determinacy might be considered valuable characteristics for both ethical-theoretical and purely practical reasons. Of course, these desiderata are interpreted slightly differently in their realistic and moralistic variants.

Universality

Much of what was said earlier can be repeated here. If a regime is to be justified publicly, then it must be reasonable for every member of the relevant community. All members of the community must be included, none may be excluded if the justification is to be adequate. As Waldron says, "If there is some individual to whom a justification cannot be given, then so far as *he* is concerned the social order had better be replaced by other arrangements, for the *status quo* has made out no claim to *his* allegiance."[45]

We must not now read Waldron's warning in a moralistic way. Rather, it should be taken to imply that, in slighting some particular individual, we would undermine the stability of the regime or, at the very least, add to the burden of compliance with its dictates. The individual in question, having been given no grounds for finding the regime a reasonable one, may consider herself at liberty, especially when she can do so without detection, to be a 'free rider' with respect to its collective benefits and burdens. As Rawls says, "[A] scheme made stable by an effective public sense of justice is . . . better . . . than a scheme which requires a severe and costly apparatus of penal sanctions, particularly when this apparatus is dangerous to the basic liberties."[46]

It may be questioned whether, within a purely practical framework, genuine universality is indeed desirable. Nagel seems to suggest that it might be superfluous, absent a concern with moralistic issues. He says: "We might, for example, seek a justification for political institutions not to everyone, but only to enough people to permit the institutions to be forcibly imposed. . . . In a sense this would be to give up the goal of establishing legitimacy."[47] To be sure. But would it not also undercut the efficacy, from a purely realistic point of view, of the regime so justified? I believe that it would, though others, notoriously, have disagreed.[48]

Douglas Rae seems to have insisted that, from the point of view of means-ends rationality, simple majority rule is, realistically, a more than adequate basis for public justification. Whereas imposition of the unanimity requirement raises the probability p^+ that regimes favored by A will not be adopted, it lowers the probability p^- that regimes disfavored by A will be adopted. On the assumption that A wants to minimize the sum of these probabilities, a majority rule requirement is preferable to a requirement of universality (or unanimity).[49] Of course, it is very controversial that A should rationally want to minimize the sum of these probabilities, especially in relation to the realm of public justification — that of constitutional fundamentals. In order to be sure that no regime that she strongly disfavors could possibly meet the standards of public justification, an individual will and should be prepared to bear losses when others veto regimes that she most favors.

Rawls has argued that certain conditions are appropriate for the use of the maximin rule. His argument seems pertinent, on purely realistic grounds, to the requirement of universality. For a delegate to the constitutional convention, "[i]t is not," in Rawls's words, "worthwhile for him to take a chance for the sake of a further advantage, especially when it turns out that he may lose much that is important to him . . . [for there are] outcomes that . . . [he] can hardly accept."[50]

We can also discount the suggestion, due to Buchanan and Tullock, that, when decision and/or transaction costs are factored into the reckoning, some requirement less stringent than universality is appropriate. The argument, again, is that these costs are greater when unanimity is required than they are when, for instance, mere majority is demanded. There are costs, so-called external costs, associated with decision making on a less than unanimous basis. Those whose views are overridden, for example, those in a minority when majoritarian procedures are employed, typically have burdens transferred or assigned to them that they would not have had to bear had they had an effective veto over collective decisions, as they would in a unanimitarian regime. While decision and/or transaction costs fall as the unanimity requirement is relaxed, these 'external costs' rise, and the optimal balance of the two kinds of costs is achieved when procedures requiring less than unanimous agreement are in force.[51] Or so it is said.

As I have already indicated, I think this line of reasoning can be ignored in the current context. After all, the realm for which universality is being proposed is a one-time constitutional convention. Three points are therefore pertinent.

1. It is not as if, by requiring universality always and in relation to all publicly enforced decisions, we were consigning citizens to bear very high decision and/or transaction costs on a daily basis and in relation to issues on which universality might be very hard to achieve (even if 'side payments' are permitted). Delegates to the constitutional convention, aware of these very difficulties, may well decide on some decision rule for *day-to-day* political life that requires mere majority rather than unanimity.
2. Furthermore, since the convention itself is a one-time event and is concerned with issues where individuals can hardly afford to be in a losing position, the increased costs associated with universality are much more appropriate.
3. With respect to 'decision costs', majoritarian techniques lose much of their advantage over unanimitarian procedures insofar as they give 'unstable' results — for example, because of 'cycling', namely, X preferred to Y, which in turn is preferred to Z, which in turn is preferred to X.[52]

The demands of universality are stringent but appropriately so, given the realm where this requirement is meant to be applied.

Salience

If a regime is to be justified, then members of the community must be motivated, by considerations that figure in the justificatory argument, actually to behave in accordance with the various requirements by which the regime is constituted. As Nagel rightly says, "[J]ustification is intended to produce not just assent to a proposition, but acceptance of and support for a set of institutions and a form of life. . . ."[53] Although he rejects this view, Gaus puts it very clearly: "[B]ecause moral justification seems to be essentially a practical matter, it also appears to have a persuasive function. That is, it ought to move people."[54]

There are many collective benefits that can be achieved and collective burdens that can be avoided by the institution of a regime only if there is more or less willing compliance with its demands.[55] "Effective coordination requires disciplined performance, which cannot be achieved by supervision alone . . .": this truism is one of the primary reasons why the requirement of salience is a reasonable one.[56] Those individuals who have not been 'moved' by some justificatory argument in favor of a regime "would have," as Barry points out, "an incentive to seek to upset it."[57] Proposals for the regulation of social interaction are meant to be socially advantageous, and therefore to have benefits that cannot be reaped unless they are actually accepted and acted on. Justifications that lack salience cannot ensure that these benefits will indeed be realized. They therefore cannot be adequate from a realistic point of view.

Of course, unmotivated individuals might be compelled to act in accordance with the demands of some regime. But, as Michael Walzer says, the problem with any such proposal "is that it presses its practitioners toward manipulation and compulsion."[58] Thinking about the matter realistically, we see it is certainly preferable, where possible, to ensure motivational salience as a means of minimizing 'compliance costs' — namely, those costs that need to be borne either as a result of non-compliance (in the form of benefits forgone or burdens not avoided) or in order to obtain otherwise unmotivated compliance (in the form of resources employed to achieve this that could otherwise have been deployed for other purposes).

Intelligibility

If a regime is to be justified, then, "since no one could rationally support a practice for which he could not see sufficient reason," "[t]he arguments for any proposal must be simple enough to be understood by any moral agent. . . ."[59] As Rawls says, "Arguments supporting political judgments should, if possible, not only be sound but such that they can be publicly seen to be sound."[60] If highly complex arguments are employed that are dependent on obscure or controversial factual claims, "the[ir] highly speculative nature and enormous complexity . . . are bound to make citizens with conflicting interests highly suspicious of one another's arguments."[61] These arguments are less likely, indeed much less likely, to command compliance.[62] As Macedo says, this requirement "offers . . . a way of accepting the infirmities of reasonable citizens and of respecting them, blemishes and all . . . [and so of] moderating the aims of philosophy so as to ensure the wide accessibility of the relevant forms of reasoning and evidence. . . ."[63]

And these infirmities arise, not for reasons that are peculiar to certain individuals or even, indeed, to classes of individuals who might be considered 'handicapped' in comparison with their fellows. They arise because of our limited capacity to perform certain kinds of calculations and/or to obtain certain kinds of information in anything remotely like 'real time' — that is, in reasonable time to implement the decision the calculations and information-gathering are relevant to. As Herbert Simon says, "human beings have neither the facts nor the consistent structure of values nor the reasoning power at their disposal that would be required" to apply certain formal techniques for decision making.[64]

It may be objected that this requirement cannot reasonably be imposed in relation to constitutional fundamentals. After all, I have already argued, in favor of the requirement of universality, and on purely realistic grounds, that we *can* discount decision costs in relation to reasoning within this domain. Since the constitutional one time only convention is an exercise concerned with matters of fundamental importance, it will not matter (enough) that decision making is much more protracted than would be appropriate in 'everyday life'. Indeed, Davis makes exactly this objection: "Requiring deliberation in 'real time' is, however, a highly conservative assumption. . . . Once a proposal passes, it is likely to remain in force in part just because giving it up is too expensive."[65] No doubt there are subtleties here. We can permit modes of decision making in the constitutional convention that would not be appropriate in other circumstances. The delegates, realizing their inappropriateness in these circumstances, will propose other methods for use in them. But what we cannot sensibly permit, even in the constitutional convention, is the use of techniques for decision making that are *too* time-consuming or *too* far beyond the cognitive powers of the ordinary moral agent. As Simon says, "[T]here is no point in prescribing a particular substantively rational solution if there exists no procedure for finding that solution with an acceptable amount of computing effort."[66] Insofar as public justification is respectful of realistic requirements, it must respect what Christopher Cherniak calls "the *finitary predicament* of [human beings] having fixed limits on their cognitive capacities. . . ."[67] It is on these grounds, certainly, that Rawls forswears an interest in the so-called ethics of creation that he associates with utilitarianism.[68]

Stability

If a regime is to be justified, then the basis of its justification should not be too sensitive to such changes in the attitudes and attributes of members of the community as can ordinarily be expected to occur within (historically) short periods of time. We want the principles (governing regimes) that some method of justification legitimates to "be the kind of principles . . . [individuals] would continue to accept in spite of changes in their prospects and other circumstances."[69] Or, as Rawls puts it, we want "stability . . . [in the sense that] those who affirm the various views supporting the political conception will not withdraw their support of it should the relative strength of their view in society increase and eventually become dominant."[70]

I can think of two reasons why stability is a reasonable realistic desideratum.[71]

1. If some system of fundamental constitutional arrangements is not stably justified, then we will have to pay, repeatedly, precisely the heavy decision costs that the allegedly one time only character of the justificatory exercise was supposed to enable us to bear in the interests of other desiderata, both realistic and moralistic. Where justification is unstable, changes in individuals' attitudes and attributes will require that the justificatory exercise be repeated in order that some new regime be justified on the basis of these new attitudes and attributes. *Ceteris paribus,* we want to repeat *constitutional* decision making as seldom as possible and thus require as much stability in our justifications as is compatible with the demand that they also be 'sensitive' to relevant changes in attitudes and attributes.[72]

2. Some of the decisions we take about appropriate social relations may be irreversible. Suppose, for instance, that implementation of some proposal results in the (avoidable but) irreversible degradation of some natural resource, so that individuals some generations distant from the time of implementation can no longer draw on this resource. This situation is especially unfortunate if the proposal was based on considerations that were appropriate for the generation of 'justifiers' but not for their descendants. A preference for stable justifications can be grounded on the irreversibility of certain decisions in relation to the reasonable expectations of future generations.[73]

Determinacy

Much of what was said earlier can be repeated here. If a regime is to be justified, then we want its regulative principles and practices to be determinate in their implications. With respect to every form of conduct ϕ that might be the object of constitutionally fundamental disagreement within the community, with some members wanting to ϕ and others wanting there to be no (legitimate) ϕing, we require that the principles constituting the regime imply some definite judgment about the legitimacy of ϕing.

As Rawls says, "This requirement springs directly from the role of its [publicly justified] principles in adjusting competing demands."[74] Since there are 'practical' as well as moralistic reasons why this role must be discharged in any human community, this requirement is 'natural enough' in the circumstances. So long as the principles of some regime are 'indeterminate' with respect to the status of A's ϕing, there will be conflict, at least potentially and very likely actually, between A and B. This conflict (a) ties up community resources in its adjudication or containment that could be employed for other, perhaps more productive purposes, and (b) prevents the realization of at least some of the benefits of cooperation that the regime is meant to supply to its citizens. There is good reason, 'realistically', to require determinacy.

The ideal of public justification is given in those desiderata that it is natural enough to impose on adequate conceptions of the underlying concept. To determine a public conception of that concept, and thus to solve the problem of public justification, we will hope to find a conception of public justification that satisfies these desiderata better than any others available to us. Unfortunately, it is not clear that there is a determinate answer to the question, Which conception fares best with respect to the ideal? This is so, in particular, because it is not clear that *any* conception can satisfy *all* the desiderata. Conceptions that fare well with respect to some desiderata will fare poorly, ipso facto, with respect to others. To determine which conception is best will therefore be no easy matter. This, anyway, in what I will try to show in Part II.

Notes

1. Opinions differ about whether moral theory ought to be concerned with the problem of determining *socially* valid principles of conduct. Benn, for instance, in *A Theory of Freedom*, p. 19, claims that "[w]ithin the modern consciousness, practical reason is located in the first instance not in the mustering of knockdown arguments to persuade or justify oneself to others but in the process of individual choice and judgment." On the other hand, Hampshire suggests (*Innocence and Experience*, p. 52) "taking public debate as the model of the operation of the mind in practical reason," clearly implying at least prima facie obligations on individuals to test their own moral judgments against those of others. But whatever the merits of 'moral individualism' of the kind espoused by Benn, compared with the 'moral collectivism' recommended by Hampshire, it is clear that, where collectively binding decisions are at issue, a collective approach to them is warranted. This is the significance of my remark that since the concept of public justification is meant, when articulated, to 'play some social role', we must discover a public conception of that concept. (Cf. also sec. 40.)

2. *A Theory of Justice*, pp. 130–31.

3. "The Politics of Justification," p. 281. Ultimately, these dual aims may reflect a Kantian distinction. Cf. Baynes, *The Normative Grounds of Social Criticism*, p. 18: "The principle of judgment is the Moral law which, through an application of the categorical imperative as a test procedure for maxims of action, specifies our duties. . . . The principle of execution, on the other hand, considers the mode of compliance or incentive through which an action is performed in accordance with the law."

4. Barry, *Theories of Justice*, p. 363.

5. Nagel, *Equality and Partiality*, p. 21.

6. *Equality and Partiality*, p. 15.

7. *Political Judgment*, p. 117.

8. Charles Taylor, *Sources of the Self*, p. 101.

9. Gauthier, *Morals by Agreement*, p. 7. Cf. Barry, *Theories of Justice*, p. 363.

10. *Equality and Partiality*, p. 21.

11. *Liberal Virtues*, p. 45.

12. Cf. Nagel, *Equality and Partiality*, p. 26.

13. *Equality and Partiality*, p. 6.

14. *Equality and Partiality*, p. 26. Nagel doesn't himself have infirmities in mind; he is concerned with the complex motivational structure of individuals that encompasses personal and impersonal perspectives, both of which are morally significant on his account.

15. Thanks to Michael Smith for helpful comments about this issue.

16. Cf. Rawls, *Political Liberalism*, pp. 48–49, n. 1.

17. *Contingency, Irony, and Solidarity*, p. 47.

18. This requirement should not be confused with Rawls's requirement (*A Theory of Justice*, p. 132), one of the "formal constraints of the concept of right," that "principles are to be universal in application." Rawls's requirement regulates the substance of the principles that are to be justified, whereas my requirement regulates the basis on which they are to be justified. On Rawls's account, "a principle is ruled out if it would be self-contradictory, or self-defeating, for everyone to act upon it." On my account, a principle is ruled out if it is not reasonable from every point of view.

19. "Theoretical Foundations of Liberalism," p. 135.

20. Cf. Fishkin, *The Dialogue of Justice*, p. 44: "An acceptable theory should [not be] . . . subject to a delegitimating charge that people were brainwashed or coercively molded so as to support the regime in the required way."

21. *Liberalism and the Limits of Justice*, p. 17.

22. *Justice and Modern Moral Philosophy*, p. 2.

23. *The Foucault Reader*, p. 47.

24. *Liberal Purposes*, p. 30.

25. *Liberal Purposes*, p. 30.

26. *A Theory of Justice*, pp. 260–61.

27. G. R. Grice, "Moral Theories and Received Opinion," pp. 11–12.

28. *A Theory of Justice*, p. 587.

29. *Politics and Ambiguity*, p. 55.

30. Macedo, "The Politics of Justification," p. 295. Cf. Gauthier, *Morals by Agreement*, pp. 170–71.

31. "Moral Conflict and Political Legitimacy," p. 232.

32. Macedo, "The Politics of Justification," p. 281. Cf. Nozick, *Philosophical Explanations*, p. 470, where such transparent argumentation is characterized as "a mutual value-theoretic situation."

33. Cf. Macedo, *Liberal Virtues*, pp. 67–68: "[P]ublic justification . . . fosters trust. . . ." Cf. Rawls, *A Theory of Justice*, p. 133: "[T]he general awareness of their universal acceptance should have desirable effects and support the stability of social cooperation."

34. "The Idea of an Overlapping Consensus," p. 4, n. 5.

35. "Kantian Constructivism in Moral Theory," p. 540. Cf. Williams, *Ethics and the Limits of Philosophy*, p. 100, and Will Kymlicka, "Liberalism and Communitarianism," pp. 196–97.

36. *Political Liberalism*, pp. 66–67.

37. *Situating the Self*, p. 169.

38. *Constructions of Reason*, p. 38.

39. Cf. Harold Brown, *Rationality*, p. 71: "In order to be rational we must proceed in accordance with appropriate rules, and we must be able to choose these rules in a rational manner. But how do we determine which rules to choose? . . . The threat of an infinite regress appears in yet another guise."

40. *Rationality*, p. 145. Cf. Cherniak (*Minimal Rationality*, p. 100), who mentions as requiring justificatory attention only those "specific counterpossibilities that there is a definite basis for thinking might now apply."

41. *The Dialogue of Justice*, p. 41.

42. Cf. Rawls, *A Theory of Justice*, pp. 133–34: "A further condition is that a conception of right must impose an ordering on conflicting claims."

43. It cannot be guaranteed, for arbitrary regimes, that one will 'dominate' the other — that is, that the set of activities with respect to which one has no determinate implications will be a proper subset of those for which the other has no determinate implications. Perhaps one has no determinate implications with respect to fewer kinds of activities than the other does even if it does not dominate the other in this sense. In this case, fine judgments may be necessary to determine the relative merits of the two regimes with respect to determinacy. Perhaps the cases the second is silent about are less significant, ethico-politically, than those about which the first has no determinate implications.

44. *A Theory of Justice*, pp. 133–34.

45. "Theoretical Foundations of Liberalism," p. 135.

46. *Political Liberalism*, p. 317.

47. *Equality and Partiality*, p. 23.

48. Rawls now seems to be one of them. Among the "general facts" characterizing the "political culture of a democratic society," Rawls includes (*Political Liberalism*, p. 38) "a third general fact . . . that an enduring and secure democratic regime . . . must be willingly and freely supported by at least a substantial majority of its politically active citizens." From the context, it is clear that Rawls's concerns here are realistic. Rawls is surely right in thinking that, as a matter of 'necessity', a "substantial majority of its politically active citizens" is more than an adequate basis for a 'realistically justified' society. This would be more than enough to guarantee social peace, for instance. But there are, as I will point out, substantial 'compliance costs' associated with anything less than full unanimity, at least with respect to constitutional essentials, and so, from the point of view of abstract theory, no reason to resile from this more stringent demand.

49. Cf. Lessnoff, *Social Contract*, p. 127, and Mueller, *Public Choice*, pp. 210–12.

50. *A Theory of Justice*, p. 154.

51. Cf. Lessnoff, *Social Contract*, p. 126, and Mueller, *Public Choice*, pp. 28–31.

52. Cf. Mueller, *Public Choice II*, p. 96.

53. *Equality and Partiality*, p. 23.

54. *Value and Justification*, p. 321. This is by no means the same as, e.g., Fishkin's requirement that "[a]n acceptable theory should be individually binding . . . [i.e.] should have an explanation for why that person is obligated to uphold the regime." Fishkin (*The Dialogue of Justice*, p. 42) is concerned with reasons that might not be motives, whereas, here at least, I am concerned with only those reasons that are also motives.

55. For a distinction between compliance and acquiescence, cf. Gauthier, *Morals by Agreement*, p. 230.

56. Peter Blau and Marshall Meyer, *Bureaucracy in Modern Society*, p. 8.

57. *Theories of Justice*, p. 7.

58. *Interpretation and Social Criticism*, pp. 62–64.

59. Davis, "The Moral Legislature," p. 308.

60. "The Idea of an Overlapping Consensus," pp. 20–21.

61. Rawls, *Political Liberalism*, p. 162. Cf. Dworkin, *Taking Rights Seriously*, p. 166: "[P]rinciples otherwise appealing are to be rejected or adjusted because they are too complex or otherwise impractical. . . ."

62. This requirement should be distinguished from a closely related one also formulated by Rawls — one that, as in the cases of universality and transparency, concerns products not processes. For instance, Rawls requires (*A Theory of Justice*, p. 132) that "each can understand . . . [the] principles [that are justified] and use them in his deliberations . . . [which] imposes an upper bound of sorts on how complex they can be. . . ." Cf. "Kantian Constructivism in Moral Theory," p. 561 and *Political Liberalism*, pp. 267–68.

63. "The Politics of Justification," p. 283.

64. *Reason in Human Affairs*, p. 17.

65. "The Moral Legislature," p. 309.

66. "From Substantive to Procedural Rationality," p. 69.

67. *Minimal Rationality*, p. 8.

68. Cf. *A Theory of Justice*, p. 159.

69. William Nelson, *On Justifying Democracy*, p. 105.

70. "The Idea of an Overlapping Consensus," p. 11. This account of stability is to be contrasted, I think, with that which Rawls articulates in "The Domain of the Political and Overlapping Consensus," p. 239, where he says: "Let us say that a political conception of justice . . . is stable if it meets the following condition: those who grow up in a society well-ordered by it . . . develop a sufficient allegiance to those institutions . . . so that they normally act as justice requires, provided they are assured that others will act likewise." This requirement seems more like mine of salience, perhaps considered in relation to a posterior mode of justification. Also closer to my conception of salience, but this time in relation to a prior mode of justification, is another matter that Rawls considers under the heading of stability (*Political Liberalism*, p. 141) — namely, "whether . . . the political conception can be the focus of an overlapping consensus."

71. Another way in which Rawls's conception of stability differs from mine is in relation to the interpretation of this desideratum as a realistic rather than a moralistic requirement. On Rawls's understanding, the (substantively different) idea of stability is what I would call a moralistic requirement. He says (*Political Liberalism*, pp. 142–43): "To clarify the idea of stability, let us distinguish two ways in which a political conception might be concerned with it. In one way we view stability as a purely practical matter: if a conception fails to be stable, it is futile to try to realize it." This, clearly, is the conception of stability that I am working with. But it is not Rawls's conception, for he continues: "[J]ustice as fairness is concerned with stability in a different way. . . . [J]ustice as fairness is not reasonable in the first place unless in a suitable way it can win its support by addressing each citizen's reason. . . ."

72. Cf. Rawls, "Kantian Constructivism in Moral Theory," p. 565: "[G]iven the way the original position is set up, we can allow, in theory, that, as the relevant general beliefs change, the beliefs we attribute to the parties likewise change, and conceivably also the first principles that would be agreed to." One way of combining stability and sensitivity is to empower a Supreme or High Court to act, in effect, as an ongoing embodiment of the constitutional convention, and to charge such a body with responding to such social and cultural changes as may require a re-articulation or interpretation of fundamental constitutional principles decided on by the constitutional convention. This is implicit in Rawls's discussion of the role of the U.S. Supreme Court; cf. *Political Liberalism*, ch. 6, sec. 6.

73. Other grounds for preferring stable to unstable justifications are suggested by Ackerman's brief discussion of the possibility of adopting an 'equal fulfilment' criterion for the distribution of resources. Cf. *Social Justice in the Liberal State*, sec. 13.2.

74. *A Theory of Justice*, pp. 133–34.

II

DECONSTRUCTION

The use of deconstruction has an intrinsically political character. The method always takes what is claimed to be authoritative, logical, and universal and breaks those claims down, exposing arbitrariness, ambiguity, and conventionality — in short exposing a power phenomenon where it was claimed that only reason existed.

STEPHEN K. WHITE, *Political Theory and Postmodernism*

6

Prima Facie Incoherence

19.   Contestability of the Concept of Public Justification?

Recall the problem. The liberal account of political legitimacy is based on the concept of public justification. No regime is legitimate for a community unless that regime is reasonable from every point of view. This concept is too vague to provide a basis for actually determining, for arbitrary specifications of regime and community, whether or not a given regime is legitimate, and therefore whether or not its demands ought to be honored or resisted. As in other familiar cases, we must interpret or articulate this concept, we must find a conception of public justification, in order to apply it to problematic cases.

There are a number of different conceptions of public justification:

- *Rawls's method of reflective deliberation* — a regime is legitimate if it would be accepted in a situation of choice whose conditions are agreed to be appropriate for choices of that kind;[1]
- *Gauthier's bargaining model* — a regime is legitimate if it serves to advance the realization of individuals' agent-relative interests, subject to the costs of achieving a cooperative surplus;[2]
- *Ackerman's conversational model* — a regime is legitimate if its distribution of burdens and benefits can be defended subject to the constraints of neutral dialogue;[3]
- *Harsanyi's utilitarian contract* — a regime is legitimate if it maximizes individuals' prospects for maximizing their net utility;[4]
- *Habermas's model of the ideal speech situation* — a regime is legitimate if its main features are the object of a consensus formed subject to universalization of the interests in play;[5] and
- *Gaus's mixed contractual/bargaining model* — a regime is legitimate if each of its citizens can accept its distribution of benefits and burdens as reflecting the outcome of a fair agreement about the division of the cooperative surplus that this regime enables them to realize.[6]

This plurality of conceptions merely reflects the plurality of different dimensions with respect to which types of public justificatory strategies might be arrayed. (See section 9.) We have conceptions that emphasize convergence from diverse starting points, such as Gauthier's and Ackerman's, and those that emphasize consensus from a common standpoint, such as Habermas's and Harsanyi's. Similarly, we have those that emphasize interactive modes of justification, such as Gauthier's, Ackerman's, and Habermas's, and those that emphasize non-interactive modes, such as Harsanyi's and Gaus's. (See Table 4.1 for details.)

Given this plurality of different conceptions, it is natural to ask, "Is there a demonstrably *best* conception of public justification?" If there were, the *problem* of public justification might be readily solved. And, if there is not, this problem may remain unsolved. Without a determinately best conception, the question of legitimacy may continue to be contested and thus may not be answered to the satisfaction of all those concerned with it. If there are competing conceptions of public justification, and if one implies that the regime is legitimate for a community, whereas the other implies that the regime is not legitimate for that community, then we may have no way of settling the question of the regime's legitimacy for the community until we discover or invent a way of settling the prior question, "Which of the competing conceptions is the better (preferably, best) conception of public justification?" (Even when there is no determinably best or public conception, we may sometimes be able to determine the legitimacy of the regime if there is nevertheless some way of identifying a regime that is 'dominant' in the sense that it is the best regime for the community *whatever* the conceptions of public justification the members of the community might happen to have.)

How could we determine which of the many different conceptions of public justification is the determinately best (available) interpretation of that concept? We could do so by determining which of these conceptions best satisfies the ideal of public justification, which is constituted, as we have just seen, by various realistic and moralistic desiderata. (The public conception of X is the conception that is best fit to play the role of X in the circumstances of X. And that is determined by how well the various conceptions satisfy the ideal of X.) The results of this chapter will, as it happens, cast some doubt on the viability of this exercise. I will try to show that, for many pairs of desiderata, one from each of the two main 'families', satisfaction of one of the pair is linked to non-satisfaction of the other. For instance, a conception that satisfies the moralistic demand for independence ipso facto fails to satisfy the realistic demand for salience. At this more abstract methodological level, liberalism thus illustrates a point often made about it as a more concrete, substantive doctrine — namely, that it "is a basket of ideals that inevitably come into conflict with one another if a serious effort is made to realize any of them fully, let alone all of them simultaneously."[7]

In fact, these results will constitute a prima facie basis for showing that the concept of public justification is an essentially contestable concept and thus, arguably, of no use in determining the legitimacy of regimes. First, the concept of public justification is an appraisive concept; to say that a regime is publicly justified is to appraise it ethico-politically. Second, the application of this concept is determined by multiple criteria. To show that a regime is publicly justified, we must use reasoning that satisfies a number of different demands, such as universality, specificity, reflexivity, salience, and so on. Finally, satisfaction of some of these demands is prima facie incompatible with the satisfaction of others. Unless there is some "overarching principle and perspective from which these [competing demands] can be put into . . . [some] objective balance,"[8] we will be unable to identify a determinately best interpretation of this concept. *But perhaps there is some such overarching principle and perspective* of the kind alluded to! If there were such a perspective, then we could appeal to it to aggregate or synthesize the various rankings of conceptions with respect to desiderata to obtain some overall ranking. That a conception J_1 (or a regime) was δ_1-superior but δ_2-inferior to another conception J_2 (or regime) would, given such a principle, represent no particularly difficult problem. Any such principle, were it to exist, would simply take the ranks $\delta_1(J_1)$, $\delta_1(J_2)$, $\delta_2(J_1)$, $\delta_2(J_2)$ and convert them into some overall ranking of the competing conceptions (or regimes).

In Part II, I have two aims: (1) to consider the failures of 'tracking' I have alluded to (sections 20 and 21); and (2) to consider and dismiss some specific suggestions that there is indeed some overarching principle that could be employed to determine some optimal overall balance among the various desiderata (Chapter 7).

20. Dimensional Failures of Tracking

There is some prospect of identifying, for each of the dimensional contrasts considered in Chapter 3 — for example, convergence versus consensus, direct versus indirect — some link to specific moralistic and realistic desiderata and, moreover, a failure of the desideratum linked to one of these types to track and/or be tracked by the desideratum linked to the other of the types. In this case, it can be shown that every conception is inadequate with respect to at least one of the desiderata that together constitute the ideal of public justification.

Abstractly, use D_i+ and D_i- to name the opposite positions along dimension D_i. (If D_1 is the dimension convergence/consensus, D_1+ might be convergence and D_1- might be consensus.) Suppose that D_i+ is linked to the desideratum δ_j and that D_i- is linked to the desideratum δ_k. (Perhaps convergence is linked to salience, and consensus is linked to transparency.) Suppose that δ_j fails to track or to be tracked by δ_k — in other words, good performance with respect to δ_j means, ipso facto, poor performance with respect to δ_k. In this case, any conception that occupies the position D_i+ ipso facto performs poorly with respect to the desideratum δ_k, whereas any conception that occupies the position D_i- ipso facto performs poorly with respect to the desideratum δ_j. Since every conception must occupy one of these positions, every conception must perform poorly with respect to one of these desiderata.[9] If this is true with respect to each such dimension, then every conception will, in fact, be *multiply* inadequate, since it must occupy a position with respect to each of seven different dimensions and so can be expected to perform poorly with respect to as many as seven desiderata.

Let us see, in more concrete terms, how this might work.

Consensus/Convergence

The moralistic requirement of transparency is likely to be easier to realize if our mode of justification is oriented to consensus. If both *A* and *B* find a regime reasonable on account of one and the same consideration *R*, then each is likely to believe, of the other's basis for finding that regime reasonable, that it is a reasonable basis; after all, it is her own basis as well. Bearing in mind the demand that public justification should be grounded in "moral reasons that can be openly presented to others," we have little difficulty in meeting this demand in the case of justificatory methods relying on consensus. Difficulties might arise, however, were convergence rather than consensus required for adequate justification. There are A and R_B such that, were A to come to realize that B finds the regime reasonable on account of R_B, A would not be able himself to find it reasonable, whatever other grounds he might have for doing so. For instance, if R_B was that B would be able to fulfill her conception of the good in that regime and if A believed B's conception of the good was depraved, then A might not be able any longer to support the implementation of such a regime, perhaps even despite the fact that in it his conception of the good might also be realizable.[10] Whereas consensus-based justification fares well in relation to the moralistic requirement of transparency, convergence-based justification may not fare so well.

On the other hand, the realistic requirement of salience may be easier to meet within a framework of justification oriented to convergence. Given empirical diversity in the psychology of relevant individuals, any mode of justification that implicitly attributes to each individual the same attitudes and attributes as it attributes to every other is likely to be grounded in counterfactual assumptions about psychology, particularly as it is relevant to motivation. If we require consensus as a basis for justification, we will need to supplement our justificatory apparatus in order to ensure compliance with the requirements we claim to have justified.[11] And while we must not suppose that all convergence-based justification is direct justification, and thus utterly immune to problems of compliance, it is nevertheless true that if our aim is convergence, we have *better* prospects for capturing the empirical diversity of human motivation.

Positive/Negative

A positive approach to public justification is better able to satisfy the realistic demand for intelligibility. If the legitimacy of a regime depends on no one having any reason to reject it, then potential citizens are asked to engage, in order to verify its legitimacy, in very searching psychological investigations of a kind that would not be necessary were a positive approach instead taken. This point rests on a principle familiar to readers of the Sherlock Holmes stories. It is difficult, in some cases impossible, to 'prove a negative'. For B to show, within a framework of negative justification, that A's commitment to a regime is or would be warranted, she would have to establish that, of all A's beliefs, desires, and preferences (or those of his 'surrogate' should an indirect mode of justification be in play), none of them constitutes a reason for rejecting that regime. Given the prodigiously complex and tangled nature of the 'web' of attitudes, this would be a Herculean feat.[12] On the other hand, for B to verify that A (or his surrogate) does, positively, have some reason for accepting a given regime, it will be enough for B to confirm, perhaps 'behavioristically', that A has this reason and, perhaps by logical analysis, that it is indeed a reason for accepting the regime. Of course, in both cases B needs to be something of a Hercules, given the vast number of individual agents involved. But while the number of individual agents involved is a constant — and so represents limits to the 'realism' of *any* justificatory story — the amount of work that needs to be done to verify, for each of these many individuals, that her commitment is a reasonable one is vastly greater for the negative than it is for the positive mode of justification.

On the other hand, a negative approach seems superior from the point of view of independence. Indeed, it seems to have been recommended by Scanlon on something like these grounds. Because what is reasonable is in some respects indeterminate, it is possible both that it be reasonable that *B* accept a regime on account of R^+ and that it be reasonable that *B* reject the same regime on account of R^-. If we adopt a positive approach to justification, we will say that the regime is justified (with respect to *B* and on account of R^+), whereas, if we adopt a negative approach, we will say that that regime is not justified (with respect to *B* and on account of R^-). Since there are cases, depending on the ideological character of R^+, in which the regime is *not* 'really' justified for *B*, we will therefore prefer the negative approach. For example, supposing that they have been taught that they are to sacrifice themselves to others, it may be reasonable for women to accept a regime that requires this of them; but it would also be reasonable, given that they have ambitions of their own, to reject any such regime. If we are to achieve independence of ideological factors that sustain a patriarchal regime, we must prefer a negative approach.

Volitional/Cognitional

Since it is allegedly obscure how beliefs can motivate behavior (even in the absence of suitably 'matched' desires), a volitional approach will probably be preferred to a cognitional one with respect to salience. Suppose someone believes that the Reasonable requires that she adjust her Rational pursuit of self-interest. She may nevertheless be unmoved to make this adjustment unless she has a desire to conform to the dictates of the Reasonable. Indeed, even Rawls seems to grant this point, referring, for instance, to principle- and conception-dependent desires, rather than, as might seem more natural, to principles and conceptions (which might themselves motivate acceptance of some regime).[13]

On the other hand, a cognitional approach may be superior with respect to reflexivity, which requires when we use particular standards and evidence to assess the legitimacy of a regime, that we be prepared to test both standards and evidence for *their* adequacy. It is much more straightforward and much less controversial to test the adequacy of beliefs than of desires, and we seem, at least currently, to have much more elaborate apparatus for doing so. For instance, it is relatively easy to determine whether it is reasonable to have the belief that the demands of the Reasonable require an individual to adjust her Rational pursuit of self-interest. But it is relatively hard to determine whether it is reasonable to have the desire to conform to the demands of the Reasonable.

Direct/Indirect

Whereas a direct mode of justification is superior with respect to salience, an indirect mode of justification is superior with respect to independence. Indeed, this contrast is so marked that it has already been the subject of much critical commentary.

When a direct mode of justification is employed, we construct an argument on the basis of what individuals actually happen to believe, desire, or prefer. If we say that A and B have, respectively, the reasons R_A and R_B for accepting a regime, then we are taken to refer to some beliefs or desires that A and B themselves actually have. But in this case, excepting weakness of will, A and B actually will act to support this regime; their reasons for doing so are also motives for doing so.

On the other hand, when an indirect mode of justification is employed, our argument is based not on A's actual beliefs and desires and B's but, instead, on the beliefs and desires of their surrogates α and β. And since *their* reasons for commitment to a regime, R_α and R_β, respectively, need not even be among the reasons that A and B might actually have, there will typically be a gap between these reasons 'for' A and B and their actual empirical motives.[14]

An indirect approach to justification is, however, obviously superior with respect to independence — precisely for the reason that it is inferior with respect to salience. The development of surrogates for A and B is typically based on precisely the wish to achieve some independence from their actual, possibly biased, and undoubtedly ideologically contaminated beliefs and desires. Whereas the empirical B may have the desire to sacrifice herself for the good of others, her surrogate β has no such desire, for that B herself has it is the product, let us suppose, of her socialization in a patriarchal society that suppresses her 'real interests' in independence and autonomy.

Economic/Political

Adopting an economic approach, we seek an optimal compromise between opposed interests; adopting a political approach, we seek a publicly defensible basis of agreement. A political approach is superior with respect to transparency, whereas an economic approach is superior from the point of view of salience.

In effect, transparency requires that each individual understand every other individual's grounds for commitment to a regime. Because politically justificatory procedures involve just the kind of public dialogue about legitimacy as will reveal to each participant the attitudes of every other participant, such a procedure does satisfy this important moralistic requirement. An economic procedure is very unlikely to. What we have, in this case, is something like (the economist's model of) the market, in which pricing mechanisms signal information about *aggregates* of demand and supply without providing, and indeed by occluding, information about particular individuals. To reach an optimal compromise to opposed interests, each individual must accommodate herself to the competing demands of many, many other individuals. But she does not, indeed could not, do this by accommodating herself one by one to each of them — in a process that would render their psychology transparent to her. She does this, rather, by accommodating herself to a vector of forces that impinges on her and acts, in this situation, like the pricing mechanism in the market. It is a summary of all that information about other individuals that she could not possibly deal with on a one-by-one basis — a summary in which all such information about individuals has been lost.[15] An economic approach is inferior to a political approach with respect to the moralistic requirement of transparency.

On the other hand, an economic approach is superior with respect to salience. If a political approach requires, as Barry puts it, that relevant individuals should "find a basis of agreement that is acceptable from all points of view,"[16] then there will, ipso facto, be considerable 'filtering' of individuals' actual beliefs and desires. In a public forum, *A cannot* say, even if he has great power, that he prefers some regime because his interests are or would be better served than those of individuals he despises.[17] He *can* say that he recommends acceptance of another regime because the interests of each are as well served as possible given competition for scarce resources. If the latter is approved for implementation, then *A* will have a motive, which he was unable to express in the public forum, for dishonoring the demands of this regime — the justification of it may not be salient for him. As Barry says, "If the terms of agreement fail to reflect differential bargaining power, those whose power was disproportionate to their share under the agreement would have an incentive to seek to upset it."[18] But no such 'gap' between justified outcomes and bargaining power can occur when the mode of justification is economic. It is precisely the role of such modes to adjust outcomes to bargaining power.

Prior/Posterior

Any method that involves reference to individuals' prior attitudes is bound to be superior with respect to reflexivity but inferior with respect to stability.

Individuals ought to be suspicious of any mode of justification that refers not to their actual attitudes and attributes but, instead, to the attitudes and attributes that they would have were they to be citizens of the regime that this mode of justification is used to justify. Knowing the capability of regimes to socialize or indoctrinate their citizens into attitudes of conformity,[19] individuals are likely to reject the standard implicit in posterior modes of justification, which therefore fail to satisfy the requirement of reflexivity. Within a framework that stresses prior justification, there is no such opportunity for manipulating individuals' attitudes and attributes. This framework is therefore superior with respect to reflexivity.

On the other hand, it seems very likely that posterior justification will be superior from the point of view of stability, and for precisely the same reason that it is inferior from the point of view of reflexivity. Any regime whose test for legitimacy is the attitudes and attributes that individuals acquire who live in it has opportunities for shaping and filtering those attitudes and attributes, indeed for controlling their development, in ways that promote stability.[20]

Interactive/Non-Interactive

Recall Benhabib's vivid image (Chapter 3, n. 74) of the geometricians working in isolation on the same problem. Because of the constraints on their reasoning, all arrive, independently, at the same conclusion. The only way in which it can be imagined that isolated, non-interacting individuals will arrive at some consensus or point of convergence is if each of them is substantially constrained in her reasoning. For instance, in Rawls's construction, the plurality of parties to the original position is indeed superfluous in view of their identity with one another. In this case, we will naturally get some determinate common answer to the problem that they are set. But this is achieved at the price of abstraction or idealization away from the concrete particularity of the individuals the parties 'represent'. Any such approach can be expected to fare poorly with respect to salience. As I have already noted, modes of justification that involve abstraction and idealization are vulnerable from the point of view of motivational salience.

On the other hand, a non-interactive approach is likely to be superior with respect to independence, again for reasons already canvassed. Because a non-interactive approach will inevitably involve techniques of abstraction and idealization, it necessarily puts some distance between the attitudes relevant to the justificatory enterprise and those, possibly corrupt, attitudes that individuals actually have.

21.   Other Failures of Tracking

For many pairs of desiderata, failures of tracking have already been noted in the literature. For other pairs of desiderata similar failures of tracking can also be established.

Universality versus Determinacy (versus Salience)

Perhaps most often noticed is a failure of superiority with respect to universality to track superiority with respect to determinacy. The wider the 'coverage' of a mode of justification, the less determinate the implications of any regime justified in that way. Noting that "[m]ore demanding [i.e., determinate] norms are less plausibly the object of agreement than less demanding norms," Cohen asks whether "the importance of accommodating moral diversity lead[s] to a thinner conception of justice . . . ?"[21] Bernard Williams comments on the almost irresistible tendency for a liberal justificatory strategy to "draw the boundaries outward to include, beyond those with whom we effectively have to make an agreement, those with whom it would be ethically desirable to make an agreement," noting that such an extension of justificatory 'coverage' brings with it "an ever thinner basis for deciding what set of rules some agent might 'reasonably reject'," concluding that what remains "is very indeterminate."[22]

The reasoning is tolerably clear. The probability that there will be some determinate proposal on which different individuals might converge from different justificatory starting points arguably varies inversely with the number of individuals in question. The more numerous the individuals, the more numerous the different starting points.[23] The more numerous the starting points, the less likely it is that there is some determinate conclusion that can be reached from each of these different starting points. (Compare: Only empty logical truths can be validly derived from every proposition.) The more adequate the justification from the point of view of universality, the more likely it is that the proposal justified be indeterminate, rather than determinate. No conception oriented to convergence can hope to satisfy both of these independently credible desiderata.

In modern pluralistic societies, the probability that a collection of individuals will share a belief or desire R varies inversely with the size of the collection. The more nearly 'universal' the group to whom a given proposal is, consensually, to be justified, the less likely it is that there will be a consideration R, which is a reason for all of them, for finding this proposal a reasonable one, and so, the less likely it is that any determinate proposal will in fact be justified to them. (In the limit, if the set of beliefs or desires shared by them is the null set, then the proposal justified to them is the 'null proposal,' i.e., the proposal that leaves unanswered, for every action ϕ, the question of the legitimacy of ϕing.) No consensualist can hope to satisfy both of these independently credible desiderata.

We could try to avoid this kind of indeterminacy without sacrificing universality. We could do so by adopting a more indirect mode of justification. We could appeal not to the actual members of some concrete community but, instead, to their abstracted or idealized surrogates. Rationalizing or otherwise 'adjusting' their beliefs and/or desires (considering only their 'real interests' for instance), we find that the surrogates have much more in common than the citizens they stand surrogate for, and therefore there is a substantial basis for justification, and therefore what can be justified to the surrogates (and hence for the citizens) has significant content, that is, it is determinate in the required sense. Of course, in this case, we face potentially embarrassing questions about the motivational salience of the justification we have provided. That A's surrogate α has some reason R_α to find some determinate proposal a reasonable one does not suffice to motivate A's compliance with the dictates of that proposal. Indeed, A might reject R_α (wrongly, to be sure, if there is, 'objectively' good reason to accept it), and so might reject the proposal. He has been provided with no motive for finding it reasonable and for conforming his behavior to the requirements that it imposes.

There seems to be a three-way 'trade-off' between the desiderata of universality, determinacy, and salience. We can 'buy' determinacy only by sacrificing either universality or, perhaps, salience. We can 'buy' universality only either by making the proposal justified less determinate or, perhaps, by depriving it of motivational salience for many of the individuals for whom (but not to whom) it is justified.

Independence versus Salience

Also frequently commented on is the failure of superiority with respect to independence to track superiority with respect to salience. The more independent a mode of justification is of possibly 'contaminated' attitudes and attributes, the less salient are the implications of any regime justified in that way. According to Tom Campbell:

> Contract theorists are . . . in great difficulty when they seek to characterise a state of nature which has sufficient similarity to empirical reality for us to see its connection with our own nature and social experience, and yet is still a situation in which any agreement reached . . . is fair, in that it is not the outcome of the sort of coercion, inequality or material ignorance which is commonplace in actual societies.[24]

Sandel offers an early and canonical formulation of this particular difficulty under the heading of "the perplexing and difficult demands of the Archimedean point — to find a standpoint neither compromised by its implication in the world nor dissociated and so disqualified by detachment."[25] Nagel, characteristically, treats this problem as a moral-psychological problem: "Objective advance produces a split in the self, and as it gradually widens, the problem of integration between the two standpoints becomes severe, particularly in regard to ethics and the personal life."[26]

The key here is implicit in what has just been said under the heading of "Universality versus Determinacy (versus Salience)." To achieve independence of possibly self-serving or self-enslaving attitudes, it may be necessary to employ more indirect means of justification and, therefore, to abstract or idealize away from those of an individual's reasons that might also be motives for conformity. Justifications that achieve a reasonable degree of independence and thus can exert 'Archimedean leverage' with respect to existing structures and practices are ipso facto likely to perform poorly with respect to their motivational salience. Independence has been 'purchased' by adopting indirect modes that themselves perform poorly with respect to salience.

Independence versus Determinacy

Also frequently noticed is the failure of superiority with respect to independence to track superiority with respect to determinacy. The more independent a mode of justification is with respect to possibly 'contaminated' actual attitudes and attributes, the less determinate the implications of any regime justified in that way. According to Sandel, "the original position achieves too much detachment from human circumstances, [so] that the initial situation it describes is too abstract to yield the principles Rawls says it would, or for that matter, any determinate principles at all."[27] Ackerman offers a vividly imagined characterization of the fundamental difficulty:

> By setting the choice set at infinity and the chooser at zero, all arbitrariness has been banished from the characterization of the choice situation. . . . [But when] the Rawlsian Zero confronts the Infinite Choice Set, it is impossible to choose any principles of justice until he is endowed by his creator with some set of principles to guide his judgment. . . . But as soon as Rawls permits the contractors to know some things and not others, the characterization problem arises with renewed force.[28]

Much the same point is relevant here as in the first two cases. To attain independence, it may be necessary to employ indirect means of justification. Such means involve abstraction and/or idealization. This not only undermines motivational salience, it also empties the basis of justification of much of its content and therefore deprives its results of much of their possible determinacy.

Other failures of tracking have also been noticed, though less frequently than the ones already considered.

Galston has recently drawn attention to the possibility that superiority with respect to reflexivity or perhaps transparency fails to track superiority with respect to stability or perhaps salience. He says: "The ability to separate ourselves reflectively from our other commitments is bound to have an effect on our ability to maintain those commitments, especially the ones resting on tradition, unquestioned authority, and faith."[29]

Jon Elster notes the possibility of some inevitable 'trade-off' between intelligibility and universality: "Since there are in fact always time constraints on discussions — often the stronger the more important the issues — unanimity will rarely emerge . . . [and yet one] can discuss only for so long, and then one has to make a decision, even if strong differences of opinion should remain."[30]

Danilo Zolo plausibly identifies a failure of tracking in relation to universality and stability:

> The most basic political mechanism which brings about security, through a reduction of the complexity of the environment, is the definition of an internal/external boundary. . . . In this way, the social group encompasses individuals and behavior patterns which are compatible with its own stability, and encourages, through what Schattschneider has called the 'mobilization of bias', the collective definition of 'extraneous' individuals and 'deviant' behavior patterns which it considers inimical to its own survival.[31]

Connolly sees in Foucault's 'genealogies' an argument establishing, in effect, a failure of tracking between reflexivity and independence. Reporting Foucault's views, he says: "Reflexivity is a trap. It obligates us to bring the self more completely under the control of historically constructed standards of reason and morality."[32]

Finally, Benhabib seems to identify two such failures of tracking: (1) between independence and universality — "the constraint of neutrality [in my terms independence] illicitly limits the agenda of public conversation and excludes particularly those groups like women and blacks who have not been traditional partners in the liberal dialogue";[33] and (2) between intelligibility and salience — "Within the constraints of institutions, decision procedures, limited by space and time and scarce resources, must be respected. To hope for the rational consensus of all under these circumstances would paralyze institutional life to the point of a breakdown."[34]

In addition to these by now well-known 'failures of tracking,' I am aware of some others.

Stability versus Salience (versus Universality)

Suppose that A will find some proposal a reasonable one on account of R, but would not do so for the reason R'. In this case, no justification of that proposal is stable with respect to this contingency: that A happens to have R when he might have had R' instead. In order to achieve stability of justification for such a proposal, we might suggest abstracting or idealizing away from such contingent facts about A's motivation. We might stipulate, instead, that a proposal be considered justified when we have found some consideration R_α that would make that proposal reasonable for A's surrogate α. Of course, it will matter, if stability is to be increased, how we understand the transformation of concrete citizens 'into' their idealized surrogates. But we usually do understand this transformation in a way that is responsive to the problem of achieving stability in our justifications. A's surrogate α is usually understood as differing from A himself at least in being more rational, better informed, and free from such defects of motivation as envy or weakness of will. But within such a framework of assumptions, there are a great many fewer 'degrees of freedom' with respect to the endorsement of some proposal than there are when it is A himself whose motives are at issue. While A himself might abandon R for R', his surrogate α perhaps cannot abandon R_α for R_α', except, perhaps, irrationally, ill-informedly, enviously, or weakly. And this makes an appeal to α's reason R_α a great deal more stable a basis for justification than any appeal to A's reason R could hope to be.

Adopting an indirect approach to public justification in other words provides a good basis for ensuring or increasing the stability of our justificatory arguments. But here too we 'buy' stability only at a price — indeed, at the same price we need to pay in order to 'buy' determinacy — at the cost of motivational salience. Indeed, the point is one I've already made. To show that A's surrogate α finds some proposal reasonable on account of R_α provides A himself with no motive to accept this proposal and to conform his behavior to its requirements.

We might try to make our justification more stable, not by adopting indirect techniques of justification, but, instead, by narrowing our justificatory ambitions. There are two cases here — one involving convergence, the other involving consensus — but the result is the same in either case.

First, consider the case of convergent public justification. If we assume a constant probability, across individuals, that any given individual will abandon some reason R for some other reason R' during some interval t–t', then it follows that the more individuals for whom a given proposal is justified at t by reference to a matrix of reasons $\{R_1 \ldots R_n\}$, the more probable it is that the justification of that proposal will not 'survive' throughout the interval t–t'. (For the more probable it is that one of the reasons in question, R_i, will be abandoned in favor of some reason R_i', with respect to which the proposal cannot be justified publicly.)

Second, consider the case of consensual justification. If we assume a constant probability, across individuals, that any given individual will abandon some reason R for some other reason R' during some interval t–t', then it follows that the more individuals for whom a given proposal is justified at t by reference to some common body of shared reasons $\mathbf{R^*}$, the more probable it is that the justification of that proposal will not 'survive' throughout the interval t–t'. (For the more probable it is that one of the reasons in question, R_i, will be abandoned in favor of some reason R_i', and that what remains of $\mathbf{R^*}$ after R_i has been 'subtracted' no longer constitutes an adequate basis for justification.)

Universality versus Transparency

The reasoning here is familiar. A mode of justification is more adequate with respect to universality the more members of some given community are considered relevant from the justificatory point of view. But the more such individuals are included in the 'target audience' of the justificatory reasoning, the more likely it is that there will be an individual A and a reason R_B such that A, knowing that R_B is among B's reasons for finding some regime reasonable, cannot himself find that regime reasonable, whatever other grounds he might have for doing so. If the regime is to be considered justified nonetheless, then this will be only by sacrificing transparency and maintaining that it is enough that each of A and B *has* her grounds for finding the regime reasonable and that it is not also required that these grounds *survive* discovery of the grounds the other has. To achieve universality, it may be necessary to suspend the requirement of transparency. (As before, this particular 'trade-off' can be avoided by adopting a more indirect approach to justification but, again, at the cost of poor performance with respect to salience.)

Universality versus Reflexivity versus Determinacy

A mode of justification is more adequate with respect to the requirement of universality the more members of some given community are taken into account from the justificatory point of view. But the more individuals are included in the 'target audience', the more likely it is that someone in this 'target audience' will find the standards and/or the evidence unreasonable. This seems particularly likely in view of the results already achieved. Any given set of standards embodies a particular conception of public justification. There are many such conceptions. Conceptions superior in one respect are apt to be inferior in another. Of course, despite these facts, there may actually be a determinately and determinably best conception of public justification, and some justificatory procedure may well embody this conception. But even in this case, many individuals will nevertheless in fact prefer other conceptions. A justification of a regime that depends on some particular set of standards thus will not satisfy the requirement of reflexivity for these individuals. Of course, individuals are *wrong* to reject these standards if they do indeed embody the determinately best conception of public justification. But, even in this case, rejection of the standards need not be *unreasonable*. After all, arguments establishing the superiority of one conception may be quite complicated and so might themselves lack intelligibility. And matters are even more straightforward if, as might be feared given these interim results, there were in fact no determinately best conception of justification. In this case, the rejection of the standards endorsed by any given conception would not only be reasonable, it would be perfectly proper.

We could perhaps ensure the satisfaction of both these requirements by adopting more indirect modes of argumentation. But, in this case, we might have to sacrifice the determinacy of the results achieved. The reasoning is familiar. Indirect means of justification involve abstraction and/or idealization that empties the basis of justification of much of its content and therefore deprives its results of much of their possible determinacy.

Stability versus Transparency

The reasoning is again familiar. A mode of justification is more adequate with respect to stability the more likely it is that individuals who do have grounds for finding a regime reasonable will continue to have grounds for finding that regime reasonable, given such vicissitudes as are likely to be relevant in historically short periods of time. But the more transparent a form of justificatory reasoning, the more likely it is that there will be an individual A and a reason R_B such that A, whatever his initial evaluation of R_B, may come to find repugnant the fact that some particular regime is justified, at least partially, with respect to R_B. The more transparent the

TABLE 6.1. The Apparent Incompatibility of the Dual Aims of Public Justification

	Universality	Independence	Transparency	Reflexivity	Determinacy
Universality	X	—	—	—	—
Salience	—	—	—	—	—
Stability	—	—	?	?	?
Intelligibility	—	?	—	—	—
Determinacy	—	—	?	—	X

justification, the less stable the regime. (As before, this particular 'trade-off' can be avoided by adopting a more indirect approach to justification but, again, at the cost of poor performance with respect to salience.)

Summing up, we see that, for every respect in which one mode of justification might be superior to another, there is another respect in which it must be inferior. We therefore have two of the three vital conditions for incommensurability and thus for essential contestability. We have a plurality of evaluative dimensions and a failure of tracking. In the next chapter I consider whether we have all three conditions that are needed for establishing the interim thesis announced at the beginning of Chapter 2 — namely, that *the concept of public justification is, in view of the incommensurability of some of the values that constitute its ideal, apparently an essentially contestable concept.*

In any event, there are plausible arguments for at least the failures of tracking set out in Table 6.1.

We thus have the expected structure of *inter*-familial failures of tracking, reflecting the so-called dual aims of the project of public justification, and perhaps the possibility, canvassed by Joseph Raz, that "[t]here may be no middle way between actual (including implied) agreement and rational justification."[35] That there might be no such 'middle way' — and therefore no public conception of public justification — is perhaps especially suggested in the facts (a) that the key realistic desideratum, that of salience, fails to be tracked by any of the moralistic desiderata — to achieve salience, we seem to have to sacrifice transparency, reflexivity, and independence, as well as universality and determinacy; and (b) that the key moralistic desideratum, that of independence, fails to be tracked by any of the key realistic desiderata — to achieve independence, we seem to have to be prepared to 'trade off' against universality, salience, intelligibility, and determinacy. The very idea of public justification may well be an incoherent idea.[36] Indeed, we seem to have the makings of what Fishkin refers to as "competing 'ideals without an ideal' rather than a solution to the priority problem that resolves all conflict among first principles."[37]

Notes

1. Cf. *A Theory of Justice,* pp. 17–18: "[T]he question of justification is to be settled by working out a problem of deliberation; we have to ascertain which principles it would be rational to adopt given the contractual situation. . . . But how are we to decide what is the most favored interpretation [of this situation]? I assume, for one thing, that there is a broad measure of agreement that principles of justice should be chosen under certain conditions."

2. Cf. *Morals by Agreement,* pp. 145–46: "Rational persons, faced with the costs of natural or market interaction in the face of externalities, agree to a different, cooperative mode of interaction. They agree to act, not on the basis of individual utility-maximization, but rather on the basis of optimization, where the optimal outcome is determined by the principle of minimax relative concession. In reaching this agreement, of course, each seeks to maximize his own utility."

3. Cf. *Social Justice in the Liberal State,* pp. 10–11: "A power structure is illegitimate if it can be justified only through a conversation in which some person (or group) must assert that he is (or they are) the privileged moral authority."

4. Cf. Rawls, *A Theory of Justice,* pp. 165–66: "[I]f we waive the problem of interpersonal comparisons of utility and if the parties are viewed as rational individuals who . . . follow the principle of insufficient reason in computing likelihoods . . . , then the idea of the initial situation leads naturally to the average principle. By choosing it the parties maximize their expected well-being as seen from this point of view."

5. Cf. *Moral Consciousness and Communicative Action,* p. 93: "Only those norms can claim to be valid that meet (or could meet) with the approval of all affected in their capacity as participants in a practical discourse" subject to the condition that "all affected can freely accept the consequences and the side effects that the general observance of a controversial norm can be expected to have for the satisfaction of the interests of each individual."

6. Cf. "Public Justification and Democratic Adjudication," p. 252: "[I]ndividuals devoted to their own ends agree on a set of substantive moral principles, which may be understood as . . . a reasonable compromise that advances the values of everyone. . . ."

7. Galston, *Liberal Purposes,* p. 195.

8. Wolf, "Two Levels of Pluralism," p. 788.

9. What of those conceptions, most notably Rawls's, that occupy, because of their 'duplex' character, with both 'embedding' and 'embedded' modes of argumentation, both of the two positions implicit in the given dimensions? The important point here is implied by something I have already said about such conceptions — namely, that the 'embedding' argument is of fundamental justificatory significance and so is likely to possess the shortcomings of arguments ranged in the way it is with respect to the dimensions. That the 'embedded' argument might be ranged differently with respect to these dimensions does not necessarily compensate for the shortcomings of the 'embedding' argument.

10. Cf. Waldron, "Theoretical Foundations of Liberalism," p. 145: Such individuals as *A* "will be repelled by the thought that their ideals share a common form with those of people they despise. . . ." *A* in this example does not satisfy Philip Wicksteed's requirement of 'nontuism': he takes an interest in the interests of his fellows. Cf. Gauthier, *Morals by Agreement,* p. 87. *A* might also be characterized as a 'fanatic', though not, perhaps, in R. M. Hare's sense. (Cf. *Moral Thinking,* ch. 10.) *A* seems prepared to 'cut off his nose to spite his face'. Surely it is odd to pass up an opportunity to fulfill one's conception of the good merely in order to prevent others from fulfilling theirs. *How* 'odd' this is depends, of course, on how 'depraved' their conceptions seem to be/actually are.

11. A consensus theorist might supplement her model of justification in either or both of two ways: (1) by arguing that empirical diversity in psychology conceals an underlying, 'essential' similarity or even identity in psychology and that the justificatory apparatus reflects this deeper reality; and (2) by developing techniques for ensuring compliance by empirically diverse individuals with the demands of her justificatory theory, for example, through mechanisms of socialization or behavior modification or enforcement.

12. Cf. Cherniak, *Minimal Rationality,* p. 51.

13. *Political Liberalism,* ch. 2, sec. 7.

14. Cf. Dworkin, *Taking Rights Seriously,* p. 153 and Gauthier, *Morals by Agreement,* p. 344.

15. Cf. Polanyi, *The Logic of Liberty*, ch. 10, esp. p. 159, and Hayek, *Law, Legislation and Liberty*, ch. 10, esp. vol. 2, p. 116.

16. *Theories of Justice*, p. 8.

17. Cf. David Miller, "Deliberative Democracy and Social Choice," p. 61: "To be seen to engage in political debate we must argue in terms that any other participant could potentially accept, and 'it's good for me' is not such an argument."

18. *Theories of Justice*, p. 7.

19. Cf. Dryzek, *Discursive Democracy*, p. 171: "[A]ny manifestation of any discourse . . . reproduces the discourse and political vision embodied" in it.

20. Macedo gives another basis for suspecting the inevitability of trade-offs between the realistic desideratum of stability and the moralistic requirement of reflexivity. He says (*Liberal Virtues*, p. 66.): "Political theorists have often, as Leo Strauss pointed out, deployed 'exoteric' versions of their theories: ones that sacrifice full disclosure in order to avoid confrontation and contention and smooth the way to a political settlement. Widespread, unreflective theory acceptance might be jeopardized by the open and candid defence of liberalism as a regime. Sacrificing political candour and open argument in order to smooth the transition to liberal peace might well be justified, if there really is a tension between candour and allegiance. . . ." But perhaps the mechanism Macedo talks about (but doesn't endorse) is the same as the one I have in mind. Perhaps a regime supported by some 'exoteric' rationalization attracts posterior allegiance.

21. "Moral Pluralism and Political Consensus," p. 11.

22. *Ethics and the Limits of Philosophy*, p. 103.

23. Of the various assumptions of this argument, this seems the most vulnerable. We could more confidently claim that an increase in the number of individuals is nowhere accompanied by a decrease in the number of starting points. But my stronger claim, in the text, seems a reasonable one in the context of public justification. Those who emphasize convergence are particularly sensitive to the pluralistic character of modern Western societies and to the difficulties posed by such pluralism for consensual justificatory approaches. The convergentist is therefore particularly badly placed to object to the idea that different people are likely to believe and/or desire different things.

24. *Justice*, p. 71.

25. *Liberalism and the Limits of Justice*, p. 17. Cf. O'Neill, "Ethical Reasoning and Ideological Pluralism," pp. 710–11.

26. *The View from Nowhere*, p. 86.

27. *Liberalism and the Limits of Justice*, p. 27.

28. *Social Justice in the Liberal State*, p. 339.

29. *Liberal Purposes*, p. 294.

30. "The Market and the Forum," p. 115. Cf. Barry, *Political Argument*, p. 261: "[B]argaining also has costs . . . [which] increase with the size of majority required for a decision. . . ."

31. *Democracy and Complexity*, p. 41.

32. *Politics and Ambiguity*, p. 108.

33. Cf. Bruce Brower, "The Limits of Public Reason," p. 13 and Gordon Graham, "Liberalism: Metaphysical, Political, Historical," p. 100.

34. *Situating the Self*, pp. 12, 47.

35. "Facing Diversity," p. 46.

36. Cf. Rawls, *Political Liberalism*, p. 102, n. 13 for the idea that a procedure might 'embed' an ideal.

37. *The Dialogue of Justice*, p. 4.

7

Overarching Principles and Perspectives?

22. Some Preliminaries

I claim to have established a case for the essential contestability of the concept of public justification, and so for the insolubility of the problem of public justification, and so for the failure of the liberal project of legitimation.

There is good reason to believe that there are multiple independent desiderata associated with the ideal of public justification and to believe that, in many cases, satisfaction of one, say moralistic, desideratum means, ipso facto, inadequate performance with respect to other, particularly realistic, desiderata. Such a prima facie case for *the contestability thesis* could be overcome were we able to discover or construct some "further overarching principle and perspective from which these [desiderata] can be put into [some] . . . objective balance."[1]

Indeed, considerations familiar to R. M. Hare's readers may seem to suggest the inevitable availability of such principles and perspectives and the superficiality of any attempt to insist on their non-existence.[2] It is Hare's view, no doubt widely shared,[3] that "at the critical level [of moral thinking] there is a requirement that we resolve . . . [conflicts of this kind], unless we are to confess that our thinking has been incomplete."[4] When we say that duties conflict, or, analogously that desiderata seem not to admit of simultaneous satisfaction, we are speaking, according to Hare, at a merely intuitive level of moral discourse – which nevertheless has its practical uses, particularly in moral education and as a bulwark against wishful thinking. Trading heavily on the idea that "*ought* implies *can*," and that conflicting requirements therefore can't both be genuine requirements, Hare concludes that these prima facie conflicts are just that: conflicts prima facie, but, necessarily, not conflicts *tout court*. He accordingly rejects a 'one-level' treatment of morality and advocates its supplementation, especially in such situations of prima facie conflict, by appeals to a second, critical level of thinking in which a more systematic approach is taken and prima facie principles are appraised, and the conflicts they generate are resolved.[5]

We need not accept the particular details of Hare's analysis in order to feel its force. That the ideal of public justification seems to require us, for instance, to achieve salience and independence, and that these demands arguably cannot be met simultaneously does suggest that there is, necessarily, some optimal way of balancing them, and others, so that what is required of us is, in fact, something that we can do.[6]

Another point is important. Any such search for overarching principles and perspectives is itself subject to a number of constraints.

First, if such a search is to play a role in solving the problem of public justification, it must yield a determinately best way of balancing the competing demands implicit in the various desiderata or, at the very least, the various ways of doing so must turn out to be 'ultimately extensionally equivalent'; that is, they must identify the same constitutional regime as the determinately best regime even if the grounds on which or procedures by which they determine this differ from one way to the other. Otherwise, we will simply have reproduced, at a 'higher level', precisely the problem we invoked such techniques to solve. Suppose that one technique gives the assignment of weights ω_1 (to the various desiderata that cannot be simultaneously satisfied and so need to be balanced), which implies, in turn, that some conception of public justification is the best conception; that another technique gives the assignment of weights ω_2, which implies, in turn, that another conception is the best conception. Unless the two conceptions are extensionally equivalent, then we may have it that, according to the first, one regime is better, whereas according to the second, another regime is better. And this constitutes no *solution* to the problem of public justification. (I return to this point in sec. 27.)

Second, any technique for determining an optimal balance among the various desiderata must itself satisfy those of these very desiderata that are relevant to its own evaluation. Otherwise, *reflexivity* will not have been attained in relation to the determination, via the conception identified by this technique, of the best regime for a given community. These kinds of techniques provide the second-order standards and evidence by which we assess the first-order standards invoked in determining the best regime for a given community. If these second-order standards do not withstand critical scrutiny, then, by reflexivity, the first-order standards ipso facto will not or should not withstand critical scrutiny, and so the conclusions they might yield cannot be sustained, and, once again, the problem of public justification is not adequately addressed. (These considerations are not decisive. We may not want, ultimately, to assign as much weight to the requirement of reflexivity as would be necessary to sustain this suggestion. Remember that some balancing of the competing desiderata will be necessary. We cannot rule out, a priori, that reflexivity may have to be sacrificed so that other, more significant requirements can be honored.)

In this chapter, I want to consider four approaches to the problem of public justification. In each case I adapt suggestions developed in other contexts. I will try to show that each of these approaches fails, and that these failures ground more firmly what has so far been suggested — namely, that "[j]ustification, as it turns out, is an essentially contestable concept."[7]

All of the proposals I want to consider are reasonably styled 'formalistic'. Each is "abstract and computational,"[8] with a preference for "explicit and univocal decision-procedures."[9] Three of them explicitly depend on the apparatus of decision theory, broadly conceived. They identify some function that determines a socially 'dominant' regime. Aside from determining the values of input to the function and of performing the calculations associated with its evaluation, these procedures require no particular human ingenuity to employ. They embody what Sheldon Wolin calls "Methodism." Martin Benjamin says:

> 'Methodism', as Sheldon Wolin calls it, is the doctrinaire demand that all rational thought and decision be modeled on the impersonality, precision, and quantifiability of mathematical or (certain forms of) scientific reasoning. . . . The aim is to devise a uniform procedure or set of rules that if correctly applied to a certain question will yield the same determinate conclusion for all — a moral algorithm. . . . This 'rationalistic conception of rationality,' as Bernard Williams suggests, is closely allied to contemporary 'administrative ideas of rationality' or 'modern bureaucratic' conceptions.[10]

The other procedure arguably does not embody this project. This procedure is Alasdair MacIntyre's, and I turn to it in section 23.

One final point. In section 3, I considered the possibility that the search for a determinately best (available) conception of public justification might in fact be unnecessary, heuristically, because the problem of public justification might admit of a 'direct' solution. Rather than searching for the best *conception* in order to employ it to identify the best regime, we simply look for that *regime* that is best on all (available) conceptions. Such a 'dominant' regime is the one that ought to be implemented and honored, and its specifications constitute a goal toward which progressive institutional restructuring ought to be oriented. In fact, all of the techniques considered in this chapter involve such a 'direct' approach to the problem, and their failure is symptomatic of the inadequacy of such an approach. Nevertheless, it is important that I repeat a point made already. None of the techniques I am going to examine in addressing the problem was in fact intended by its advocates to play such a role. For instance, Gauthier does not intend that the principle of minimax relative concession (see sec. 26) be employed to determine a socially valid balancing of competing desiderata for public justification. I canvass the possibility of using this device for this purpose only because some of its features recommend it as a candidate for such use. When I consider this device under the heading "Minimax Relative Concession à la Gauthier and Gaus," I do so purely for expository convenience and to give credit where it is due; I do not do so by way of suggesting that this device, being unfit for solving *my* problem, is unfit for the purposes for which it was originally deployed. On this question I have, and venture, no interesting opinion.

23. MacIntyre's Strategy

MacIntyre's proposal for dealing with incommensurabilities is simple enough. Suppose that we have two rivals, X and Y. They might be rival scientific paradigms or rival moral traditions. In the case at hand, they might be rival regimes or types of regimes. These rivals might be difficult to compare in any straightforward way on account of apparent incommensurabilities. Perhaps X is superior to Y with respect to the standard δ_1, whereas Y is superior to X with respect to δ_2, where δ_1-superiority fails to track or to be tracked by δ_2-superiority. We have, then, a prima facie case of incommensurability.[11]

What does MacIntyre suggest that we do when faced with apparently incommensurable alternatives? He suggests that we compare the power of each of the rivals to explain the strengths and weaknesses both of itself and of the other, as judged by standards 'internal' to the tradition or theory being assessed, and that we select that rival as the better of the two that makes a better job of providing these kinds of explanations. If, in other words, we could show that $X >_x Y$ and that $X >_y Y$, then, surely, we could claim the unequivocal superiority of X. MacIntyre says:

> [T]he rational superiority of that tradition to rival traditions is held to reside in its capacity not only for identifying and characterising the limitations and failures of that rival tradition as judged by that rival tradition's own standards, limitations that that rival tradition itself lacks the resources to explain or understand, but also for explaining and understanding those limitations and failures in some tolerably precise way. Moreover it must be the case that the rival tradition lacks the capacity similarly to identify, characterise, and explain failures of the . . . [first] tradition.[12]

In searching for a 'dominant' regime, and thus for a 'direct' solution, this translates into the requirements that we identify a regime

a. from whose perspective we can explain the failures of other regimes with respect to the particular conceptions of public justification that they themselves are meant to embody;
b. from whose perspective we can explain the successes and failures, on its own terms, of that very regime with respect to the conception of public justification that *it* is meant to embody; and
c. that is superior to other regimes in these regards.

Can we identify any such regime as is envisaged here? If we can, then we can solve the problem of public justification.

First, a preliminary question. Why have I identified MacIntyre's method of commensuration of prima facie incommensurables with the possibility of a 'direct' solution of the problem of public justification — namely, of discovering a regime that is superior with respect to every conception? Consider what we would have, if we found a regime X that satisfied the three demands associated with MacIntyre's method. We would have a regime that is superior to its rival Y both in its own terms and in Y's terms. X can explain those failures of Y that are failures by the standards implicit in Y itself (condition (a)), whereas Y cannot explain those failures of X that are failures by the standards implicit in X itself (condition (c)). And X can explain those of its own failures that are failures in its own terms (condition (b)). We therefore seem to have shown that X is superior to Y both in its own terms and in its rival's terms, in other words, that it is superior whichever set of standards is employed, that it is a 'dominant' regime in the sense specified. *Q.E.D.*

Can we employ MacIntyre's strategy to discover a 'dominant' regime? I do not believe that we can, for reasons I have already sketched in section 3 and here elaborate.

Consider what's involved in formulating the 'ground plan' for some preferred political regime within a framework that includes a particular conception of public justification, where that conception is given by some particular assignment of weights w to the various desiderata $\delta_1 \ldots \delta_n$ that jointly constitute the ideal of public justification. Certainly, what the theorist will strive for is a more or less deductive derivation of the description of the regime from the conception plus such broadly empirical claims as are marked by it as appropriate to its own implementation.

In this case, there will *either* be no 'failures' in the conception's own terms for some rival approach to identify and explain, *or* whatever 'failures' in its own terms might be discovered will be due either to empirical inadequacy or to logical flaws. (There may be failures in terms other than its own; the conception may be an inferior conception. But MacIntyre does not and cannot permit reliance on this kind of information.) But, in this case, it is hard to see how the rival's explanation of these 'failures' could be superior, as required by condition (c), to the explanation of these 'failures' that could be provided in terms of the conception itself. Both the conception and its rival(s) will agree in deprecating factual error and invalid reasoning. In this respect, neither can be shown to 'dominate' the other, and so neither of the regimes can be established as the 'dominant' regime.[13]

Of course, there is always the possibility that these 'failures' are 'systematically self-serving' in the sense that they have the effect of 'covering up' or deprecating such weaknesses of the regime as are inevitable given the assignment ω of weights to desiderata. Perhaps an empirical claim is invoked in the derivation of the regime's principles which implies that some desideratum that is going to be scanted in that regime (because it is assigned low weight by ω) is anyway unrealizable in concrete circumstances. Or perhaps a logical error is made that seems to permit the characterization of the regime both as satisfactory in relation to δ_i and as satisfactory in relation to δ_j, despite the fact that simultaneous satisfaction of these desiderata is not possible, at least to the extent implied.

In these kinds of cases, we might think that the conception's rivals *can* better explain its failures than it can itself, and that while it may be true that every (respectable) conception will deprecate errors of fact and failures of validity in reasoning, some conceptions lend themselves more readily to, indeed perhaps even provide fertile ground for, mistakes of this kind. On this account, that regime is dominant over others, even by the standards they themselves are taken to embody, which provides the least temptation to error of this kind.

I do not think much of this suggestion. First, we need to distinguish between the 'logic of the situation' and the psychology of a regime's advocates. It is surely of no relevance — absent a finding about situational logic — that the advocates of one regime are more prone to errors in the assessment of facts and in reasoning than are the advocates of a rival regime. *Modulo* the proviso, there are no grounds to judge a regime by its advocates.

But what of the proviso? Perhaps a regime's advocates fall into error precisely because the regime drives them to do so. Perhaps *their* failings merely reflect and indeed are the causal consequences of *its* failings.[14] If citizens of one regime are less prone to these failures of judgment and reasoning than citizens of other such regimes, then their regime is indeed the 'dominant' regime, and the determination that it fulfills these conditions constitutes a 'direct' solution to the problem of public justification. That regime is best, in short, which is least productive of 'false consciousness'.[15]

Frankly, I do not see how regimes of the various kinds at issue could be distinguished reliably in this way. Remember that we are considering variants on broadly liberal themes. It is inconceivable that, relative to any of the concrete conceptions of public justification that are under consideration — Rawls's, Gauthier's, Ackerman's, and so on — a regime could be implemented that would be grossly defective from the point of view at issue. It is not as if we were comparing Rawls's favored regime with Hitler's or Stalin's.

To be sure, there may well be some differences even among broadly liberal regimes in the extent to which they depend on or generate 'false consciousness' among their citizens. Indeed, Rawls suggests that 'utilitarian' regimes are likely to depend more than his own preferred regime on 'false consciousness' for their stability.[16]

But, even granting the soundness of arguments by Rawls and others, these arguments do not provide grounds for the demonstration of 'dominance'. The reasoning here is simple enough. Suppose that a regime X is better, though not 'grossly' so, than a second regime Y in the degree to which it generates and/or depends for stability on 'false consciousness'. These are grounds, *ceteris paribus,* for considering X superior to Y, but are they grounds that, as required for the demonstration of 'dominance', are recognized as such from the point of view both of that conception of public justification underlying X and of that conception underlying Y? Within broad limits, surely not. Superiority with respect to 'false consciousness' is equivalent, in effect, to superiority with respect to reflexivity. And while this desideratum is an important one, it is one whose satisfaction is known to be at odds with the satisfaction of the realistic requirements of universality, salience, and stability. (See Table 6.1.) To say that superiority in this respect *ought* to be sufficient to determine 'dominance' *simpliciter* therefore presupposes, and so certainly does not bypass, a determination of the best conception of public justification.

This kind of approach is not a technique for the 'direct' determination of a best regime. Whether it will work or not depends entirely on the quality of the argumentation given in favor of the proposal that superiority with respect to 'false consciousness' implies superiority *simpliciter.* In other words, we will need to determine a best conception of public justification *before* we can appeal to this line of reasoning. Engaging in such reasoning therefore is not a way of mounting a 'direct' attack on the problem of public justification. MacIntyre's strategy therefore fails: "Each system of thought had its own set of standards internal to it and there was no third set of neutral standards to which appeal could be made."[17] This must be our interim conclusion.

24. The Majoritarianism of Ackerman and Gaus

Gaus and Ackerman both face the problem of what Ackerman calls "good-faith disagreement."[18] This is what I call the 'problem of public justification'. What both envisage is that the resources necessary for achieving unanimity will 'run out' long before this problem has been solved. While unanimitarian techniques might provide guidance in characterizing the rough general outlines of a satisfactory regime, they are inadequate to determine what needs to be determined if there is to be a public basis for the adjudication of disagreements. As Gaus says, "[O]nce the . . . argument proceeds beyond abstract basic principles its claims to have provided a public justification will be increasingly contested—and rationally so."[19] The problem in this situation, as Ackerman says, is posed by the question, "What decision rule should be used when liberal statesmen disagree about the best way to compromise the liberal ideal . . . ?"[20] Even if "our citizens are fated to disagree about the *substance* of second-best compromise . . . [it nevertheless] does not follow that they are fated to reach a conversational impasse when the question arises as to the *procedure* that offers the best way of resolving their substantive disagreements."[21] Like his citizens, our constitutional delegates disagree about a substantive question, "Which regime is best?" But perhaps, as Ackerman suggests, they could nevertheless agree on some procedure to determine which regime they ought to honor. According to Ackerman, some such procedure is indeed available for this purpose. It is simple majority voting, which, as Ackerman reports, Kenneth May has shown "is the *only* decision procedure that satisfies four simple conditions that we will call *universal domain* (U), *anonymity* (A), *outcome indifference* (O), and *positive responsiveness* (P)."[22] If these conditions are all the conditions and the only conditions that individuals have reason to require in a method of aggregating their preferences for regimes, then, absent formal difficulties, this is a method they could agree to use to identify a dominant regime.

Step I: Violations of Extremal Restriction

Unfortunately, formal difficulties are readily at hand. Imagine that regimes are arrayed as follows in the order of their 'recognition' of realistic desiderata: $X>Y>Z$. Of course, some individuals who assign heavy weights to realistic desiderata will rank the conceptions in accordance with this array—that is, $X>Y>Z$. And other individuals who weight moralistic desiderata heavily may rank these conceptions in the reverse order, $Z>Y>X$, given the failures of tracking already noted. But some individuals may rank regimes only partly in terms of their 'unidimensional' similarity to the particular regime they actually most prefer. Someone who weights realistic requirements heavily might nevertheless rank the regimes $X>Z>Y$ precisely because she also 'feels the tug' of the moralistic requirements that she nevertheless does not weight so heavily.[23] But in this case, a majoritarian social decision function provably fails to define a transitive social ordering over these individual rankings and thus fails to solve the problem of public justification.[24] These rankings violate the extremal restriction requirement, which is apparently a necessary (as well as a sufficient) condition for the definition of an ordering of alternatives via majoritarian techniques.[25]

What this means, crudely, is that so long as there are all three kinds of rankings mentioned in the last paragraph, there is potential for a cycle of voting, in which X defeats Y which defeats Z which, in turn, defeats X, so that which one is undefeated and therefore legitimated depends on the exact order in which the comparisons are made. And this, of course, opens up the pairwise procedure of majoritarian voting to manipulation by those who can control the agenda. Suppose that we have three individuals. A's conception of public justification implies that, between regimes X and Y, $X>Y$; that between Y and Z, $Y>Z$; and that between X and Z, $X>Z$. B's conception implies that, between regimes X and Y, $Y>X$; that between Y and Z, $Z>Y$; and that between X and Z, $Z>X$. C's conception implies that, between regimes X and Y, $Y>X$; that between Y and Z, $Y>Z$; and that between X and Z, $Z>X$. To find a socially valid preference for regimes, we need to 'reduce' the three-way comparisons to two-way comparisons. Suppose we determine the overall 'winner' by first determining the X-Y majority and then determining the majority between the X-Y winner and Z. X is the first-round winner and then is beaten by Z in round two. But what if we had first compared X and Z and then compared the winner, Z, with Y. In this case, Y wins the 'play-off' and is thus the overall winner. Which regime comes out best overall depends not solely on the choice of decision function, majority on a two-way comparison, and on the individual preferences that are 'input' into it, but also on a factor that can only be considered 'conventional', namely, the *order* in which the two-way comparisons are made. Such a procedure is therefore unacceptable in the context of constitutional decision making where there is a great deal at stake, and delegates would be reluctant to make outcomes dependent on purely conventional decisions about agendas.

Given a profile of individual orderings that includes orderings like $X>Z>Y$, this non-existence result can be derived. But should we *take* this profile? In one sense nothing turns on whether we include orderings like $X>Z>Y$ in such a profile. I can and will show how to get the same general conclusion on the basis of a profile that does not include them (see "Step II"). Still, their inclusion perhaps needs to be defended. How could individuals fail to rank alternatives in accordance with their similarity to their most preferred option? The simplest point is, I think, the best. To say that these orderings are not psychologically plausible, or perhaps even possible, is, in effect, simply to insist on 'privileging' orderings that respond in simple ways — either directly or inversely — to some allegedly unidimensional arrangement of regimes. But the legitimacy of any such 'privileging' depends, of course, on exactly the point I have been concerned to dispute: that the issue that arises in relation to regimes is indeed a 'unidimensional' one; such an issue is at least bidimensional (moralistic and realistic desiderata), and rankings such as $X>Z>Y$ clearly respond to its bidimensional character. There are therefore no grounds for ignoring the possibility, indeed the reality, of individuals of the kind I've described.

The result therefore stands. Majoritarian techniques cannot reliably give a transitive social ordering of regimes and therefore cannot provide an adequate basis for constitutional decision making: transitivity and being proof against agenda-manipulation are clearly desirable characteristics of any procedure that is adopted in that context.

Step II: The Inadequacy of Condorcet Winners in Constitutional Contexts

But what if all individuals did rank regimes in such simple ways as are illustrated in Table 7.1? These individuals, obviously, "agree that [X] is at one end of the scale, [Z] at the other, and [Y] in the middle, which means they agree entirely on how the political spectrum is arranged."[26] As William Riker says, such "single-peakedness implies transitivity and hence ensures the existence of a Condorcet winner"[27] or, in other words, of "an option which can beat all others in [all combinations of majoritarian] pairwise voting."[28] There seems to be no difficulty in defining a social deci-

TABLE 7.1. Some Specimen Orderings of Regimes

	X	U	Y	V	Z
A	1	2	3	4	5
B	=2	1	=2	3	4
C	=3	=2	1	=2	=3
D	4	3	=2	1	=2
E	5	4	3	2	1

sion function that determines, based on individuals' orderings, which regime ought to be selected by those individuals as the socially 'dominant' regime.

Care is needed even here. All that is guaranteed by the single-peakedness of individuals' orderings is the existence of a 'Condorcet winner' — a regime, in other words, that will be preferred *by a majority* of individuals, in pairwise comparisons, to every other regime. But in the realm of public justification and in relation to the desideratum of reflexivity, this is clearly inadequate as a basis for instituting the Condorcet winner. Remember that individuals are imagined as choosing among distinct constitutional regimes; they are delegates to a constitutional convention. Remember too that solutions to the problem of public justification are subject to the requirement of reflexivity. To show that the Condorcet winner is the regime that ought to be instituted, it is not enough that it is preferred according to a majoritarian social decision function. It will also be necessary to show that the majoritarian social decision function is itself satisfactory, and clearly it is not — despite the fact that it satisfies May's four conditions. In this context, these conditions are palpably inadequate as a basis for commanding assent to its use.

First, majoritarian decision making is best adapted to "conflictual choices in which no mutually beneficial opportunities are available,"[29] It remains to be seen that the situation of constitutional choice does involve inevitable conflict rather than the possibility of mutually beneficial compromises. Indeed, it is a general feature of Condorcet winners that they do not always represent what might be thought of as an optimal compromise[30] but sometimes have "some characteristics of a 'tyranny of the majority'," in which a majority imposes a solution that ranks very highly for each of *them* in favor of an alternative that "ranks *relatively* high on all preference scales."[31]

Imagine that *A, B, C, D,* and *E* in Table 7.1 represent *types* rather than individuals. Then, depending on the demography, the 'Condorcet winner' for these types might in fact be *X*. If there were, for instance, twice as many type-*A* individuals as there were individuals of all the other types combined, then the regime *X* would indeed be the 'Condorcet winner'.[32] Type-*A* individuals prefer *X* to every other regime in pairwise comparisons, and, given their numbers, their preferences always prevail if pairwise majoritarian comparisons are employed to determine collectively enforced outcomes.

Of course, this regime ranks very poorly, for instance, on the orderings of type-*E* individuals, who are required to make much larger concessions than type-*A* individuals if this regime is adopted. Indeed, type-*A* individuals concede nothing and type-*E* individuals concede 'everything' in relation to their preferred regimes if the regime *X is* adopted for the community. But how, in this case, can rational, willing compliance with the demands of this regime be expected from type-*E* individuals? They are victims of majority tyranny, and we can expect them to claim and will think it reasonable if they claim, in Gaus's words, that "the proposal does not constitute a reasonable bargain."[33] Where an 'optimal compromise' is forgone, some "are to accept the greater advantages of others as a sufficient reason for lower expectations over the whole course of . . . [their lives]. This is surely an extreme demand." Within the constitutional realm, delegates would surely "recognize that it would be highly unwise if not irrational to choose principles which may have consequences so extreme that they cannot accept them in practice."[34]

Second, for the constitutional realm, it is unclear that any merely majoritarian decision procedure is appropriate, whatever its merits in other realms and quite independently of whether it succeeds in finding a solution that might plausibly be thought of as an 'optimal compromise'. First of all, we need not be concerned, in this realm, about decision and transaction costs, and so we may prefer, given the prospects for vote-trading and so on, to insist on otherwise more 'costly' unanimitarian procedures. Certainly, when vote-trading is permitted, there are favorable prospects: "Each voter increases his ability to *control* those *events* (issues) about which he feels most intense in exchange for a loss of control over those events about which he cares little."[35] Given that delegates to a constitutional convention *can* be expected to care a very great deal about those issues about which they feel most strongly, control over the disposition of such issues is surely to be prized. In such a situation, "the rejected alternatives have outcomes that one can hardly accept."[36]

In summary, the answer to my question is no: there is no prospect, despite the assumed single-peakedness of individuals' orderings of regimes, of a direct solution of the problem of public justification using the techniques recommended by Ackerman and Gaus. A majoritarian social decision function can be *defined* but could not be *adopted*, by delegates to a constitutional convention, as a device for identifying an 'optimal' regime. Use of such a function undermines prospects for determining an 'optimal compromise' that imposes lesser 'strains of commitment', and for insuring against outcomes that are utterly unacceptable. (The two points are two sides of a single coin.) David Miller says: "This, we might say, is *the* problem posed by social choice for democracy — that is, in general, there is no fair and rational way of amalgamating voters' preferences to reach a social decision."[37]

25.   Hurley's Social Knowledge Functions

Here, some observations of Hurley may give hope. She suggests that, when a social decision function is reinterpreted as "a social knowledge function . . . and the social choice conditions as conditions on ways of arriving at beliefs about what should be done on the basis of the beliefs of citizens," "an explicit and principled epistemological basis [is provided] for rejecting or restricting trouble-making conditions" — that is, conditions generating non-existence results.[38] Let's consider her important arguments.

Hurley's main point is that "[c]ertain social choice conditions . . . are rendered attractive by non-cognitivist presuppositions" (crudely, that individuals' orderings of regimes are 'mere preferences' and not subject to rational discussion) and that "among the conditions which produce intransitivities [i.e., imply non-existence] are some which there is independent reason to regard as incompatible with" an alternative, cognitivist conceptualization of "social choice conditions as conditions on ways of arriving at beliefs. . . ."[39] In particular, the conditions **U** (unrestricted domain) and **I** (independence of irrelevant alternatives) — which according to Hurley must be considered together since "much of . . . [Condition **I**'s] power derives from its application across such a domain" as is implied by **U**[40] — must be violated because "a social knowledge function sensitive to tracking concerns . . . must be sensitive to external information about the reliability of beliefs . . . [and] this sensitivity . . . violates condition" **I** and thus apparently permits the evasion of the non-existence theorem.[41] The basic idea seems to be that the cognitivist demand, that an individual's beliefs about what is best (in my case, what is the best regime) should 'track the truth' and thus be responsive to argumentation and the presentation of evidence, (a) restricts the domain of variants to some subset of those permitted by **U**, and (b) is to be expressed, within a decision-theoretic framework, as the exploitation of information in ways precluded by **I**. In either case, the conditions sufficient for a non-existence proof seem no longer to obtain, and the existence of a social knowledge function therefore seems to be demonstrated.[42]

In assessing Hurley's approach, we find that much depends on what we take her to be trying to show. There are two possibilities: (1) so-called social knowledge functions, interpreted à la cognitivism, are to be *substituted* for social decision functions, interpreted à la non-cognitivism, in order, in our case, to determine a 'dominant' regime; (2) so-called social knowledge functions, interpreted à la cognitivism, are to *supplement* other devices for determining a 'dominant' regime. In the first case, I think it is reasonable to insist that if the question at issue is best interpreted à la cognitivism there is either no need to recruit any so-called social knowledge function to determine a 'dominant' regime, or that conditions sufficient for a non-existence proof still obtain. In the second case, I think that it is reasonable to insist that, in the realm of public justification, there is no proper role for a merely supplementary use of so-called social knowledge functions. Let me consider these points.

1. Individuals order regimes in various ways. The 'natural' reading of these orderings is subjectivist and non-cognitivist: they simply reflect individuals' preferences for regimes. Is there a way of reinterpreting them à la cognitivism and so of treating them as subject to further constraints that might, for instance, undermine the claim that they require, for their adequate representation, the full strength of condition **U**? Hurley thinks there is. She thinks that such orderings should be interpreted not as expressions of subjective preferences but, instead, as judgments about which regime would be best for the community, in which case they admit, as they do not on a purely subjective interpretation, of truth and falsity and of being disciplined by the demands that they be responsive to 'debunking' and, more generally, that they 'track the truth'. The problem here, I think, is that if there are considerations adequate to play any 'debunking' role, then it is not clear why the machinery of social decision theory, adapted to cognitivist assumptions, should have any role to play in the determination of a 'dominant' regime. In this case, our appeal, in order to identify such a

regime, is to the considerations that can play a 'debunking' role and not to any aggregative machinery. Of course, absent these considerations, there are no grounds for restricting or disciplining individuals' preferences, and we therefore have the conditions for the demonstration of non-existence. My main point, however, is the opposite. In the presence of such considerations it may well be true that we can guarantee the existence of a social knowledge function, but in their presence we have no need for the use of any such device, not, at least, as a substitute for rational argumentation.

2. This brings me to the second interpretation of Hurley's project and the one, I believe, fairer to her own intentions. Perhaps the argument is meant to go something like this. If there are considerations adequate to play a 'debunking' role in relation to individuals' opinions about the 'dominant' regime, then these considerations can themselves be recruited for use in arguments aiming to identify that regime and ensure the existence of a social knowledge function that can be used, when conditions demand, to supplement rational argumentation. For instance, these considerations might enable us to restrict the range of individuals' rankings of regimes and, perhaps, to narrow the field of alternative regimes that have to be considered. But perhaps constraints of time and other resources force us to make some collective decision about the 'dominant' regime . . . *before* the considerations and the arguments they give rise to enable us actually to reduce the candidates to a singleton. In this case, because the considerations have enabled us to satisfy the conditions necessary for the existence of a social knowledge function, we could appeal to that function to identify a 'dominant' regime, though not, perhaps, the one we would ourselves have identified if our argumentation had continued.

In this second case, the role of the social knowledge function is not to substitute for rational argumentation; it is, instead, to augment or supplement such argumentation, particularly when constraints of time and other resources force a decision on us before a proper course of rational argumentation can be completed.[43] If this is Hurley's point, then I think that it is, in general, a good one. But in the realm of public justification such a supplementary use of social knowledge functions has, I think, no legitimate role to play. We have imagined this realm precisely as one where, because it is a one-time event and because the decisions to be taken are so important, constraints of time and other decision costs are largely irrelevant. In this case, we can appeal directly to whatever considerations Hurley has in mind as a basis for 'debunking' rather than, even in a purely supplementary way, employing the social knowledge function whose existence these very conditions seem to guarantee.

In other words, I believe that Hurley's arguments have no bearing on the case at hand: they are either otiose or inappropriate. They are otiose if the social knowledge function is intended as a substitute for rational argumentation or inappropriate if it is intended as a supplement for such argumentation. (In section 34, I describe a 'community of interpreters', which might be the institutional embodiment of the social knowledge functions that Hurley seems to have in mind.)

Of course, Hurley's work does have much to teach us. Foremost, perhaps, is that we need not, in the face of plurality, abandon all hope of treating the matter at issue in cognitivist terms. But doing so will not, on the account that I favor, involve any commitment to some 'social knowledge function'. It will, instead, involve commitment to a genuinely discursive institutional approach. (See Chapter 9.)

26. Minimax Relative Concession à la Gauthier and Gaus

Remember the problem. *A* prefers *X*, *E* prefers *Z*, and so on. (See Table 7.1.) Suppose that we propose to compromise, to find some regime that all could reasonably accept as the best they could hope to have given the facts (a) that there is no general agreement about which regime is best, and (b) that there is nothing more to be said from the point of view of 'reason' about which regime is best. (Condition (b) follows from the assumption of incommensurability — namely, that *A*'s preference for *X* is reasonable *given* his conception of public justification, that *E*'s preference for *Z* is reasonable *given* her conception of public justification, and that there is nothing effective that can be said that ought to carry weight both with *A* and with *E* about which of these conceptions is the right one.) The problem is that of identifying what it would be reasonable for all to accept. As Gaus says:

> Assume that a variety of public moralities advance the values of everyone: call the set of such proposals *P*. Unless harmony obtains, for any proposed public morality *p*1 that is a member of *P*, some person will reasonably object that from his valuational perspective *p*1 advances his values less than some other member of *P*, and so he gives up too much if *p*1 is chosen. For any proposal, we must expect the less advantaged to claim that the proposal does not constitute a reasonable bargain.[44]

Translating this into terms relevant to the present discussion, we get that, for each proposal that some particular regime be implemented, someone will claim that this regime is too unlike her preferred regime for its acceptance to be reasonable from her point of view. (Perhaps the proposed regime satisfies desiderata of public justification that she considers insignificant in comparison with those that it does not satisfy.) The absence of 'harmony' in Gaus's sense is simply the absence, in my terms, of a regime in which both realistic and moralistic desiderata are satisfied simultaneously and to the maximum degree, and it implies that there will *always* be some individual who will have prima facie grounds for complaint no matter what regime is implemented. As Gaus says, faced with this problem, we "require some criterion as to what constitutes an acceptable compromise."[45] Given such a criterion, we might be able to identify a regime that, while it required some (many, all) individuals to accept a regime that was not 'optimal' from their points of view, nevertheless it was the best all individuals could expect given the absence of 'harmony' and the divergence of opinions about the best balance of competing demands. Such a regime would be 'dominant' not in my original sense; it would not be the best regime by every set of standards. Such a regime could still reasonably be called 'dominant' in an extended sense; it is the best *compromise* by every set of standards (*given* certain constraints).

As already indicated, the criterion of majoritarian voting will not do. One of the grounds for rejecting the 'Condorcet winner' is that such a regime does *not* always represent such an acceptable compromise. Sometimes a majority imposes a solution that ranks very highly for each of *them* in favor of an alternative that "ranks *relatively* high on all preference scales."[46] For instance, under certain circumstances, the highly realistic regime *X* might be the 'Condorcet winner' — if, for instance, type-*A* individuals sufficiently outnumbered individuals of other types.

On the other hand, the regime Y is, arguably, the one, unlike X (or Z), that "ranks relatively highly on *all* preference scales." Certainly, both type A and type E individuals make equal concessions if this regime is adopted. (Similarly, type B and type D individuals make equal, but now smaller, concessions if this regime is adopted. Let us ignore type C individuals, who of course make no concession.) Furthermore, the regime Y is ranked third or better by all the different types of individuals. It is therefore arguably the 'optimal compromise' in a way that, whatever the imagined demographic circumstances, the regime X is not.

In fact, the technical idea of 'minimax relative concession', relied on by Gauthier and adopted by Gaus, is intended to formalize the notion, in this general sense, of an 'optimal compromise'.[47] Indeed, the basic idea is already implicit in what I have said. When individuals must agree in order to obtain some cooperative benefit, then that substantive agreement is rationally defensible with respect to which individuals' concessions are minimized. The 'optimal compromise' is the situation in which "the greatest or *maximum* relative concession it requires, is as small as possible, or a *minimum,* that is, is no greater than the maximum relative concession required by every other outcome."[48]

Indeed, Gaus adapts this idea to more or less precisely the 'problem of public justification'. Within a broadly contractualist framework, Gaus imagines each party proposing "a code of public morality that is best from his perspective" and asks how we could determine an 'optimal compromise'.[49] In particular, he considers an array of 'public moralities', ranged along the dimension from conservative to socialist and including a substantively liberal public morality at roughly the midpoint, and argues that, subject to certain conditions, "it can be shown that the solution endorsed by minimax relative concession will always be the option closest to the median position on the left-right spectrum."[50] This result answers to roughly the same reasoning already presented informally. For a community consisting of individuals of types $A, B, C, D,$ and $E,$ the median regime Y is, as 'intuition' would suggest, the 'optimal compromise' in the sense that it requires of each individual that she (be prepared to) make some compromise, in order to honor the opposed opinions of others, and yet it requires that she make no greater (relative) compromise than is necessary to find some regime that all can reasonably endorse.

As Gaus is careful to note,[51] using such a technique in a constitutional setting demands recognition of the *multi*dimensional character of decision making in such a setting. As he says, "It does not seem particularly plausible to insist that all the relevant disagreements among the main ideologies . . . can be reduced to a [single] simple . . . dimension."[52] He nevertheless presents a compelling argument that, when multidimensionality is recognized, the 'optimal compromise' is still the 'median regime', that is, "the point defined by the medians of all dimensions."[53] If we rank regimes in relation to such first-order values as liberty and equality, then the optimal compromise is the regime that is at the median with respect to liberty *and* at the median with respect to equality. With respect to the problem of public justification, the optimal compromise is the regime that is at the median with respect to moralistic desiderata *and* at the median with respect to realistic desiderata.

Certainly, this is an ingenious approach to multidimensional collective decision making. But Gaus himself points to, though he doesn't perhaps adequately emphasize, its most notable failing—namely, that the regime that is 'at' medians on each of a number of dimensions may not in fact exist. The superposition of these points in a multidimensional space of values may necessarily be unoccupied. Gaus gives the following example, using 'first-order' values of environmental concern and liberty/equality. He says: "For example, the median environmental position may include policy prescriptions inconsistent with some personal liberties endorsed by the median position on the left-right dimension."[54] While we can *talk about* the superposition of the medians, we're not *referring,* when we do so, to any regime that could actually be coherently implemented.[55] Indeed, this seems very much in prospect in relation to the problem of public justification. It may not be just an unfortunate contingency (as it might be in relation to environmentalism versus liberalism) that a coherent regime that is at the median with respect to the moralistic desideratum of independence is not at the median with respect to the realistic desideratum of salience and vice versa. Holding one of these demands constant, we may have no way of satisfying the other (to the relevant degree).

Gaus himself does not want "to suggest that the nature of a justified morality can somehow be mechanically produced by aggregating the prescriptions of the median positions."[56] But in this case, the technique of minimax relative concession does not represent, in itself, a solution to the problem of public justification.

27. The Question of Extensional Equivalence, and Other Issues

Some time ago Riker wrote:

> The moral and prudential standoff among methods would not in itself occasion difficulty for democratic theory if "most of the time" most methods led to the same social choice from a given profile of individual values. But this is not the case. Between any pair of methods there may be agreement on the choice from a large proportion of possible profiles. But it is not enough to consider agreement between pairs of methods. One ought instead to compare outcomes among all commonly used and frequently proposed methods. So far as I know, no one has attempted such a comparison. But it seems a safe conjecture that, if such a comparison were made, the proportion of social profiles from which all the compared methods produced identical results would be tiny. How, then, can it be said that any particular method truly amalgamates individual values when different methods—all with distinguishable but nevertheless justifiable claims to fairness—amalgamate quite differently?[57]

How, indeed? I claim to have done, in this chapter, what Riker said ought to be done. I claim to have made a systematic comparison of a number of methods that might be used to identify a 'dominant' regime. Furthermore, I think Riker was right to suspect that any such investigation would 'show up' the pretensions of social choice theory, and related methods, to determine a socially valid ordering of rival regimes.

There are therefore limits on political decision making when it involves the use of any of the techniques of social decision theory. (See sec. 7.) In each case, we encounter the circumstances of politics (antecedent disagreement and mutual dependence) but could hope to succeed in addressing these circumstances only if certain conditions were satisfied which are not in fact satisfied.

MacIntyre's strategy would have worked if we had already known how to weight the various competing desiderata, but it cannot work given that we do not know how to do this — and are using that technique precisely in the hope of finding out how to do so.

Majoritarian voting would have worked if the issues at stake were not constitutional issues or if the extremal restriction requirement were indeed satisfied by profiles of orderings of regimes. Since these conditions are not satisfied, this technique cannot be deployed in this context.

Hurley's social knowledge functions could have been deployed to identify a 'dominant' regime if the relevant issues could have been treated within a cognitivist framework, but if they can, such techniques as Hurley's are not in fact required.

Finally, the idea of minimax relative concession and Gaus's 'median position result' could have been deployed to identify a dominant regime if there were reason to believe that the n-dimensional median position in fact identifies a coherent set of principles, but since it is unlikely to do so, these techniques cannot be employed in this context.

As Charles Dodgson long ago observed, "A really scientific method for arriving at the result, which is, on the whole, most satisfactory to a body of electors, seems to be still a *desideratum*."[58]

Notice, furthermore, that the situation would not be improved very much if we assumed that these techniques could in fact be deployed in the context of constitutional theorizing. Here we run up against a problem already flagged for attention — namely, the possible proliferation of so-called dominant regimes. For instance, it is already implicit in what I have said in sections 24 and 26 that, relative to a particular demographic profile, the technique of majoritarian voting will identify the 'dominant' regime, if there is one, as the 'Condorcet winner', whereas techniques associated with the idea of minimax relative concession will identify the dominant regime, if there is one, as the 'median' regime with respect to some (speciously) unilinear 'objective' ordering of regimes. Since the Condorcet winner is likely to be distinct from the median regime, we have simply reproduced, at a 'higher level', the very problem we invoked these techniques to solve. We now have that, according to one technique, the Condorcet winner is the 'dominant' regime, whereas, according to another technique, the median regime is the 'dominant' regime, and so we are no further forward in our attempts to discover which regime *is* the 'socially dominant' regime. We thus reproduce, at a more abstract level, the classic negative results of social choice theory.

Is there, then, no prospect of solving the problem of public justification? Some have certainly drawn this conclusion, though not from such systematic considerations as those displayed here. In Chapter 8, I consider two such broadly 'skeptical' responses to continued difficulties in identifying a 'dominant' regime. In Chapter 9, I will show how, if at all, this problem might be solved. And solving it certainly seems necessary. Reiman is right when he claims that "[u]nless truths of morality can be identified by reason, moral conflicts are only clashes between people with different unverifiable beliefs . . . [and since, in that case,] victory goes to the side with the power . . . right becomes indistinguishable from might."[59]

Notes

1. Wolf, "Two Levels of Pluralism," p. 788.

2. Cf. Hare, *Moral Thinking,* p. 26, where, in relation to moral conflicts (i.e., conflicts of duties), he says that "superficiality is perhaps more quickly revealed by what is said about this problem than in any other way."

3. Cf. Larmore, *Patterns of Moral Complexity,* p. 10: "Modern moral philosophy . . . has stubbornly assumed that moral conflicts must be only apparent, that there must be some single higher-order principle that captures our most basic intuitions." Cf. also Gaut, "Moral Pluralism," p. 20: "[T]here seems to be an assumption, rarely argued for, that the correct theory must be prioritist," i.e., function to resolve all such conflicts. For pertinent discussion, implicitly critical of Hare's position, cf. Steiner, *An Essay on Rights,* ch. 4, sec. C.

4. *Moral Thinking,* p. 26.

5. Cf. *Moral Thinking,* ch. 2.

6. Hare canvasses a number of responses to the 'moral conflicts' that he considers. The one he does not even mention — that there might be 'moral gaps', in other words, that there might in some cases be no right answer to the question "What should we do?" — is, of course, the one I have been concerned with. Indeed, there is much to be said for the view, adapting Hare's own diction, that "a 'modernist' approach, as opposed to a 'post-modernist' one, is perhaps more quickly revealed by what is said about this problem than in any other way." The 'modernist' more or less dogmatically insists on 'completeness', that is, the absence of 'moral gaps', whereas the 'post-modernist' insists, on the contrary, on their possibility, even indeed on their reality.

7. Herzog, *Without Foundations,* p. 18.

8. Hampshire, *Morality and Conflict,* p. 115.

9. Larmore, *Patterns of Moral Complexity,* p. 10.

10. *Splitting the Difference,* p. 108.

11. Cf. MacIntyre, *Three Rival Versions of Moral Enquiry,* p. 7: "[W]ithin each partisan camp there has emerged a rough and ready agreement as to what weight is to be assigned to different types of reasons in different types of context, but there is no general . . . consensus on this. . . . Yet at the same time there is an equally rough and ready general . . . consensus . . . as to what is to be accounted as at least some sort of relevant reason for upholding and advancing any particular conclusion."

12. *Three Rival Versions of Moral Enquiry,* p. 181.

13. Cf. Fishkin, *The Dialogue of Justice,* pp. 80–81: "The difficulty is that proponents of each procedure . . . can make precisely symmetrical claims: each can derive first principles from his own preferred account of the moral point of view. The basis for any particular principle supported in this way is open to reasonable disagreement precisely because the rival procedures embody slightly different rival conceptions of moral reasonableness, each making the same fundamental claim."

14. Cf. MacIntyre, *Three Rival Versions of Moral Enquiry,* p. 146: "For it may well be the case . . . that a philosophical or theological position may be so organized, both in its intellectual structures and in its institutionalized modes of presentation and enquiry that conversation with an opposing position may reveal that its adherents are systematically unable to recognize in it even those errors, defects, and limitations which ought to be recognized as such in the light of their own and its standards."

15. This requirement is clearly implied in Rawls's formulation of the "full publicity condition" on conceptions of justice. He says (*Political Liberalism,* p. 68) that when this condition is satisfied, "[t]he political order does not . . . depend on historically accidental or established delusions, or other mistaken beliefs resting on the deceptive appearances of institutions that mislead us as to how they work." Cf. *A Theory of Justice,* p. 133 and n. 8.

16. Cf. *A Theory of Justice*, sec. 76.

17. *Three Rival Versions of Moral Enquiry*, p. 109. MacIntyre is speaking of the appearances in relation to the conflict between Aristotelian and Augustinian systems.

18. *Social Justice in the Liberal State*, p. 274.

19. "Public Justification and Democratic Adjudication," p. 257. Gaus isn't worried, as I am, that it will prove impossible, lacking a determinate public conception of public justification, to justify even 'constitutional fundamentals'. Gaus is worried, however, that what is justified is so 'indeterminate' in my sense that it will be incapable of guiding action and resolving disputes. It is at this stage, different from the one I have in mind, that Gaus invokes majoritarian methods. Cf. *Justificatory Liberalism*, Part III.

20. *Social Justice in the Liberal State*, pp. 273–74.

21. *Social Justice in the Liberal State*, p. 275. Cf. Gaus, "Public Justification and Democratic Adjudication," pp. 277–78: "Arguments stressing procedural equality will be particularly attractive at this stage. . . . And this leads us to some version of one person, one vote representative democracy."

22. *Social Justice in the Liberal State*, p. 277. Cf. Ackerman, *We the People*, p. 277: "If, then, a proposal deserves a place on the higher lawmaking agenda, its support in the country should not only be deep and broad. It should be in a position to decisively defeat all the plausible alternatives in a series of pairwise comparisons — in the terms of the trade, it should be a Condorcet-winner."

23. It is sometimes, indeed customarily, said of such an individual that her preferences are not 'single-peaked'. But this characterization depends on privileging the preference orderings of the individuals who do respond directly or inversely to a particular arrangement from most to least satisfactory along some allegedly unitary dimension. It is only when we privilege the array $X>Y>Z$ that we consider that the ordering $X>Z>Y$ has two peaks, a higher one at X and a lower one at Z. If we were to privilege this latter ordering instead, then it would be the former that fails to be single-peaked. (I owe these points to Jerry Gaus.) Fortunately, it is possible to make the points about majoritarian techniques that I want to make without essential reference to the concept of single-peakedness.

24. Although some theorists have rejected transitivity, in this particular case, we *can* satisfy the demand, in defense of that requirement, that the "arbitrary outcomes arising from cyclic preference orderings violate some basic ethical norm" (Mueller, *Public Choice*, p. 193). Clearly, transitivity is a minimal necessary condition for the identification, using some method of aggregation, of a collectively best regime. If a method produced a non-transitive ordering of regimes, then we might have, indirectly, both that $X > Y$ and that $Y > X$, and so might be unable to derive, via such a method, a decisive answer to that question, for individuals who disagree about which of these regimes ought to be instituted. Any method of aggregation that fails to determine a transitive ordering ipso facto fails really to address what I have called the 'problem' of public justification. Furthermore, as Ackerman notes (*We the People*, p. 277), the requirement that the social ordering be transitive precludes the manipulation of the agenda by the parties who determine this ordering. Being proof against agenda-manipulation is surely a desirable property of any device that is intended for use in a constitutional context. Cf. William Riker, *Liberalism Against Populism*, p. 132.

25. Cf. Mueller, *Public Choice II*, pp. 76–77.

26. Riker, *Liberalism Against Populism*, p. 128. That these individuals' rankings of regimes are single-peaked is plausible, indeed compelling. Miller provides helpful commentary ("Deliberative Democracy and Social Choice," pp. 63–64): "What does single-peakedness reveal about voters' preferences? It shows that they understand the choice before them in the same way, even though they adopt different positions on the spectrum. . . . A single dimension of choice underlies the various positions, and this is sufficient to guarantee that the rank orderings will be single

peaked." But surely this is just the situation in the case at hand. All (potential) citizens understand the choice among regimes as lying on the spectrum from most realistically satisfactory to most moralistically satisfactory; each such individual has a favored point on this spectrum; and each individual ranks alternatives to this favored regime by their similarity to it along this unidimensional array of possibilities. We do have single-peakedness in this case.

27. *Liberalism Against Populism*, p. 126.

28. Iain McLain, *Public Choice*, p. 155.

29. Mueller, *Public Choice*, p. 214.

30. The array of profiles in Table 7.1 is somewhat misleading in this regard since, were *A, B, C, D*, and *E* the only voters, as opposed to the only types, the Condorcet winner is also plausibly identified as the optimal compromise — a coincidence that is due both to single-peakedness and to a uniform distribution of voters over types. Once we distribute voters over types more realistically, however, we see that there is no guaranteed coincidence of Condorcet winners with optimal compromises. If the distribution is skewed *A*-ward, then there will be a departure, *A*-wardly, from the 'optimal compromise'. (Of course, the notion of an 'optimal compromise' is not being thought of in aggregative terms. To determine it, we look at moving from each type in the direction of the other types, a matter that is unaffected by the number of individuals per type.)

31. Mueller, *Public Choice*, p. 61.

32. Cf. Ackerman, *We the People*, p. 357, n. 13: "Andrew Caplin and Barry Nalebuff have proved that, under a wide variety of plausible configurations of voter preference, an option that wins 64 percent of the vote is sure to be a Condorcet-winner."

33. *Value and Justification*, p. 344.

34. Rawls, *A Theory of Justice*, p. 178.

35. Mueller, *Public Choice*, p. 52.

36. Rawls, *A Theory of Justice*, p. 154.

37. "Deliberative Democracy and Social Choice," p. 58.

38. *Natural Reasons*, p. 336.

39. *Natural Reasons*, pp. 335–36.

40. *Natural Reasons*, p. 234.

41. *Natural Reasons*, p. 339.

42. Condition **U** provides for the possibility that we will have to consider, in determining a socially valid ordering of regimes, all combinatorially possible individual orderings. Condition **I** requires that the social ordering of *X* with respect to *Y* depend entirely on individuals' orderings of *X* with respect to *Y* and, specifically, that it not depend on individuals' orderings of *X* with respect to *Z* or on their orderings of *Y* with respect to *Z*. Condition **I** in effect ensures the purely ordinal character of the information relevant to determination of the social ordering of alternatives and is arguably inappropriate if the problem of determining such an ordering is thought of in a cognitivist context. Certainly, cardinal information, for example, in the form of 'degrees of confirmation', might be available in this case. (Of course, the bare possibility that cardinal information might be available is not enough for Hurley's results. Such information has actually to be available for the non-existence theorem to be overturned. And it is likely that it is not. Certainly, it arguably will not be available if 'degrees of confirmation' depend on multidimensional evaluations of the kind we're considering here.)

43. Cf. Rawls, *Political Liberalism*, p. 240: "One difficulty is that public reason often allows more than one reasonable answer to any particular question. . . . Everyone appeals to political values but agreement is lacking and more than marginal differences persist. Should this happen, as it often does, some may say that public reason fails to resolve the question, in which case citizens may legitimately invoke principles appealing to nonpolitical values to resolve it in a way they find satisfactory."

44. *Value and Justification,* pp. 343–34.

45. *Value and Justification,* p. 344.

46. Mueller, *Public Choice,* p. 61.

47. Cf. Gauthier, *Morals by Agreement,* ch. 4, sec. 3 and Gaus, *Value and Justification,* secs. 21.3, 28.

48. *Morals by Agreement,* p. 137; the derivation of this principle from the 'reasonable conditions' I mention in the text is at pp. 141–45.

49. *Value and Justification,* p. 440.

50. *Value and Justification,* p. 449.

51. *Value and Justification,* sec. 28.3.

52. *Value and Justification,* p. 457.

53. *Value and Justification,* p. 461.

54. *Value and Justification,* pp. 461–62, n. 54.

55. This particular example is somewhat misleading, of course. The values that are incompatible are not at or even near the medians for their dimensions but, instead, near the 'high' end in both cases.

56. *Value and Justification,* pp. 461–62, n. 54.

57. *Liberalism Against Populism,* p. 235.

58. Quoted by Mueller, *Public Choice II,* p. 384.

59. *Justice and Modern Moral Philosophy,* p. ix.

8

Responses to and Diagnosis of Prima Facie Incoherence

28. Liberalism and Postmodernism

Let us review the situation. I am concerned with the problem of public justification—with identifying a political regime that is, in some sense, 'dominant', that is, a regime that everyone would find reasonable, *whatever* her thinking about what is necessary if a regime is indeed to be a reasonable one. This problem is thrown up by the multiplicity of competing demands that are relevant to the judgment that a given regime is reasonable, and by the many different ways in which these demands might be 'balanced' by different individuals. Some individuals might, quite reasonably, prefer a regime that satisfies moralistic requirements. Other individuals might, quite reasonably, prefer a regime that satisfies realistic requirements. Perhaps no regime satisfies both kinds of requirements. But unless all individuals prefer the same regime, none is 'dominant', and the demand for public justification cannot be met.

In the last chapter I considered some techniques, in the tradition of 'Methodism', that might be deployed to solve this problem. (Most were not actually designed for that purpose.) Since none of these techniques in fact seems to work in this context, perhaps we should conclude, as Miller says, that "there is no fair and rational way of amalgamating voters' preferences to reach a social decision."[1] Apparently left open by this (interim) result are important questions about the nature of justification in a political context—namely, "Who decides what is and what is not an argument, by what criteria, and what constitutes the force of a better argument?"[2]—so that, as Edward Said puts it, the very idea of justification becomes "at once the object of struggle and the tool by which the struggle is conducted."[3] In the face of these conclusions, some theorists despair of establishing a basis of public justification and, in this chapter, I consider their responses to the apparent incoherence of the idea (secs. 29 and 30).[4] I also try to diagnose the failure of some approaches to the problem and to suggest an alternative approach (secs. 31 and 32).

We owe to Rorty the insight that there are, arguably, affinities between the liberal justificatory project, particularly in the version articulated by Rawls, and meta-philosophical developments associated with a 'postmodernist' repudiation of some *transcendent* perspective with respect to which actual principles and practices can be evaluated.[5] As Rorty says, "reflective equilibrium," in Rawls's sense, "is all we need try for – . . . there is no natural order of justification of beliefs, no predestined outline for argument to trace."[6] I think Rorty is right about this, but I will not press the point here.[7] What I do want to say is that, whether Rorty is right or not on the substantive (meta-) philosophical point, there is certainly something to be gained, in evaluating the liberal project from looking, as I will do in this chapter, to the work of self-identified 'postmodernists' and their critics. We will find much to confirm their suspicions and conclusions.

If, with Jane Flax, we conclude that "[t]he 'essential contestability' . . . of the constituting notions of Enlightenment metanarratives has been exposed"[8] by the kinds of demonstrations essayed in Chapter 7, then we must expect to encounter, as Hilary Lawson puts it, "[t]he two apparently contradictory tendencies towards anarchy and towards conservatism [that] are found in . . . post-modernism." According to Lawson, results like my (interim) results "threaten anarchy by removing the stability of reality and truth, but they endorse conservatism by appealing to the only thing that is left, namely, what we already have."[9] While I do not believe that a 'postmodernist' perspective is inevitably poised uneasily between anarchy and/or nihilism on the one hand and conservatism and/or traditionalism on the other hand, I nevertheless examine some common responses to demonstrations of the kind provided here under the two headings "Anarchism" and "Authoritarianism." (These responses are likely to be mixed, perhaps somewhat promiscuously, in the work of individual theorists, however.)

29. Anarchism

I have chosen the epithet 'anarchism' on account of its own ambiguity, for there are responses to the failure of the liberal project that reflect at least four different senses in which we do indeed use this epithet and its cognates:[10] (1) sometimes, we mean by 'anarchy' a social situation in which individuals' relations with one another are based entirely on agreements that they have freely entered into and that they themselves alone enforce; (2) sometimes, we mean by 'anarchy' a social situation in which individuals' relations with one another are wholly dependent on the force that each can personally command; (3) sometimes, we mean by 'anarchism' a program of resistance to domination; (4) sometimes, we mean by 'anarchy' a chaotic social situation in which there is little or no discernible social order. Whether any of these usages has any philosophical validity, all are common in ordinary speech, and each is reflected in a kind of response to the failure of the liberal justificatory project.

According to the account I have been surveying, the legitimacy of a regime consists in the public justification of that regime. If the very idea of public justification is itself essentially contestable, then the very idea of legitimacy is perforce contestable, and we might reasonably conclude that, demonstrably, *no* regime is legitimate for *any* community.[11] But this is tantamount to "the anarchist alternative" to (methodological) liberalism, namely, that there is "no publicly justified morality at all"[12] and that the "coercive backing" of the state apparatus to coordinate and regulate human interactions "is a dispensable evil in that sufficient coordination among human beings can be achieved without it."[13] (This is 'anarchism' in the first of my four senses.)

On this account, the failure of liberal methodology simply reveals the fundamentally authoritarian character of liberalism itself, a point already pressed by such precursors of 'postmodernism' as Theodor Adorno and his colleagues.[14] As Leonard Krieger puts it, "Liberals, in this view, created a new form of authority by stressing the voluntary submission of putatively free individuals to . . . constraints which were actually reified forms of authoritarian control by a dominant social group."[15] And the abandonment of liberal aspirations is, in effect, the rejection of all state authority.

Such a broadly 'anarchist' response to the failure of liberal methodology is also, then, arguably 'postmodernist' in character. Zygmunt Bauman puts well the main points:

> The post-modern period is distinguished by having abandoned the search itself, having convinced itself of its futility. Instead, it tries to reconcile itself to life under conditions of permanent and incurable uncertainty; a life in the presence of an unlimited quantity of competing forms of life. . . .[16]

As Benhabib says, "[L]ike Doestoevsky and Nietzsche before them, postmodernists seem to say 'God is dead; everything is allowed.'"[17] Or, on Flax's account, "Postmodernists are a- or even antipolitical. They are relativists; if we take them seriously, any political stance will be impossible to maintain or justify."[18]

Indeed, Flax's remarks indicate one source of instability in any substantively anarchistic response to the apparent failure of the liberal project. Presumably, the claims that "coercive backing . . . is a dispensable evil" and that "all traditions have equal rights"[19] are themselves substantive political claims that are thus put in doubt by our apparent inability to justify propositions precisely of this kind.[20] Perhaps this potential difficulty would not matter very much for a community that already embodied anarchistic ideals. But 'our' communities do not. If anarchism is the substantive position that 'follows from' the failure of the liberal justificatory project, then it will have to be implemented in the context of already existing political arrangements. Consider the proposal that we transform our political relations to eliminate all forms of statist coercion. The legitimacy of this proposal for a given community depends on its justifiability for that community and is thus itself thrown into doubt by the failure of the project of public justification. (It is a common complaint against broadly 'postmodernist' tendencies that they subvert *all* theorizing. See sec. 30.)

Perhaps substantive anarchism is *not* the appropriate response to the alleged failure of the liberal project. Many theorists have suggested that the employment of force is not eliminated but merely 'decentralized' if liberalism fails. (This is 'anarchism' in the second of the four senses earlier distinguished.) Whether this is, substantively, what 'anarchists' have usually had in mind is disputable.[21] But it is the response that many commentators on 'postmodernism' identify as a characteristic, if often unacknowledged, implication of the 'postmodernist' critique. As Lois McNay puts it, "By abandoning any normative perspective, it is not clear how a postmodern position of *laissez-faire* could ensure against an environment of hostility and predatory self-interest in which the more powerful repress the less privileged."[22] At the very least, "[s]ince postmodernists believe there is no truth, conflict will only be resolved through the raw exercise of power. . . ."[23] On this account, "modern politics cannot be a matter of genuine moral consensus . . . [but, rather, is] civil war carried on by different means."[24]

And, indeed, it is truly "civil war carried on by different means" and not simply what many theorists, postmodernists or otherwise, accept as the nature of politics realistically conceived—namely, the balancing of competing interests (in the face of the impossibility of genuine moral consensus). If the failure of the justificatory project reveals the impossibility of uncoerced moral consensus, then the failure of the project of 'social choice' likewise reveals the impossibility of an uncoerced balancing of competing interests. All that is left is force and fraud.

In the absence of publicly justified political arrangements, we might easily fall into an attitude of laissez-faire that is simply an inducement to potential oppressors.[25] In view of this possibility, we may feel, as McNay puts it, a certain "reluctance to endorse an entirely deregulated libertarianism"[26] of the kind that might well 'follow from' the collapse of the liberal project. Many 'postmodernists' have suggested, instead, that the appropriate response is broadly 'oppositional'. As Foucault says, "[T]he real political task in a society such as ours is to criticize the workings of institutions which appear to be both neutral and independent: to criticize them in such a manner that the political violence which has always exercised itself obscurely through them will be unmasked, so that one can fight them."[27] (This is the third of the senses of 'anarchism' distinguished earlier.) But this kind of response, it is widely believed, is unstable and arguably incoherent. Many critics have complained of what Habermas has called Foucault's 'totalizing critique'. Richard Bernstein says:

> Critique—even genealogical critique—must preserve at least one standard by which we engage in the critique of the present. Yet when critique is *totalized,* when critique turns against itself so that all rational standards are called into question, then one is caught in a performative contradiction.[28]

According to Gianni Vattimo:

> [T]he plain espousal of equality, if it is genuinely disenchanted, has no rational arguments with which to oppose the reduction of reality . . . to a pure play of forces. . . . Why, in the end, if there are no metaphysical principles, should we prefer rational argumentation to physical confrontation?[29]

Of course, we needn't insist on the impotence of critique within such a framework. As McNay says, "Oppositional truths destabilize the concept of an absolute truth by indicating that there are other truths yet to be developed. . . ."[30] Although there may be no possibility of public justification, there may still be contestation, unless we are robbed even of that. This is what some suggest. Absent a basis for objectivity, we will be deprived of any decent motive and certainly of any legitimate reason even for purely oppositional politics.[31] Once my political opinions are shown to be unsustainable via publicly justificatory argument, "I may no longer be able to remain committed to them." Benjamin asks, "Will not this approach . . . destroy all conviction and leave [me] . . . vulnerable to the 'passionate intensity' of those whose aggrandizing belief in one or another world view and way of life has not been tempered by the external standpoint?"[32]

Perhaps, in the end, we are left with *nothing* as a basis for politics in any substantive sense, even including that of the 'anarchist'. Only chaos is left. (This is 'anarchism' in the fourth sense.) But this will not do, as even Jacques Derrida, the arch-postmodernist, is said to realize. Bernstein reports:

> Derrida has an acute sense that, at least since the "rupture" we call Nietzsche, we can no longer be content with self-satisfied appeals to moral and political foundations, first principles and *archai*. We are compelled to question these. But he is equally acute in his realization that such questioning doesn't "solve" anything. We cannot assume a permanent frozen stance of *an-arché*. For this is another fixed metaphysical position. We cannot escape responsibility, decision, and choice.[33]

But *how* are we to exercise responsibility and make choices if we are deprived of the consolations of reason? We are to do so, on some accounts, on an authoritarian basis.

30. Authoritarianism

Once again, my choice of epithet is based, at least in part, on the ambiguity of the chosen term. Roughly, it is my intention to point to a variety of alternative, non-argumentative sources of political legitimacy. We have the authority of the Hobbesian sovereign or the charismatic authority of 'The Leader', which resides not necessarily in the success of any publicly justificatory argument but, instead, in 'his' capacity to secure peace and to ensure conformity with 'his' dictates.[34] We have, as well, the authority of tradition, which sanctions practices that cannot be justified by any argumentative means. And, finally, we have the authority of such gods as might concern themselves with the affairs of human beings and who might, from time to time, legislate or command for us.[35] Ernest Gellner says: "Tradition opposes rationality on behalf of custom, Authority does so on behalf of a special but also possibly unique Source of Revelation."[36] In any event, at least the notion of traditional authority is, indeed two slightly different such notions are, current in the debate about 'postmodernism' — and thus about the apparent failure of the liberal project.

On the one hand, we have that notion of traditional authority that is associated with the idea of (cultural) evolution. It figures prominently in the work of such (methodologically) conservative political theorists as Hayek. On this account, theorists of public justification have failed on account of hubris. They have tried to do what cannot be done, namely, provide a *discursive* justification of political arrangements. But while their failure is salutary — it reminds us of the impotence of what Hayek calls 'constructivist' approaches — it is not fatal to more broadly political projects of legitimation.[37] From the failure of the project of public justification, we need not conclude that "any political stance will be impossible to maintain or justify."[38] Whereas the kind of 'reason' meant to be embodied in public justification cannot be relied on, we nevertheless *can* rely on the authority of tradition. This authority is, in turn, derived from broadly evolutionary considerations.

According to Hayek, "rules of conduct . . . have evolved because the groups which practised them were more successful and displaced others."[39] From this it presumably follows that rules long current in some community should be honored on account of their relative past success in the regulation of human behavior. Adapting an idea of James March, we might say this:

> Ideas of *selected* [legitimation] emphasize the process of selection among . . . organizations [and polities] through survival or growth. Rules of behavior achieve [legitimacy] not by virtue of conscious [discursive justification] by current role players but by virtue of the survival and growth of social institutions in which such rules are followed and such roles are performed.[40]

No such approach to the problem of political legitimacy is going to be easily undermined. Some comment is nevertheless called for.

First, there are notorious difficulties with any argument seeking to infer superiority (with respect to 'fitness') even from the fact of differential survival. For one thing, many traits are not (directly) subjected to selective pressures at all but survive, or fail to, because they are linked (whether genetically in the case of organisms, or institutionally in the case of social practices) to other traits that *are* subject to selective pressures.[41] From the fact that a social practice has survived, nothing about its superiority can readily be concluded,[42] and nothing, therefore, about its legitimacy, if this is defined in terms of its evolutionary superiority.

Second, traits *are* subject to selection pressure in a sense that could, but needn't necessarily, provide a basis for establishing their superiority (and hence their legitimacy in the case of social practices) only if there is some possibility of differential selection, for example, between variants. This requires the co-existence of variant forms in the same general setting.[43] But this condition may rarely have been satisfied in the case of institutions and social practices, where uniform impositions are very common. And even where variants have co-existed, it seems likely that one will have prevailed over others on account of its discursively demonstrated superiority or on account of the power of its supporters, rather than on the basis of its superior 'adaptation' to the environment. In either case, survival demonstrates nothing (extra) about superiority and hence legitimacy.

This broadly traditionalist alternative to discursive justification is addressed to the same problem, that of legitimation. It relies, however, not on 'reason', but on evolution. While this approach cannot be dismissed, it is not obvious that it can succeed. While the general idea of social evolution is clear enough, the kinds of data are usually lacking that are required to establish legitimacy via such an idea.

On the other hand, we have Gellner's "traditionalists-sceptics, men who embrace tradition because they despair of reason [and of evolution] and prefer contingent, baseless stability to flux and uncertainty."[44] On this account, we do not *argue* for the legitimacy of various practices on the basis of their differential survival in competition with other similar practices. Rather, we *assume* the legitimacy of existing practices and limit our discourse to their interpretation.[45] As Walzer says, "A given society is just if its substantive life is lived in a certain way — that is, in a way faithful to the shared understandings of the members."[46] Such a fideistic reliance on tradition is clearly articulated by Roger Scruton:

> A conservative is 'for' certain things: he is for them, not because he has arguments in their favour, but because he knows them, lives with them, and finds his identity threatened (often he knows not how) by the attempt to interfere with their operation. His characteristic and most dangerous opponent is not the radical, who stands squarely against him, armed with myths and prejudices that match his own, but rather the reformer, who always acting in a spirit of improvement, finds reason to change whatever he cannot find better reason to retain.[47]

Whether such an approach provides a real alternative to the seemingly failed project of public justification of course depends on its own coherence and plausibility. The most important point is that, in the circumstances of politics, an unargued appeal to 'tradition' is likely to be futile, merely opening up new sources of disagreement rather than disclosing latent grounds of reconciliation.[48] Benhabib gives a thorough account of this problem:

> The ['traditionalist'] social critic cannot assume that . . . she will find a single set of criteria on which there is such consensus that one can simply assume that by juxtaposing these criteria to the actual carrying out of the practice one has accomplished the task of . . . [legitimation]. So the first defect of situated criticism is a kind of "hermeneutic monism of meaning", the assumption namely that the narratives of our culture are so univocal and uncontroversial that in appealing to them one could simply be exempt from the task of evaluative, ideal-typical reconstruction.[49]

'Our' traditions simply are not homogeneous enough to provide a basis of legitimation via interpretation. Anyone who says they are is "insensitive to the dark side of appealing to 'we' when it is used as an exclusionary tactic — as the 'rationalization' for fostering intolerance."[50]

Furthermore, even assuming the univocity of 'our' traditions, we must acknowledge that such an approach is "incapable of dealing with the problem of the effects of *social domination* on beliefs and understandings."[51] This is, of course, simply the requirement of independence in a different guise. Suppose that we propose determining some disputed issue by interpreting 'our' traditions and thus bringing them to bear on this difficulty. Assume that 'our' traditions are univocal and easily shown to be so with respect to this issue, implying that it should indeed be resolved in some particular way. (This is a 'charitable' assumption, given the points made in the preceding paragraph.) As Connolly says, "[T]o adopt without revision the concepts prevailing in a polity is to accept terms of discourse loaded in favor of established practices";[52] in this case, as Foucault puts it, we "run the risk of letting ourselves be determined by more general structures of which we may well not be conscious, and over which we may have no control."[53] The achievement of independence therefore seems to require some movement away from 'our' traditions, even when they 'speak' with a single voice. But in this case, it is hard to see how an interpretive appeal to 'our' traditions could actually constitute a mode of legitimation. Legitimacy depends on independence, and independence is not sought let alone achieved by purely interpretive approaches to the problem of legitimacy.

(Of course, all this is a bit of a parody. Many interpretivists recognize the polyvocality of 'our' traditions and the difficulties we are likely to encounter when we try to articulate them to current concerns. And they recognize too the embeddedness, in 'our' traditions, of the very standards that we might use to 'distance' ourselves from other aspects of those traditions. But there is point to my parody. I use it as a springboard for introducing, in section 34, a more sophisticated notion of interpretation.)

What is the upshot of these considerations? The liberal justificatory project has apparently failed. The very idea of public justification is itself contestable and hence of little or no use in the legitimation of regimes. That we should therefore embrace some or other form of substantive anarchism is a claim that cannot itself be sustained in the absence of some viable mode of legitimation. That we should therefore give ourselves over to the authority of tradition is also a judgment that cannot readily be accepted. If we interpret tradition's alleged authority *instrumentally,* as deriving from the social-evolutionary superiority of established practices and principles, the case will be hard to make. If we instead interpret tradition's alleged authority *intrinsically,* as the only viable alternative to social disorder, problems of interpretation block any ready reliance on this mode of legitimation.

Liberal modes of justification do not seem to work; alternative modes of legitimation do not seem to work either. What has gone wrong? This diagnostic question is the subject of sections 31 and 32.

31.   Substitutionism and Its Inadequacy

Even as they acknowledge one or another particular 'failure of tracking', most proponents of the project of public justification by and large ignore the threat to that project which is posed, if not by any particular result of this kind, then, at least, surely by the sum of them. Indeed, few seem to be aware of more than one or two of the particular results that I have summarized in Chapter 6, especially Table 6.2.[54] Opponents of this project, on the other hand, take its impossibility, more generally the "Impotence of Reason" which it allegedly demonstrates,[55] to have been established by these kinds of results and thus embark on what Hayek calls a "rationalist revolt against reason."[56] In my view, both proponents and opponents are wrong in the postures they assume. Proponents are wrong to be complacent in the face of well-known difficulties, whereas opponents are wrong in jumping so quickly from demonstrations of prima facie incoherence to a conclusion of impossibility *simpliciter.* In this case, as in many others, 'Ramsey's Maxim' is appropriate — namely, "that the truth lies not in one of the two disputed views but in some third possibility which has not yet been thought of, which we can only discover by rejecting something assumed as obvious by both the disputants."[57]

What is this 'third possibility'? And what, which must be rejected, is assumed by both parties to the dispute about public justification?

Let me take the second point first; I consider the first point in section 32.

Taken for granted by both proponents and opponents of the project of public justification is what I call a 'substitutionist' approach to this project.[58] By this I mean an approach based on the substitution, in attempting to determine the 'dominant' regime, of some analytical device for the collectively disciplined judgments of concrete, historically situated individuals.[59] Both proponents and opponents are to this extent still in the grip of this characteristically 'modernist' idea.

For instance, we might apply the majoritarian voting techniques recommended by Ackerman and Gaus, or employ the so-called social knowledge functions that Hurley alludes to, or, perhaps, adopt the idea of minimax relative concession advocated by Gauthier and Gaus to enable us to calculate some optimal balance of competing demands and thus to identify, 'algorithmically', the 'dominant' regime for a given community. At least at the point the procedure is actually employed,[60] there is, in each case, substitution of the procedure for the (continued) discussion of pertinent issues. Faced with the problem of 'good-faith disagreement' about concrete details of constitutional arrangements, Ackerman and Gaus suggest that individuals vote and that proposals favored by a majority be adopted. In this case, individuals supply 'input' to and are, presumably, bound by the 'output' from the machinery of majoritarian voting. In much the same circumstances, Hurley suggests that, discussion being cut short by constraints of time and other resources, individuals' opinions be treated as judgments of fact and supplied as 'input' to a social knowledge function that, presumably, delivers as 'output' a collectively valid judgment of fact on any issue in dispute. And, finally, both Gauthier and Gaus suggest that, when compromise is required, an optimal fair compromise can be identified, mechanically, by gathering information about individuals' maximum and minimum acceptable concessions and then calculating on this basis. All these techniques are "abstract and computational"[61] and exhibit a marked preference for "explicit and univocal decision-procedures."[62]

That such techniques can be deployed in the circumstances of politics is what many proponents of the project of public justification complacently assume: they are wrong to do so. That the failure of such techniques to solve the problem of public justification shows the insolubility of that problem is what many opponents of this project quickly conclude: they too are wrong. For it is what both assume — namely, that the problem can be solved, if at all, by and only by such substitutionist techniques — that lies beneath their opposed errors of judgment. In fact, the problem of public justification *can* be solved, *contra* the anarchists and authoritarians who think it can't be; and yet the problem *can't* be solved by substitutionist means, *contra* the complacent attitudes of many methodological liberals when faced with prima facie difficulties. This, anyway, is what I argue in Chapter 9, where I try to develop a non-substitutionist approach to the problem of public justification. In the meantime, it will be helpful to say more about substitutionism and to sketch an alternative, *political* approach (see sec. 32).

How are we to characterize a broadly substitutionist approach to the problem of public justification? This question is important at least in part because, to develop a better alternative, we will need to know what to avoid.

First, as already indicated, a substitutionist approach is "abstract and computational," with a preference for "explicit and univocal decision-procedures." Each of the 'analytic devices' considered — majoritarian voting, social knowledge functions, and minimax relative concession — reduces the individual to a source of 'input' in some canonical form, data which are then computationally manipulated by the theorist to produce some 'conclusion' that anyone else using the device and applying it to the same data would also, perforce, have produced.[63]

Second, the substitutionist approach is therefore Procrustean in reducing a given problem to the dimensions of some canonical specification of relevant problem situations.[64] Whatever the issue might be that remains unresolved when techniques of majoritarian voting or minimax relative concession are employed, the 'input' to those techniques is cast into the same form as it would be were some quite different problem at issue. Any opinions or feelings of the individuals actually affected that do not fit these canonical forms are, of course, 'irrelevant' and never figure as 'input' to these techniques.

Third, it is systematic and abstracted from concrete particularity. As Williams says, "Theory looks characteristically for considerations that are very general and have as little distinctive content as possible . . . ,"[65] aiming to provide, as Bernstein puts it, a "permanent, ahistorical matrix" for our calculations.[66] Each of the 'analytical devices' I have considered depends, for its own contours and alleged validity, entirely on the highly abstract, indeed quasi-mathematical argumentation that allegedly supports it. (Gauthier's defense of minimax relative concession has the form of a theorem in decision theory, broadly construed. There is no mention of any but the most abstract 'facts' about individuals and their situations.) Whereas 'input' to these devices may itself be concrete and historically grounded, their own workings are otherwise unaffected by the historical settings in which they are employed. (We use the same techniques of majoritarian voting, if those are the ones we are using, in all the various situations where their use might be prescribed by our theory of social decision making.)

Fourth, a substitutionist approach is pre-emptive in the sense that it seeks to settle disputed questions 'once and for all'.[67] Bernstein refers, for instance, "to the old positivist hope that we can once and for all (in principle) decide what to count as legitimate and illegitimate (or meaningless) discourse."[68] And so too do proponents of minimax relative concession think that we can determine, once and for all, what kinds of techniques ought to be employed in any particular situation in which compromise appears to be necessary and/or possible.

Fifth, and finally, such an approach clearly embodies "the 'command economy of thought' represented [in a previous epoch] by the Church."[69] It constitutes an attempt to gather information to 'the center', to 'process' this information wholly at 'the center', and to issue directives from 'the center' to those who have supplied the information. It does not recognize the possibility that a more decentralized, less Procrustean approach might have merit. (See the Preface and sec. 41.)

Such an approach nevertheless is attractive in many ways. It would be odd in the extreme if it were not. After all, as Walzer says, "Something like this is what most philosophers, since Plato, have been after. . . ."[70]

First, the substitutionist approach honors, indeed seems designed to honor, such important moralistic desiderata as transparency and reflexivity. Any 'calculation' performed with the aid of majoritarian techniques, for instance, is reasonably transparent to members of the community concerned with the outcome of that calculation, and the arguments supporting the use of such techniques are themselves, at least to a first approximation, familiar and seemingly sound.

Second, substitutionist techniques explicitly "challenge the idea that 'might makes right'."[71] Some care is needed here, of course, for we must not claim, in defense of substitutionism, that it altogether eliminates the effects of power in all its various senses. For instance, majoritarian voting techniques will typically reward political groups that are powerful, if in no other sense, then at least in the sense of having many members. Still, the use of such techniques is a substitute, not just for individuals' judgments, but just as importantly, for what might be called blatant displays of naked power, typically in the form of force (i.e., violence) or the threat to employ it. And this, surely, is a *valid* substitution in the circumstances of politics.

Third, a substitutionist approach is responsive to exactly the difficulties in which the problem of public justification is grounded—namely, the absence of antecedent agreement about what to do, indeed about how to decide what to do. Given a 'moral algorithm' of the kind sought by substitutionists, "rational individuals need not debate over what criteria should be applied" in the case of political disputes any more than they need to in the case of disputed claims about some mathematical problem.[72]

These are some of the considerations that tell in favor of a substitutionist approach. Unfortunately, as is already evident in the conclusions of Chapter 7, this approach is fundamentally flawed, and an alternative is required.

For one thing, precisely because of its abstraction and Procrustean tendencies, a substitutionist approach is unable "to deal with the indeterminacy and multiplicity of contexts and life-situations with which practical reason is always confronted."[73] As Benjamin puts it, such an approach "will require a degree of idealization and abstraction that limits its usefulness for many of the practical concerns that give morality its point."[74]

Second, a substitutionist approach is, arguably, politically suspect because of "the abstract and disembodied distorting and nostalgic ideal of the autonomous male ego which the universalist tradition privileges."[75] In its abstraction from concrete particularities, and absent an attested and determinate theory of human nature that deals adequately with prima facie human diversity, any substitutionist approach is bound to substitute some 'model-conception' or 'device of representation' that isn't entirely adequate to the empirical diversity of human types. (See sec. 8.) Indeed, this point is already implicit in my own observations about 'failures of tracking' between, say, independence and salience or independence and universality.

Of course, there is the more specific issue raised by Benhabib and others. This is directed as much to the *style of theorizing* as it is to the particular character of the 'model-conceptions' that are substituted, for example, in original position argumentation, for concrete (and, particularly, sexed) individuals. This broader issue of method is what Susan Hekman, for instance, has in mind when she says that "feminists have shown that this dichotomy between masculine abstraction and feminine contextuality has been the central means of excluding women from the sphere of rationality and maintaining their inferiority."[76] What she means, I think, is not just that the parties to the original position reflect, in the characteristics attributed to them, traits and aptitudes that, in our cultures, are correlated with male gender roles. She means as well, and perhaps primarily, that the very idea of substituting 'model-conceptions' for concrete individuals is itself the kind of 'move', in theorizing, that men are more likely to make than women.

More generally, the substitutionist approach is hostile to plurality, diversity, and otherness. Its techniques "are implicitly totalitarian because totalizing . . . normalizing because normative."[77] This is a nearly unavoidable concomitant of any abstracting, Procrustean approach to the reconciliation of disagreement. In seeking to prescribe for all individuals, despite their concrete differences, any such approach must rely on 'norms' whose alleged relevance to those who do not actually fit them is therefore normalizing, in the sense Foucault seems to have in mind. Connolly provides a useful account:

> Each theory gravitates toward an ontology of concord. . . . Otherness — that which does not fit neatly into the form assumed by self or society — is not treated as that which might not fit because even a good order (or self) must itself produce elements which do not synchronize with its structure.[78]

Another aspect of this difficulty is the dependence of substitutionist approaches on the surely contrary-to-fact assumption that it is possible to identify fixed and determinate inputs to the processes of calculation that they recommend. As Bernard Manin puts it, "what must be criticized . . . is . . . the assumption that individuals in society possess an already formed will, already know exactly what they want" and that theorists therefore need only to calculate on the basis of information about what people want.[79]

Finally, given its abstractive, distanced, and idealizing character, a substitutionist approach may not be able to identify a regime as the 'dominant' regime, whose demands are salient for the community for which it is proposed. This difficulty is embodied in what I call the 'problem of recognition'. Suppose, for example, that some such social knowledge function as Hurley envisages could indeed be deployed to perform the balancing act required in order, despite the plurality of partly competing desiderata, to identify some regime as the 'dominant' regime for a given community. Since this result is the product of the theorist's labors and involves an appeal to esoteric theoretical machinery, it cannot be guaranteed that, when it is presented to the individuals in question, it will indeed be recognized by them as a valid result that ought to bind them. As Marilyn Freidman says, "[M]oral and political theorists who propose methods for achieving an unbiased, or *impartial,* standpoint . . . typically provide no independent criteria for recognizing whether or not impartiality has been achieved by the specified methods."[80]

In fact, the substitutionist approach naturally lends itself to expression, in the context of public justification, in a particular way. If you are trying to decide once and for all, if you seek to pre-empt concrete decision making, if you want to give general rules that are applicable to a variety of situations, then, naturally, you will favor a project of indirect justification. For this project expresses precisely the theorist's desire to substitute her judgment, made, she thinks, from some privileged perspective, for the judgment of the actors on whose behalf her judgment is supposedly being made. Iris Marion Young puts the point very well.

> Impartial reason must judge from a point of view outside of the particular perspectives of persons involved in interaction, able to totalize these perspectives into a whole, or general will. The impartial subject need acknowledge no other subjects, whose perspectives should be taken into account and with whom discussion might occur. Thus the claim to be impartial often results in authoritarianism. By asserting oneself as impartial one claims authority to decide an issue in place of those whose interests and desires are manifest. From this impartial point of view one need not consult with any other, because the impartial point of view already takes into account all possible perspectives.[81]

32.   A Political Alternative

When it comes to the identification of a 'best' regime or a public conception of public justification, the basic problem in relying on substitutionist techniques is precisely that they do aim to substitute, for the collective judgment of a community of concretely situated individuals, some device or method that, however subtle, is meant to give some kind of mechanical aid in solving this problem. For such an approach, I therefore propose to substitute one that, is itself political. After all, as Barber reminds us, "Politics is what men do when metaphysics fails . . . it is the forging of a common actuality in the absence of abstract, independent standards."[82] Or, as Connolly says:

> When groups range themselves around essentially contested concepts, politics is the mode in which the contest is normally expressed. . . . Politics involves the clash which emerges when appraisive concepts are shared widely but imperfectly, when mutual understanding and interpretation is possible but in a partial and limited way, when reasoned argument and coercive pressure commingle precariously in the endless process of defining and resolving issues.[83]

What is a 'political' approach to the problem of public justification? A fuller answer to that question is implied in Chapter 9, where I develop one in some detail. Some sketchy preliminary indications will be helpful, however.

First, the substitutionist approach involves abstracting from differences in order to render into the canonical form everyone's 'input' into the device that will synthesize or amalgamate it. While some differences are honored — the ones that are expressible in the canonical language — others are altogether ignored, and, more importantly, the 'bearers' of those differences are not themselves called upon to address and resolve them: that is the work of the theorist, employing whatever devices are available in this kind of case. On the other hand, the political approach involves acceptance of difference and of the fertile 'opposition' of differences. Anne Phillips provides a very nice formulation:

> The mistake has been to see this process as one of delving behind the so-called accidents of being to come up with a purified core. The problem is better approached from the opposite direction: of being able, partly through comparison with those who are different, to reconceptualize what we had considered our core attributes as if they were accidents themselves . . . and enter imaginatively into an experience that is different from our own.[84]

Second, whereas the substitutionist approach looks for once and for all solutions to problems, the political approach emphasizes the perpetually provisional character of any solutions it might happen to throw up. As Nancy Fraser puts it, the political approach "must substitute . . . a temporality of its own: one of patient, enduring, interminable work, Penelopean or Sisyphean labor."[85] The results of applying political techniques are, in other words, perpetually provisional. As O'Neill says, "The vindication of such principles is recursive rather than foundational."[86] Rather than trying to find some perspective that is proof against every conceivable source of bias and prejudice, the political approach, knowing that its labors may have to be repeated later, engages "concrete notions of specific *partialities,* that is, biases whose manifestations in normative thinking can be specifically identified and corrected."[87]

Third, whereas the substitutionist approach is generalizing and abstractive, the political approach gives great weight to concrete cases and specific decisions — to 'paradigms' conceived in terms of principles and purposes, rather than the application of pre-existing rules. Indeed, there may be advantages in proceeding in this way. As Wong points out, "It is sometimes easier to come to an agreement on more specific instances covered by these principles than it is to come to an agreement on the more abstract and general levels."[88] Since a political approach is oriented in this way to cases, it asks us "to see justification in »theoretical inquiry» as like, for example justification in courts of law — not a matter of the application of atemporal principles of rationality, but a series of appeals to the customs, precedents, procedures, and institutions which make a particular system possible."[89]

Fourth, and finally, rather than trying to find substantive answers, the political approach contents itself with trying to find procedures that individuals can use to find their own answers. It is an institutional approach rather than a theoretical approach because it embodies its insights institutionally rather than in the form of devices of calculation. The political approach accepts Rawls's pure proceduralism as applicable to the case of politics and, in particular, to the problem of public justification. It tries to set up a procedure whose outcomes are, by the fact that they are its outcomes, right answers to questions about public justification. It embodies, in Benhabib's formulation, "a radically proceduralist model of the public sphere, neither the scope nor the agenda of which can be limited a priori, and whose lines can be redrawn by the participants in the conversation."[90] But more on this important point in Chapter 9.

Notes

1. "Deliberative Democracy and Social Choice," p. 58.
2. Richard Bernstein, *The New Constellation*, pp. 220–21.
3. *The World, the Text, and the Critic*, p. 216.
4. Cf. Hampshire, *Innocence and Experience*, p. 13: "Philosophical confusion, and the general scepticism resulting from it, can lead to despair, to a sense that there is no solid ground to stand on when one is thinking of political conciliation and of the decencies of public life." (Hampshire is not among those who do in fact despair.)
5. Cf. his essays "Postmodernist Bourgeois Liberalism" and "The Priority of Democracy to Philosophy" in *Objectivity, Relativism, and Truth*.
6. *Objectivity, Relativism, and Truth*, p. 193.
7. Cf. my paper "Transcendence and Conversation."
8. "The End of Innocence," pp. 450–51.
9. "Stories about Stories," p. xxvi. For a much earlier presentation of related ideas, cf. William W. Bartley, "Rationality versus the Theory of Rationality," p. 5, where he mentions "the two main philosophical positions that have grown from the claim that rationality is logically limited: *skepticism* and *fideism.* . . ."
10. Miller, "Anarchism," p. 11, distinguishes "[f]our main currents in anarchist thought. . . ." These do not quite correspond, however, to the four senses of the epithet I am going to distinguish.
11. This is not quite right. There may be communities so united in their understanding of the various demands associated with the ideal of public justification that the idea of public justification is not in dispute among them. And, for communities of this kind, there may well be regimes that, demonstrably, are publicly justified and therefore legitimate. Still, this is unlikely to occur in modern pluralistic societies of the kind most pertinent to our inquiries.
12. Gaus, "Public Justification and Democratic Adjudication," p. 259, n. 11. (Gaus is not endorsing this view.)
13. Gerald MacCallum, *Political Philosophy*, p. 80.
14. Cf. Frank Hearn, *Reason and Freedom in Sociological Thought*, p. 14: "Horkheimer and Adorno sense in the Enlightenment project a dark side, a tendency to establish a repressive order based on reason."
15. "Authority," p. 158.
16. *Legislators and Interpreters*, p. 120.
17. *Situating the Self*, p. 209.
18. "The End of Innocence," p. 446.
19. Paul Feyerabend, *Science in a Free Society*, pp. 82–83.
20. Cf. Rorty, *Objectivity, Relativism, and Truth*, p. 202: "The view that every tradition is as rational or as moral as every other could only be held by a god. . . ."
21. As MacCallum says (*Political Philosophy*, p. 81), "Some anarchists appear to be complaining of any reliance [on] . . . schemes utilizing any orders and commands whatever. . . ."
22. *Foucault and Feminism*, p. 8.
23. Flax, "The End of Innocence," p. 446. (Flax is not endorsing this view.)
24. MacIntyre, *After Virtue*, p. 253.
25. Cf. Roger Trigg, *Reason and Commitment*, p. 135: "[A] subjectivist may want to make everyone accept what he says, and he may resort to force precisely because he believes rational argument is impossible."
26. *Foucault and Feminism*, p. 163.
27. "Human Nature: Justice versus Power," p. 171.

28. *The New Constellation,* p. 151.

29. *The Transparent Society,* pp. 95, 119. Cf. Bauman, *Legislators and Interpreters,* p. 141: "How can one argue the case for or against a form of life . . . when one feels that one's argument cannot any more legislate . . . ?"

30. *Foucault and Feminism,* p. 137.

31. I reject this suggestion. Cf. "Transcendence and Conversation."

32. *Splitting the Difference,* p. 99.

33. *The New Constellation,* p. 215.

34. These are so obviously 'masculinist' ideas that it would be fatuous to employ my usual term 'her'.

35. Cf. Hampshire, *Innocence and Experience,* pp. 143–44: "Suppose a person claims that her church, through the valid orders of its pope, bishops, and priests, is the repository of moral truth which comes directly from God . . . [and so says] that her morality . . . leaves no place open for fair negotiations about institutions and practices involving substantial moral concerns, as her faith defines them."

36. *Reason and Culture,* p. 58.

37. Justification is a mode of legitimation, but there are, on this account, other modes as well.

38. Flax, "The End of Innocence," p. 446.

39. *Law, Legislation and Liberty,* vol. 1, p. 18.

40. "Bounded Rationality, Ambiguity, and the Engineering of Choice," p. 149.

41. Cf. Stephen Jay Gould, *The Panda's Thumb,* ch. 3.

42. Cf. Gould, *An Urchin in the Storm,* p. 31: "[T]he parts of organisms . . . [are] integrated into systems constrained by history and rules of structure, [they are] not . . . a set of tools, each individually honed to benefit organisms in their immediate ecologies." This is one of the reasons why survival of a trait is not evidence of its superiority to other imaginable alternatives.

43. Cf. Simon, *Reason in Human Affairs,* ch. 2.

44. *Reason and Culture,* p. 59.

45. Cf. Vattimo, *The Transparent Society,* pp. 93–94: "This . . . alternative is to be preferred, we are told, in the name of a duty to be faithful to the . . . tradition, for which no further argument is offered."

46. *Spheres of Justice,* p. 313.

47. *The Meaning of Conservatism,* pp. 12–13. The epithet 'fideistic' is Bartley's; cf. n. 9 above.

48. Cf. Macedo, *Liberal Virtues,* p. 31: "But those who invoke tradition, convention, or social practice really provide no help to any political position so long as the very diversity of traditions, conventions, and practices is the root of our predicament."

49. *Situating the Self,* p. 226. Cf. Bernstein, *The New Constellation,* p. 244.

50. Bernstein, *The New Constellation,* p. 247. Cf. Dryzek, *Discursive Democracy,* p. 18.

51. Susan Moller Okin, *Justice, Gender, and the Family,* pp. 42–43.

52. *The Terms of Political Discourse,* p. 2.

53. *The Foucault Reader,* p. 47.

54. Fishkin is a notable exception; cf. the series of essays culminating in *The Dialogue of Justice.* But his views are not as widely discussed as I think they ought to be.

55. Gellner, *Reason and Culture,* p. 179.

56. *Law, Legislation, and Liberty,* vol. 1, p. 32.

57. Quoted in Kekes, *A Justification of Rationality,* pp. 90–91.

58. I think there is more than merely a verbal resemblance between my contrast between substitutionist and political approaches to the problem of public justification, on the one hand, and Benhabib's contrast (*Situating the Self,* p. 153) between substitutionalist and interactive universalism.

59. Cf. Stephen Toulmin, *Cosmopolis,* p. 172: "If critics such as Lyotard see the absence of a foundational system as substituting 'absurdity' for 'rationality,' this objection shows only that their attack on Cartesianism shares Descartes' prejudice in favor of 'systems'."

60. Of course, Hurley definitely and Ackerman and Gaus arguably use their techniques as a way of supplementing a discussion that has become 'bogged down', so it is not as if the significance of judgment and discussion is ignored by these theorists.

61. Hampshire, *Morality and Conflict,* p. 115.

62. Larmore, *Patterns of Moral Complexity,* p. 10.

63. Cf. Michael Oakeshott, *Rationalism in Politics,* p. 15: "The art of research has . . . three main characteristics. First, it is a set of rules; it is a true technique in that it can be formulated as a precise set of directions which can be learned by heart. Secondly, it is a set of rules whose application is purely mechanical; it is a true technique because it does not require for its use any knowledge or intelligence not given in the technique itself. . . . Thirdly, it is a set of rules of universal application; it is a true technique in that it is an instrument of inquiry indifferent to the subject-matter of the inquiry."

64. Cf. Jean Elshtain, *Public Man, Private Woman,* p. 300: "Those with a need for absolute certainty must force intractable human material into the mold of their hubris in order that life mesh with abstraction." Cf. also Young, "Impartiality and the Civic Public," p. 61: "It constructs total systems that seek to engulf the alterity of things in the unity of thought . . . to eliminate otherness."

65. *Ethics and the Limits of Philosophy,* pp. 116–17.

66. *Beyond Objectivism and Relativism,* p. 8.

67. Cf. Benhabib, *Situating the Self,* p. 81: "Like Walzer, Habermas sees the attempt of the political theorist to provide citizens with a normative yardstick as a preemption of their right to democratic politics."

68. *Beyond Objectivism and Relativism,* p. 198.

69. Bauman, *Legislators and Interpreters,* p. 35.

70. "The Virtue of Incompletion," p. 225.

71. Flax, "The End of Innocence," p. 456.

72. Brown, *Rationality,* pp. 12–13.

73. Benhabib, *Situating the Self,* p. 3.

74. *Splitting the Difference,* pp. 75–76.

75. Benhabib, *Situating the Self,* p. 3.

76. Hekman, *Gender and Knowledge,* p. 16.

77. Nancy Fraser, *Unruly Practices,* p. 56, reporting the views of Foucault.

78. *Politics and Ambiguity,* p. 10.

79. "On Legitimacy and Political Deliberation," p. 351.

80. "The Impracticality of Impartiality," p. 645.

81. "Impartiality and the Civic Public," p. 62.

82. *The Conquest of Politics,* p. 209.

83. *The Terms of Political Discourse,* p. 40.

84. *Engendering Democracy,* p. 58.

85. *Unruly Practices,* p. 72.

86. *Constructions of Reason,* p. 21. Cf. Lyotard, *The Postmodern Condition,* p. 61: "Consensus is a horizon that is never reached." According to Benhabib (*Situating the Self,* p. 6), such an approach involves "an interactive form of rationality rather than . . . the timeless standpoint of legislative reason."

87. Freidman, "The Impracticality of Impartiality," p. 646.

88. "Coping with Moral Conflict and Ambiguity," p. 778.

89. Rorty, "From Epistemology to Hermeneutics," p. 16.

90. *Situating the Self,* p. 12.

III

RECONSTRUCTION

There is no theoretically neutral, pretheoretical ground from which the adjudication of competing claims can proceed. It is all too easy to conclude further that therefore . . . there can be no rational way of settling the difference between them.

ALASDAIR MacINTYRE, *Three Rival Versions of Moral Enquiry*

9

'Solving' the Problem

33. A Political Solution

I propose a broadly 'political' solution to the problem of public justification —
namely, of identifying a 'dominant' regime for a given community in the face of the
variant conceptions of public justification likely to be current in that community (at
least if it resembles ours). What does a 'political' solution look like in this case?
That depends on what the problem looks like in this case.

The problem is this. We have no standard that is commonly accepted and that is
adequate to determine, within any reasonable range, which constitutional regime is
the best — or, alternatively, for a given regime, whether or not it is legitimate. Actually, we have many such standards, many conceptions of the concept, but no *public*
conception. If we understand the idea of public justification as being applicable, primarily, to the domain of constitutional fundamentals (see sec. 8), and thus to have
special application to the deliberations of delegates to a constitutional convention
(and, by extension, justices of a Supreme or High Court), we cannot imagine that
constitutional decision making will be very orderly in a convention whose delegates
(or on a Court whose Justices) do not share even a determinate and determining set
of standards for evaluating the proposals that are put to them. Some order must be
introduced if they are to proceed profitably in articulating a constitutional framework of institutions for their community.

How are we to solve this this problem? In two stages, I believe. First, we must
do some pre-constitutional theorizing to see if we can determine how the convention might work. Second, we must, in making this prior determination, strive to
equip the delegates to the convention so that they will be able, at the same time as
they try to articulate concrete and substantive proposals for basic constitutional
devices, to refine further whatever principles of procedure we have, pre-constitu-
tionally, endowed them with and so to arrive, though perhaps only transiently, at
some public conception of public justification. The pre-constitutional theorizing I
refer to will result, or so I will argue, in the convention being structured so that delegates constitute "a community of interpreters"[1] of the concept of public justification,
which, it is hoped, will arrive, though indirectly, at a public conception of that concept. The convention, in other words, will be so structured as to constitute "[a] liv-

ing tradition . . . an historically extended, socially embodied argument, and an argument precisely in part about the goods which constitute that tradition."[2] By concen-
trating on institutions, rather than calculative mechanisms, such an approach is
arguably Wittgensteinian in "realigning the question, 'What makes rational justification possible?' as the question 'What sorts of human practices make it possible?'"[3]

In order to indicate how pre-constitutional theorizing might proceed, it will be
helpful first to say something about how a community of interpreters might indirectly refine a concept to which each member of that community is committed. I
will then argue that 'reasonable' individuals will favor the establishment of such a
community among the delegates to a constitutional convention whose role is determining the basic political structure for the concrete community whose members the
delegates represent. My general strategy (though not my specific understanding of
it) has much in common with Reiman's suggestion that "[t]he social contract theory
takes as its point of departure a situation that could be real." As he says, "People
could, at some point sit down and decide among themselves what sort of society
they want to have or what principles of justice they want to guide their activities."
But where Reiman says "people *could* . . . sit down," I say that "people *should* sit
down" and decide on constitutional fundamentals for their society. And I mean real
people making real decisions. I therefore don't follow the common path that
Reiman delineates when he says this: "When philosophers cast this situation into a
theoretical device for assessing the justice of social systems, they necessarily transform it into a hypothetical situation."[4] No such transformation is envisaged on my
account.

34.   'Normal Discursive' Constitution Making

The title of this section is very tendentious. The allusion is to Rorty's notion of
"normal discourse," which, he says, "is that which is conducted within an agreed-
upon set of conventions about what counts as a relevant contribution, what counts
as answering a question, what counts as having a good argument for that answer or
a good criticism of it."[5] Clearly, I am going to describe in this section a "community
of interpreters" who are *not* engaged in normal discourse in exactly this sense. But
they are nevertheless engaged in the kind of discourse that Kuhn's "normal scientists" are engaged in when they progressively 'articulate' the paradigm they share a
commitment to. Kuhn says:

> In its standard application, the paradigm functions by permitting the replication of
> examples any one of which could in principle serve to replace it. In a science, on
> the other hand, the paradigm is rarely an object for replication. Instead, like an
> accepted judicial decision in the common law, it is an object for further articulation
> and specification under new and more stringent conditions.[6]

In both cases, Kuhn's and mine, there *is* agreement, much as Rorty says. But in both
cases, there is also diversity in the interpretation, specification, and articulation of
what is, at a more abstract 'level', the object of agreement. According to Bernstein,

"The sharing of criteria by communities of scientists allows for, and indeed requires, interpretation, weighing, and application of these criteria to specific choices and decisions."[7] My usage is more faithful than Rorty's to the Kuhnian original in two senses. It emphasizes the importance of articulating to concrete phenomena a vague and perhaps only implicitly specified paradigm; and it highlights the way in which the articulation of a paradigm depends on the availability of a plurality of interpretations of it. Kuhn says:

> The considerable effectiveness of such criteria does not . . . depend on their being sufficiently articulated to dictate the choice of each individual who subscribes to them. Indeed, if they were articulated to that extent, a behavior mechanism fundamental to scientific advance would cease to function.[8]

It is, in fact, just this "behavior mechanism" that I want to articulate in this section.

It is obvious from what has already been said that, for my particular understanding of interpretive communities, I am indebted to Kuhn's analysis of normal and revolutionary epochs in science and, especially, to his idea that "individual variability in the application of shared values may serve functions essential to" rational inquiry.[9] In fact, implicit in this idea is what I call the 'wave model' of communal cognitive judgment.[10] How does this work in general and, in particular, in the case of constitutional decision making?[11]

First, any community of interpreters/artisans is engaged simultaneously in producing artifacts and in forming judgments about their relative merits in relation to some multidimensional system of standards that underlies the 'founding concept' that community is engaged in interpreting. In the case of the constitutional convention, the delegates are engaged in devising constitutional devices — for example, bills of rights, procedures for the election of officials, institutional means of ensuring an adequate separation of powers, and so on. They are also involved in forming judgments about the suitability of these devices relative to the ideal of public justification. The concept of public justification is, *ex hypothesi,* the 'founding concept' of the 'community' of delegates.

Second, each member of this community takes herself to be engaged in publicly interpreting the founding concept — that is, in trying to decide how, *for the community,* it ought to be interpreted or embodied. She does not take herself to be engaged simply in trying to determine what the concept 'means' to her; she is, instead, a "strong evaluator" in Charles Taylor's sense.[12] In the case of the constitutional convention, each of the delegates takes herself, when she proposes the adoption of some particular constitutional device, to be committed, ipso facto, to the view that this device is an appropriate one for the community as a whole, and not just one whose adoption would suit her particular purposes or reflect her particular attitudes.[13]

Some care is needed here. The obvious and explicit activities of the community are productive rather than interpretive. Its members are making artifacts that are meant to *embody* the community's 'founding concept'. Their interpretive activities, in which they explicitly reflect on this concept, are perhaps largely subsidiary to this primary project. The activities of delegates to a constitutional convention are likely to be even further removed than this from direct and explicit interpretive reflection on the community's founding concept. They will be engaged, primarily, in constructing constitutional devices, and, insofar as they do reflect on this activity, much of their thinking and discussion will be concerned with 'first-order' values like liberty, equality, community, and so on, rather than with the (arguably 'second-order') values embedded in the ideal of public justification. Still, their 'first-order' reflections and their productive activities taken together *imply* answers to interpretive questions about the concept of public justification.[14]

Third, each member of the community is committed, as a result of socialization, to evaluate the artifacts produced in the community in terms of various and sometimes competing desiderata, and subject to certain 'paradigmatic constraints'. Any given individual will learn, during socialization, both that certain desiderata are relevant in judging the relative merits of products and thus in interpreting the founding concept these products are taken to embody, *and* that certain products are exemplars of what the community is trying to produce and therefore of the founding concept they are trying to interpret and embody.[15] Taken together, the paradigmatic products constrain, but do not uniquely determine, a system of weightings with respect to the desiderata. For instance, given that some particular product is exemplary, it may not be possible, consistently with this judgment, entirely to discount the desideratum δ_j, since it is, let us suppose, precisely in relation to its superiority with respect to δ_j that the product is superior to other artifacts the community has produced. As Dworkin says, "[T]the paradigms will be treated as concrete examples any plausible interpretation must fit. . . ."[16]

In the case of the constitutional convention, certain historically exemplary enactments and the reasoning that led to their adoption will be considered paradigmatic of what the community of delegates is trying to fashion. (Such enactments may be "icons" in Jaroslav Pelikan's sense.[17]) As Rawls says, "Throughout the history of democratic thought the focus has been on achieving certain specific liberties and constitutional guarantees, as found, for example, in various bills of rights and declarations of the rights of man."[18] That these devices are considered paradigmatic for members of that community will somewhat constrain, without of course uniquely determining, their own activities. As Rawls says, "The successful practice of its ideas and principles over [time] . . . places restrictions on what can now count as an [interpretation] . . . , whatever was true at the beginning."[19] For instance, First Amendment guarantees of freedom of speech and of the press, and Fourteenth Amendment guarantees of equal protection and due process will be recognized by the delegates as paradigms of what must pass the test of public justification, whatever that might turn out to be, if anything at all does. No matter how one weights the various desiderata associated with the ideal of public justification, one will want to ensure the rights enshrined in these enactments.

'Negative paradigms' may also play an important role in articulating the concept of public justification. As Macedo says, "Confronting an occasional fanatic . . . reminds us of what in the world we stand for as liberals."[20] Indeed, these kinds of considerations may be more important than those embodied in 'positive paradigms' such as the First Amendment. This, I think, would be Hampshire's view: "There is a basic level of morality, a bare minimum, which is entirely negative. . . ."[21] Certainly, the *fatwa* against Salman Rushdie, the Nazi Race Laws, Constitutional recognition of antebellum slavery, and so on, are all concrete examples of what can *not* be justified publicly in communities such as ours.

Fourth, although all members of the community share such commitments, there is nevertheless considerable diversity within the community both in the interpretation of the desiderata (and therefore in their application in judging concrete products) and in the relative importance that is assigned by various individuals to any given desideratum in comparison with others. (This is the point on which my account of normal discourse seems to differ from Rorty's.) Each member of the community can be thought of as forming judgments, from time to time, about the overall relative merits of various products as concrete embodiments of the founding concept the community is interpreting in producing these artifacts. It is nevertheless not guaranteed, and indeed typically it will not be the case that different individuals make the same judgments about such artifacts. Perhaps A prefers X to Y, that is, thinks that it is a better example of what they are trying to achieve or a better concrete embodiment of the founding concept they are trying to interpret, whereas B prefers Y to X.[22] Such differences are typically due to underlying differences in weights assigned to desiderata. Perhaps A weights δ_i heavily whereas B weights δ_j heavily. A's preference for X then simply reflects the fact, perhaps accepted as such by B, that $X >_i Y$; and, similarly, B's preference for Y may simply reflect the fact that $Y >_j X$.

For instance, in the constitutional convention, some delegates might prefer 'absolutist' and others weaker interpretations of the protections afforded under the broad general heading 'freedom of speech'. Perhaps those who prefer weaker interpretations do so because they believe that 'absolute' protection of such a freedom is at least potentially (socially) destabilizing. Those who prefer an 'absolutist' interpretation do so, on the other hand, because they believe that only on such an interpretation can real transparency of governmental processes be realistically in reach.

In fact, fifth, this diversity in judgments is important in maintaining what Kuhn calls an "essential tension" between conservative and innovative attitudes toward productive and interpretive tasks. A might prefer X to Y because, on his interpretation, X better reflects the weighting of desiderata that is implied in judgments that certain products are exemplary artifacts. B might prefer Y to X because, on her interpretation, Y better reflects a weighting of desiderata that stresses hitherto unemphasized values (which all nevertheless agree are values). Without A's 'conservatism', what is valuable in the community's historical achievements might be too easily abandoned.[23] Without B's 'radicalism', the community might remain attached to past achievements long after they had ceased to be applicable in changing circumstances. As Kuhn says, "Within the group some individuals may be more traditionalistic, others more iconoclastic, and their contributions may differ accordingly."[24] In this respect and in others, the "community of interpreters" resembles Wilhelm von Humboldt's "social union of social unions," in which, as Rawls says, a society not only "accommodate[s] a plurality of conceptions of the good but also . . . coordinate[s] the various activities made possible by human diversity into a more comprehensive good to which everyone can contribute and in which each can participate."[25]

For example, in the case of the constitutional convention, one delegate's advocacy of an 'absolutist' interpretation of the demand for freedom of speech may reflect assignments of weights, with heavy weighting given to transparency, which are implicit in the various historical enactments and proposals accepted by the community as paradigmatic examples of what they are trying to achieve. Another delegate's advocacy of a weaker interpretation of this demand may reflect her assessment of the contemporary importance, given changing social circumstances, of ensuring greater stability in relation to constitutional essentials.

Sixth, what sometimes happens when there are differences of opinion within the community is that a 'wave' of interpretations sweeps through the community and, after it has passed, anchors the judgments of its members in a new set of paradigms and articulates a new and richer interpretation of the founding concept they are each trying to embody in their productive activities.[26] Consider the following scenario.

At a given time, each member of the community has a conception of the community's founding concept that reflects her best understanding, given her own character and social position, of the implications, with respect to relevant desiderata, of the community's accepted paradigmatic products.[27] Call A's conception of this concept ω_A, B's ω_B, and so on. (This diversity reflects the diversity of opinions within the concrete historically situated community whose members the delegates in fact represent.)

At any given time, each such individual is presented with an array of newly created artifacts, each of which is intended to embody, concretely, the founding concept of the community. Each of these products has, with respect to each of the desiderata that ground the community's founding concept, a certain rank, call it $\mu_i(X)$, that is, X's rank with respect to the desideratum δ_i.[28] Let $\mu^*(X)$ summarize, though it will not aggregate, the ranking of X with respect to *all* the relevant desiderata (μ^* takes the form of a matrix). Each individual's *overall* judgment about how well X does indeed embody the founding concept of the community will therefore depend on two factors, μ^* and ω_i. Such a judgment will depend on X's performance, objectively assessed, with respect to each of the various desiderata, and, since weights need to be assigned to these desiderata before an *overall* assessment of its performance can be determined, on the individual's understanding of the relative importance of these desiderata, that is, on her conception of the founding concept, ω_i.

For instance, delegates to the constitutional convention are presented, from time to time, with proposals that certain constitutional devices be accepted as part of the 'ground plan' for the regime that they are engaged in 'designing'. Each of these devices will be evaluated with respect to each of the desiderata that jointly constitute the ideal associated with the 'founding concept' for their community — that of public justification. The proposal that an 'absolutist' interpretation of freedom of speech be adopted will rank highly, let us suppose, with respect to transparency. The workings of a regime incorporating such a device will, *ceteris paribus,* be more transparent than those of a regime not incorporating it. And such a proposal will also, let us suppose, rank poorly with respect to stability. Regimes incorporating such a device may be more readily destabilized than those not doing so. (In this case, μ^* can be thought of simply as an expression of these supposed facts and others like them.)

Because ω_i is a variable, there will be a variety of different judgments within the community about how well X embodies the community's founding concept. Because each member of the community takes herself to be interpreting its practices, that is, to be saying what she thinks all members of the community are or ought to be committed to, each member will try to develop grounds, which will count with the other members, in support of her particular evaluation of X. For the members of the community, it is true, as Benhabib says, that "the ground of the validity of [their] . . . judgments is their universal communicability with the hope of winning the assent of all."[29] If A judges, relative to $\mu^*(X,Y)$, that the artifact X is a better exemplar than Y of the founding concept of his community, he will try to develop evidence supporting this claim, or to remove incompatibilities between X and other accepted exemplars (i.e., paradigms), and so on.[30] Perhaps he succeeds, to a certain extent, in this task. If he does, he improves X's overall relative standing.[31] Perhaps he improves it enough so that B, who, given ω_B, previously had no adequate reason for judging X superior to Y, does now make this judgment.

As Connolly says, "The pressure of opposing interpretations, when each sees other interpretations as capable of some degree of rational defense, is seen by each to contribute to his 'own use or interpretation of the concept in question.'"[32] Perhaps A and B, now working together, so improve X's relative standing that other individuals now have reason, given their conceptions, to accept that X is better than Y as an embodiment of their community's founding concept. As Polanyi says, "An aggregate of individual initiatives can lead to the establishment of spontaneous order . . . if each takes into account in its action what others have done in the same context before."[33] And that is, of course, exactly what our 'interpreters' are here imagined as doing. In this case, as Rorty says, "[P]olitical progress results from the accidental coincidence of a private obsession with a public need."[34] Indeed, our 'interpreters' are plausibly described as identifying something like that elusive 'general will' of Jean-Jacques Rousseau.[35]

Remember that, if any artifact is a paradigm of the community's founding concept, every individual's conception of that concept must be able to accommodate this fact. And this may require some adjustment of weightings in certain cases. If an 'absolutist' interpretation of freedom of speech is adopted and largely on the grounds of the importance of the requirement of transparency, then no acceptable assignment of weights to desiderata can entirely scant this particular requirement, whatever might have been the case before the acceptance of this new device as a paradigm of what the community understands as a publicly justifiable feature of its fundamental constitutional apparatus.

In fact, some such wave as I have described may have swept over the United States Supreme Court, over a period of nearly two-hundred years, in relation to the protection of political speech and done so largely, though not exclusively, in favor of an 'absolutist' interpretation of this right. Indeed, the debate about this matter seems to have been conducted largely in terms of the very requirements already mentioned, namely, transparency (not "to restrict the free and informed public use of our reason in judging the justice of the basic structure") and stability (the danger that "volatile and destructive social forces may be set going by revolutionary speech").[36]

TABLE 9.1: The Wave of Acceptance Schematically Illustrated

	A	B	C	D	E	F
t_1	$\omega_A{}^\bullet\mu_1=$ YES	$\omega_B{}^\bullet\mu_1=$ No	$\omega_C{}^\bullet\mu_1=$ No	$\omega_D{}^\bullet\mu_1=$ No	$\omega_E{}^\bullet\mu_1=$ No	$\omega_F{}^\bullet\mu_1=$ No
$A \otimes \mu_1 \Rightarrow \mu_2 > \mu_1$						
t_2	$\omega_A{}^\bullet\mu_2=$ YES	$\omega_B{}^\bullet\mu_2=$ YES	$\omega_C{}^\bullet\mu_2=$ No	$\omega_D{}^\bullet\mu_2=$ No	$\omega_E{}^\bullet\mu_2=$ No	$\omega_F{}^\bullet\mu_2=$ No
$(A+B) \otimes \mu_2 \Rightarrow \mu_3 > \mu_2$						
t_3	$\omega_A{}^\bullet\mu_3=$ YES	$\omega_B{}^\bullet\mu_3=$ YES	$\omega_C{}^\bullet\mu_3=$ YES	$\omega_D{}^\bullet\mu_3=$ No	$\omega_E{}^\bullet\mu_3=$ No	$\omega_F{}^\bullet\mu_3=$ No
$(A+B+C) \otimes \mu_3 \Rightarrow \mu_4 > \mu_3$						
t_4	$\omega_A{}^\bullet\mu_4=$ YES	$\omega_B{}^\bullet\mu_4=$ YES	$\omega_C{}^\bullet\mu_4=$ YES	$\omega_D{}^\bullet\mu_4=$ YES	$\omega_E{}^\bullet\mu_4=$ No	$\omega_F{}^\bullet\mu_4=$ No
$(A+B+C+D) \otimes \mu_4 \Rightarrow \mu_5 > \mu_4$						
t_5	$\omega_A{}^\bullet\mu_5=$ YES	$\omega_B{}^\bullet\mu_5$ YES	$\omega_C{}^\bullet\mu_5$ YES	$\omega_D{}^\bullet\mu_5$ YES	$\omega_E{}^\bullet\mu_5$ YES	$\omega_F{}^\bullet\mu_5$ No
$(A+B+C+D+E) \otimes \mu_5 \Rightarrow \mu_6 > \mu_5$						
t_6	$\omega_A{}^\bullet\mu_6=$ YES	$\omega_B{}^\bullet\mu_6=$ YES	$\omega_C{}^\bullet\mu_6=$ YES	$\omega_D{}^\bullet\mu_6=$ YES	$\omega_E{}^\bullet\mu_6=$ YES	$\omega_F{}^\bullet\mu_6=$ YES

More generally, a wave may sweep through the community until, when all are engulfed, X is accepted as another paradigm of the community's achievements, and adjustments accordant with its status as such are now made to each member's system of weightings or interpretations of the community's founding concept.

In Table 9.1:

- ω_I is the individual I's assignment of weights to the various desiderata.
- μ_i is the 'objective' merit with respect to these desiderata of the object of concern at the time t_i.
- An individual's decision to accept or reject an artifact as an embodiment of her community's founding concept is dependent on the value, for her, of $\omega_I{}^\bullet\mu_i$. If this value reaches I's 'threshold', she accepts (says 'YES').
- $\otimes$ marks the work of individuals in improving an artifact that has objective merit μ_i so that it comes to have objective merit μ_j.

And what if a proposal does not stimulate the formation of a 'wave' of support? Mueller provides helpful commentary:

> Should an initial proposal fail to command a unanimous majority, it is redefined until it does, or until it is removed from the agenda. Thus, the political process . . . is one of discussion, compromise, and amendment, continuing until a formulation of the issue is reached benefiting all.[37]

In a related, legal context, Dworkin provides a good summary of some of these points:

> Each judge's interpretive theories are grounded in his own convictions about the "point" — the justifying purpose or goal or principle — of legal practice as a whole,

and these convictions will inevitably be different, at least in detail, from those of other judges. Nevertheless, a variety of forces tempers these differences and conspires toward convergence. Every community has paradigms of law, propositions that in practice cannot be challenged without suggesting either corruption or ignorance. . . . The practice of precedent, which no judge's interpretation can wholly ignore, presses toward agreement; each judge's theory of what judging really is will incorporate by reference, through whatever account and restructuring of precedent he settles on, aspects of other popular interpretations of the day.[38]

Through a series of such incidents, the community's founding concept may be increasingly 'articulated', or *specified* — because it is to be 'articulated', that is, *attached,* to so many concrete exemplars — so that what was once a vague concept is now at least a partial public conception of that concept. (Perhaps only partial because the conception still permits further interpretation.[39]) In at least one pertinent sense, the community has achieved 'objectivity' in the interpretation of its founding concept.[40] As Rawls says:

It is inevitable and often desirable that citizens have different views as to the most appropriate political conception; for the public political culture is bound to contain different fundamental ideas that can be developed in different ways. An orderly contest between them over time is a reliable way to find which one, if any, is most reasonable.[41]

It is in this way that a 'dominant' regime for a given community might be identified simultaneously with the articulation of the concept of public justification *into* a full-blown public conception of that concept and *onto* concrete exemplars of publicly justified social arrangements. As Galston says, "There is no philosophical alternative to 'commonsense pluralism' and no political substitute for deliberative opportunities to express and to harmonize (to the extent possible) the different emphases that are bound to emerge among individuals in free societies."[42] It is in this way that the constitutional convention might function as a community of interpreters/artisans simultaneously engaged in developing and discussing proposals for the concrete institutional embodiment of its founding concept — of publicly justified institutions — and in identifying, in this indirect, quasi-inductive way, a public conception of that concept, a conception implicit in the concrete exemplars of that concept which they develop.[43]

Constitute the constitutional convention that is to decide on political fundamentals for a given community as a community of interpreters/artisans each of whom seeks, in her own characteristic way, to articulate publicly the founding concept of that community — the concept of public justification — and to do so in two ways: by fashioning artifacts that are taken to embody it, in this case constitutional devices for the governance of the community, and by interpreting its demands so that they can be used for guiding both her productive activities and her judgments about the artifacts she and others produce. Endow the delegates to the convention with a commitment to the desiderata that constitute the ideal of public justification but ensure a certain diversity in their understanding of these desiderata and how they ought to be

weighted. Present the delegates with certain paradigmatic examples of publicly justified constitutional devices — for example, First Amendment guarantees of freedom
of speech and of religion; Fourteenth Amendment guarantees of due process and
equal protection. Ensure that the delegates are able to communicate freely with one
another and that none is able simply to coerce the rest to accept her interpretation of
their founding concept, and hope that there is otherwise enough by way of common
cultural background and shared ethical assumptions to make possible the development of what I have called a 'wave' of support, even transiently, for some particular
interpretation of the concept of public justification.[44]

(I can dispel an air of unreality that no doubt lingers here by supposing that the
work of such a one-time only constitutional convention is carried on, after its decisions are implemented, by a body of judicial arbiters, embodied in the form of a
Supreme or a High Court, so that what the delegates decide about constitutional
fundamentals can itself be interpreted and reinterpreted as need be, and the merely
partial public conception of public justification that they in effect identify can also
be further articulated as necessary.[45] This is suggested, for instance, by Rawls's
analysis of "The Supreme Court as Exemplar of Public Reason."[46] Rawls describes
a body very like the 'community of interpreters' whose lineaments I have sketched.
He says:

> [1] [T]he idea of public reason does not mean that judges agree with one another,
> any more than citizens do, in the details of their understanding of the constitution.
> [2] Yet they must be, and appear to be, interpreting the same constitution in view of
> what they see as the relevant parts of the political conception and in good faith
> believe it can be defended as such. [3] The court's role as the highest judicial inter-
> preter of the constitution supposes that the political conceptions judges hold and
> their views on constitutional essentials locate the central range of the basic free-
> doms in more or less the same place.[47]

Several of the elements of the 'wave model' appear here, marked in the text by
numerals in square brackets — namely, [1] the diversity of interpretations of the
founding concept; [2] the aim of each interpreter to provide a public interpretation;
and [3] the role of paradigms in disciplining the reflections of the interpreters.
(Much the same thinking is implicit in Ackerman's idea of "higher law-making,"
"when a mobilized majority of American citizens hammer out a considered judgment on a fundamental matter of principle" "by talking together about the deepest
values of dualist democracy."[48])

My account is arguably, though perhaps not obviously, an example of 'pure proceduralism'[49] and thus, I think, answers Benhabib's plea for "a radically proceduralist model of the public sphere."[50] That regime is the 'dominant' regime, whatever it
is, which is accepted as such by the delegates to a constitutional convention organized as I have indicated; their acceptance *makes it* the 'dominant' regime.[51] As
Rawls says, "[T]hey recognize no standpoint external to their own point of view as
rational representatives from which they are constrained by prior and independent
principles. . . ."[52]

That this approach is an example of 'pure proceduralism' perhaps needs to be argued, rather than accepted as obvious, because it is not, perhaps, an example of 'pure proceduralism' in Rawls's canonical formulation. Let us distinguish, then, between 'substitutive' pure proceduralism and 'participative' pure proceduralism. In the latter case, which is the one relevant to the wave model, the particular procedure must actually be implemented in order to determine the outcome that is justified by its use. In the former case, it will be enough to 'reason analytically' *about* the procedure to determine what the outcome of actually implementing it would be. (This distinction therefore reflects the distinction between substitutionist and political approaches — secs. 31 and 32.) Rawls's notion of pure proceduralism now seems to be the former, at least in respect of original position argumentation.[53] He says:

> There exists no practicable way actually to carry out this deliberative process and to be sure that it conforms to the conditions imposed. Therefore, the outcome cannot be ascertained by pure procedural justice as realized by deliberations of the parties on some actual occasion. Instead the outcome must be determined by reasoning analytically. . . .[54]

My notion is certainly not this notion. On my account, it will not be enough to determine the legitimacy of some constitutional proposal to try to 'reason analytically' about what the delegates to the constitutional convention might or might not decide about it. Indeed, the idea that the theorist *could* do this is itself an example of hubris in my view. How could we tell what points might be made by the delegates, what order they might be made in, how effectively each of these points might be pressed or countered, and so on?[55] On my account, the only way to discover whether a proposal is justified is actually to submit it to the delegates to such a convention and wait for them to deliver some determinate judgment about it. The matter can only be decided participatively; it cannot be decided substitutively.

In any event, I repeat: that regime is the 'dominant' regime, whatever it is, which is accepted as such by the delegates to a constitutional convention organized as I have indicated; their acceptance *makes it* the 'dominant' regime. And what makes being accepted by such delegates criterial for being the 'dominant' regime? Whether the 'wave model' constitutes an adequate basis for identifying a 'dominant' regime, and thus for solving the problem of legitimacy, depends on whether the idea of a 'community of interpreters' can be accepted to play this role by 'reasonable' individuals in something like Rawls's quasi-technical sense — that is, by individuals who are willing "to propose fair terms of cooperation and to abide by them provided others do . . . [and] to recognize the burdens of judgment. . . ."[56]

And what makes this the appropriate test? Simply this. That individuals are 'reasonable' in Rawls's sense is a condition for politics. Unless this is so, there are no prospects for the peaceful and honest resolution of those disagreements that arise in the 'circumstances of' politics. Unless this is so, we find ourselves beyond the 'limits on' politics, and only force and fraud can help us secure our interests. (See sec. 7.) It is "natural enough" in the present circumstances to let acceptance by reasonable individuals be the test. As I will suggest in section 35, 'reasonable' individuals would indeed commission delegates to a constitutional convention to act as 'trustees' for their interests. Suppose that delegates in this sense then identified some particular regime as the dominant regime for the community they collectively represent. Since each delegate acts to safeguard the interests of the individual(s) she represents, none of these individuals could have any reason to reject the regime the delegates have identified as the dominant one. After all, it would be unreasonable to do so, since rejecting this regime would be tantamount to a refusal to abide by fair terms of cooperation, and that would be unreasonable in Rawls's sense. We have, schematically,

individuals qua electors $\Rightarrow$ delegates $\Rightarrow$ A REGIME $\Leftarrow$ individuals qua citizens

or, verbally, individuals commission delegates who select a regime that binds the individuals, now thought of as citizens of that regime.

Of course, setting such a test is crucial to my project. Remember that reflexivity is a desideratum for public justification. I therefore hope to be able to show, of any standard for determining whether some system of governance is publicly justified, whether that standard is itself publicly justified. One especially pertinent way of attempting this is to consider the matter from the point of view of 'reasonable' people.[57]

35. Pre-Constitutional Theorizing

What do things look like, then, from the point of view of 'reasonable' people? 'Reasonable' people contemplating the circumstances of politics will recognize that they need to identify a 'dominant' regime for their community.

Being 'reasonable', they know that they do not currently inhabit such a regime, however satisfactory their actual regime might be from their own points of view. They know that others have different conceptions of public justification than they do and so are likely to make different judgments about the legitimacy of their current regime. And they know, being 'reasonable', that since all individuals must contend with the 'burdens of judgment', most individuals are not unreasonable in judging their current regime as they do. Furthermore, 'reasonable' individuals will also know, in particular, that none of the 'analytical' machinery associated with substitutionist ethico-political theorizing is adequate to the task of identifying a 'dominant' regime for their community. A 'reasonable' case to this effect has been made. (See Chapter 7.)[58]

Being 'reasonable', such individuals will want to enjoy the benefits of publicly justified social arrangements and will be willing to play their roles in securing these benefits if others are also willing to do so. But since others are, *ex hypothesi,* also 'reasonable', *they* will be willing to bear the burdens of securing the benefits of publicly justified social arrangements, and so *all* will be willing to bear these burdens. Of course, a 'reasonable' individual wants to be as little disadvantaged as possible in the deliberations that are to take place in the constitutional convention. She will not want to be represented at that convention by a delegate whose interests are opposed to her own, or who is required to present her case in some format or vocabulary that, in her view, only poorly expresses the force of the considerations she considers important.

'Reasonable' individuals therefore know that they do not currently inhabit a publicly justified regime, want to inhabit just such a regime, and want to do so on terms they can themselves accept. How would they go about identifying such a regime? They would do so, I submit, by commissioning delegates to a constitutional convention and laying down certain ground rules for the conduct of that convention.

Two questions: (a) Why don't 'reasonable' individuals themselves determine the lineaments of a 'dominant' regime for their community? (b) Why, if they are going to commission delegates to act on their behalf, don't they let the delegates themselves determine the ground rules they will be bound by?

Re (a), there are many pertinent considerations. First, even 'reasonable' individuals who inhabit a regime that is not publicly justified have various 'first-order' concerns and must give their primary attention to these concerns if, within the limits associated with their current regime, they are to survive and perhaps even flourish.[59] This is, perhaps, a broadly realistic consideration. Second, given the large populations of contemporary societies, representation by delegates is undoubtedly a practical necessity. Certainly, I assume the fallibility and finitude of all individuals. But, in this case, John Dryzek's remarks are pertinent:

> Given this imperfect information-processing capacity, the "all-channel network" characterizing universal participation in all decisions will impose strict limits upon group size. After all, the number of links in such a network increases with (roughly) the square of the number of members.[60]

Third, even a 'reasonable' person, indeed perhaps especially a 'reasonable' person, will know that she is not necessarily as well equipped to press her own case as someone else might be, especially when constitutional fundamentals are at stake, requiring, for effective argumentation, persuasive skills and knowledge of history and theory that many ordinary people, however 'reasonable', will not possess in sufficient measure.

Re (b), 'reasonable' individuals will know that, while their interests might be better represented by others than by themselves, their interests might also be betrayed by the delegates they commission. 'Reasonable' individuals will therefore ensure that these delegates are 'reasonably' constrained in their activities so that they, the individuals represented by them, will in fact have adequate motives for compliance with the requirements of the regime identified by the delegates as the 'dominant' one for their community. On Rawls's account, and on mine, delegates are "trustees" engaged "in securing the interests of the persons they represent." "As such . . . [they] are to do the best they can for those they represent. . . ."[61] It is to ensure that a delegate adequately discharges her role as a 'trustee' that her own activities are 'reasonably' constrained.

To determine the character of a constitutional convention set up to identify a 'dominant' regime, it will be necessary (though not perhaps sufficient) to answer two fundamental questions: (1) who are the delegates? and (2) how are the delegates to conduct themselves? How would 'reasonable' individuals answer these questions?

1. Who Are the Delegates?

As already indicated, the delegates to the convention are *not* the individual members of the community. The delegates are, instead, persons who are in the broadest sense articulate and effective advocates, in terms they themselves can recognize, for the views of the many main *types* of individuals who are members of the community for which constitutional fundamentals are being chosen.[62] As Dryzek says, "[N]o party with substantial influence should be excluded, for any such party may subsequently sabotage any agreement reached."[63] This is a realistic consideration. Young provides some moralistic guidance.

> Specific representation for oppressed groups . . . promotes justice better than a homogeneous public. . . . First, it better ensures procedural fairness in setting the public agenda and hearing opinions about its items. Second, it . . . better assures that all needs and interests in the public will be recognized. . . .[64]

Notice furthermore that there are many members of the community who will not be able to defend their own opinions about constitutional fundamentals, and their foundations in public justification, in an articulate and effective way. Since these individuals might be disadvantaged by schemes of constitutional fundamentals that might be chosen if they were left to 'conduct their own defense', and since 'reasonable' individuals want to do as well as possible, they will prefer to be represented by delegates with certain attitudes, aptitudes, and other attributes rather than to represent themselves. As Fishkin says, "[E]ffective voice must be given to interests across every significant cleavage in the society."[65]

What the main types of individuals are in a given community is bound to be controversial. Still, we will want to ensure that each of the main understandings of public justification that are actually current in the community are represented in the convention, since it is precisely the purpose of the convention to determine which of these understandings, or which synthesis of them, is most reasonably construed as the public understanding of that concept. Satisfying this demand alone will presumably ensure that a fair range of other important views are also represented. Among those that must be properly represented are, presumably, all the 'reasonable' comprehensive religious and/or philosophical conceptions that are current in the community, each of the main occupational groups, each of the main groups having or claiming special needs and/or entitlements, and so on. All those groups, *inter alia,* which are sometimes pejoratively referred to as 'special interest groups' will have to be represented in the constitutional convention. (On Young's account, such groups are "defined not primarily by . . . set[s] of shared attributes, but by a sense of identity."[66])

There is a danger, of course, that to ensure that each of the main types of individuals is represented, a great many individuals will have to be delegates to any legitimate constitutional convention.[67] (Indeed, the 'universalism' of much ethical theorizing might stem from denying that there are any such types.) Is there any way, short of constituting the entire community as a 'committee of the whole', of avoiding the kind of 'normalization' that is implicit in the representation by one individ-

ual of numbers, perhaps large numbers, of individuals whose views on various matters differ from one another?[68] (Constituting the entire community as a 'committee
of the whole' would, of course, be unworkable in modern large-scale societies.) To
answer this question, it is helpful to remember that the decisions taken by constitutional delegates are wholly and solely decisions about constitutional fundamentals.
(See sec. 8.) While individuals may differ in many ways, and in many ways that
may be relevant to, indeed crucial for, the nature of their political arrangements,
only those differences are relevant that are relevant in the constitutional realm — that
is, that might make a difference to how so-called constitutional fundamentals are
settled.[69] Given this proviso, the stipulations I have sketched seem to cater more
than adequately for *relevant* diversity within moderately pluralistic societies and to
do so within reasonable constraints on the total size of the body of delegates. Those
differences in attitudes that are likely to be relevant to constitutional fundamentals
are going to be determined, largely, by comprehensive ethical and/or religious commitments and socioeconomic status, and it will therefore be enough, at a first
approximation, to ensure the 'representativeness' of the body of delegates if these
particular differences are indeed represented (while others are ignored as irrelevant
to the task at hand). (This is another function of the Supreme or High Court — as the
continuing embodiment of the one-time only convention. Given easy access to it,
those who believe that their [constitutionally fundamental] interests were not adequately represented at the convention can make a case to this effect and hope to see
it accepted and its implications implemented.[70])

Two points require clarification.

1. Clearly, we want 'reasonable' members of a given community themselves to
participate, insofar as this is possible, in identifying a 'dominant' regime for their
community. On the moralistic side, this is demanded if we are to honor "each person's claim to moral independence,"[71] if, like Anna Yeatman, we "problematize a
subject speaking on behalf of another and . . . put a premium on subjects finding
their own 'voice'."[72] On the other hand, looking at matters realistically, we must be
concerned, especially from the point of view of salience, with any form of argumentation that appeals to so idealized a surrogate for a given individual that that individual finds the course of argumentation utterly impotent motivationally.

This approach requires the commissioning of delegates; it does not demand, and
indeed rejects the idea, that individuals might represent themselves in the constitutional convention. Do I resile from my anti-substitutionist insistence that individuals
must be allowed to, indeed be all but compelled to, *speak for themselves?* I do not
think I do. Insofar as 'reasonable' individuals themselves commission and constrain
the activities of the delegates, any legitimate demand for self-representation is in
fact adequately catered for. If A is willing to be, indeed insists on being, represented
for certain purposes by α, then we dishonor his "claim to moral independence" if
we refuse to recognize α as his rightful delegate. The appointment of delegates does
not compromise a *political* understanding of the project of public justification.

2. I suggest that the delegates must be articulate and effective. Is this an 'unreasonable' restriction? After all, U.S. Senator Roman Hruska apparently once said of a
poorly qualified nominee for the Supreme Court that even the mediocre were entitled to representation on that body. More seriously, it is often claimed that some

specifications of the attitudes, aptitudes, and other attributes of such surrogates do prejudice the prospects, indeed are mechanisms for prejudicing the prospects, of those they allegedly but do not really 'represent'. Whether this charge is well founded depends on what the parties specify as the 'rules of order' for the conduct of the constitutional convention, and so must await further clarification in subsection 2. What can be said here, though, is that if they think that their own strengths lie in emotive self-presentation or even indeed in non-verbal expression, 'reasonable' individuals are unlikely to commission delegates to represent them who are lacking in these skills. I said, originally, that I wanted the phrase "articulate and effective" to be understood in the broadest relevant sense. I meant what I said. If 'reasonable' individuals want to recruit performers and not merely orators as delegates to represent them in the convention, then that is exactly what they will do. As Fishkin is right to point out, "[t]he most effective strategies of communication will . . . sometimes be 'symbolic' or even completely nonverbal."[73]

Among the other attitudes of the delegates will be, especially, whatever knowledge about public justification and its problems is pertinent to the development of appropriate constitutional apparatus for the concrete individuals whom they represent. This, again, is appropriate in light of the problem that the delegates are recruited to solve. Whereas 'reasonable' individuals who belong to the relevant community might be ignorant of political history and theory insofar as it is relevant to the development of constitutional fundamentals, their delegates, aside from their articulate and effective advocacy, or perhaps as part of it, are knowledgeable about these matters. And this knowledge will include, in particular, such historical knowledge, and its theoretical analysis, as is pertinent to the identification of paradigms. This is knowledge that is likely to be crucial if the delegates are to discharge their duties. The individuals who commission them will therefore ensure that they have it.

2. How Are the Delegates to Conduct Themselves?

'Reasonable' individuals want the delegates to identify a 'dominant' regime, that is, to devise constitutional devices for the community they represent at the same time as they, the delegates, determine indirectly a (probably only partial) public conception of public justification. 'Reasonable' individuals will therefore determine rules for the conduct of business in the constitutional convention that are appropriate for this project. (Notice that these rules must be "self-enforcing" in Jules Coleman's sense — namely, "compliance is the dominant strategy for each individual."[74] The reason is obvious. With respect to the constitutional convention, there are no pre-existent agencies of enforcement. Indeed, the convention is conducted precisely in order to identify the form and limits of legitimate authority. If the rules do not enforce themselves, they will not be [legitimately] enforced at all.[75])

A Kantian maxim articulated by O'Neill is of crucial importance in relation to the conduct of the delegates. She says: "Incipiently free and rational beings . . . can and must regulate their communicating by maxims that do not undermine or stultify their incipient communication."[76] Delegates are free to propose whatever constitutional devices they wish to champion, whether verbally or otherwise. And they are free to champion these devices in whatever way, short of violence, that they wish.

Explicit advocacy of favored conceptions can also be expected. If the community includes 'Rawlsians', and they are represented in the convention (as they should be), then we can expect that both Rawlsian procedures and Rawlsian substantive proposals will receive an airing in the convention. Similarly for other prominent conceptions. Certainly, despite (or because of?) prior *dis*agreement about the relative merits of these conceptions, the delegates will be ready, indeed anxious, to hear them expounded.[77]

As Rawls says, "[R]easonable persons see that the burdens of judgment set limits on what can be reasonably justified to others, and so they endorse some form of liberty of conscience and freedom of thought."[78] Ackerman helpfully connects the question of the right of access to the forum with the statistician's distinction between false positives (opinions admitted that don't survive scrutiny) and false negatives (opinions refused a hearing that would have survived scrutiny). Indeed, he provides a rationale for O'Neill's imperative. He says:

> [A]n occasional false negative seems far worse than frequent false positives. Consider the consequences: . . . If the movement crosses the initial threshold in a relatively weak condition, it is unlikely its initiative will survive the obstacle course that awaits on the higher lawmaking track. . . . The consequences of a false negative are much worse. The heart of dualism is the belief that a mobilized citizenry may, on appropriate occasions, take the law into its own hands and give governors new marching orders. If established institutions successfully block the new movement at the threshold, they betray the Constitution's foundational commitment to popular sovereignty.[79]

Discourse must be facilitated, not impeded, by the rules that regulate the conduct of delegates. On the other hand, certain 'rules of order' are likely to be accepted, perhaps like those identified, in a Habermasian framework, by Robert Alexy[80] — namely,

1. Every subject with the competence to speak and act is allowed to take part in a discourse.
2. a. Everyone is allowed to question any assertion whatever.
   b. Everyone is allowed to introduce any assertion whatever in the discourse.
   c. Everyone is allowed to express his attitudes, desires, and needs.
3. No speaker may be prevented, by internal or external coercion, from exercising his rights as laid down in (1) and (2).

(To this list I would add a rule of 'responsiveness' — crudely, that each individual must respond appropriately to those questions or assertions that are or could be taken to be addressed to her. Without such a rule, we risk a Babel that never composes itself.[81]) Rawls says: "[R]ules of order are essential for regulating free discussion. Without the general acceptance of reasonable procedures of inquiry and precepts of debate, freedom of speech cannot serve its purpose."[82] 'Reasonable' people will understand this need and cater for it.

When delegates present 'arguments' for or against proposals, they needn't honor 'neutrality' in Ackerman's sense,[83] nor, when they disagree, need they, as Larmore recommends, "retreat to neutral ground, with the hope of either resolving the dispute or of bypassing it."[84] Some 'reasonable' individuals might of course want their delegates to adopt such courses of action, but others probably will not, and any general requirement that all do so would "undermine or stultify . . . incipient communication" and so could not be accepted by all 'reasonable' individuals as a basis for the regulation of the conduct of the delegates.[85]

On the other hand, since 'reasonable' individuals are committed to the peaceful resolution of disputes, it will necessarily be among the 'rules of order' that no delegate may coerce any of the others as a means of recruiting them to her cause. This, in any event, would be inconsistent with the notion that the delegates are involved, in part, in articulating the concept of public justification. It is undisputed, at the level of the shared concept, that coercion is not a form of justification. We don't need a public conception of this concept to tell us that.

There will be problem cases where we are uncertain whether the intervention of a particular delegate or group of delegates is indeed coercive in nature. For instance, are we to preclude 'offers that you can't refuse', that is, implied or explicit threats, for example, to withdraw services or cooperation? What about the differential bargaining power of the delegates, an attribute explicitly excluded by Rawls?[86] I do not myself see how bargaining by the delegates can be precluded a priori, and therefore I do not see how it can reasonably be prohibited by the 'rules of order' imposed on the delegates. In particular, delegates are determining the constitutional fundamentals for a concrete community whose members themselves have differential bargaining power and who must have some motives for compliance if stability is to be attained. And stability *is* a reasonable desideratum for the project of public justification. Furthermore, some 'reasonable' individuals might believe that bargaining power *is* relevant to the identification of a 'dominant' regime; followers of Gauthier certainly will, and I have already said that they might be represented in the convention.[87] If this attitude is itself a reasonable one, then its expression in the constitutional convention cannot reasonably be precluded. Of course, the delegates might themselves decide, in a manner Nagel identifies,[88] that even if bargaining is not prohibited by 'standing orders', it must nevertheless be precluded if they are to have any chance of succeeding in their task. Perhaps they find that there can be no prospect for unanimity so long as certain kinds of considerations are permitted to 'count' in their deliberations, and, unanimously preferring the prospects of some unanimously sanctioned substantive result, they agree to 'prescind' from these considerations. In that case, they will themselves amend their 'standing orders' to reflect this collective judgment.

Indeed, more generally, delegates shall have the power, subject to *their* unanimous consent, to amend in any way the 'standing orders' imposed on them by the 'reasonable' individuals who originally commissioned them. Two points are relevant here.

First, renegotiation of the terms of discussion is entirely appropriate. We cannot assume some fixed prior understanding of these terms without accepting what we must in this context reject as question-begging — namely, that we know what constitutes an adequate basis for public justification. Since this is just what the delegates are charged with discovering, we cannot assume that it already lies before them in the form of rules of discourse that have some initial plausibility but that might turn out to restrict them too much or too little. Since they are 'making it up as they go' — and, indeed, have been given just that job — they must be permitted to alter all those features of their situation that, in O'Neill's terms, might "undermine or stultify their incipient communication," and, given their (and our) finitude and fallibility, there is no reason to assume that such factors could be identified once and for all.

Second, there is, I think, a ready answer to the question why, in this case, the unanimity rule should be 'entrenched' as thoroughly as my remarks suggest (namely, "subject to *their* unanimous consent"). The answer is this. This rule should be 'entrenched' because no 'reasonable' individual could agree to any less stringent 'decision rule' for use among the delegates. Imagine, for instance, that *A*, a 'reasonable' individual, allows other 'reasonable' individuals to talk him into accepting a two-thirds majority rule for the deliberations of the delegates. It might happen that *A*'s delegate α is on the losing end of a two-thirds vote for the enslavement of *A* and others of his ilk, or if this would be 'unreasonable', for measures that would severely disadvantage *A* in comparison with other otherwise similar individuals.[89] This substantive outcome is not something that a 'reasonable' individual ought to be prepared to tolerate if it is avoidable. No such outcome could ensue were a requirement of unanimity in force among the delegates. No 'reasonable' individual will therefore agree to any other basis for constitutional decision making than the rule of unanimity. As Rousseau long ago noted, "the more grave and important the questions discussed, the nearer should the opinion that is to prevail approach to unanimity."[90]

To be sure, it has often been suggested, as Barry does, that "the unanimity principle is inequitable in that it enables those not affected by a proposal to claim a ransom in virtue of their power to . . . veto it."[91] But Barry's point, however apt elsewhere, has no legitimate application to the realm of public justification. More or less by definition, there are no issues to be considered by the delegates that do not affect all of the individuals whom they represent. The *realm* of public justification is constitutional fundamentals, and there can be no question here of individuals extracting ransoms even though they are "not affected by a proposal."

Also relevant to the status of the 'decision rule' is the fact that "a unanimity rule . . . encourages strategic behavior." Mueller says:

> If *A* knows the maximum share of taxes *B* will assume rather than go without the public good, *A* can force *B* to point *C* on the contract curve, by voting against all tax shares greater than t_C. All gains from providing the public good then accrue to *A*. If *B* behaves the same, the final outcome is dependent on the bargaining strengths of the two individuals.[92]

As Coleman points out, "embedded in all institutional arrangements that provide the opportunity for mutual gain is a bargaining game over relative shares."[93] And this is so, according to Coleman, even in situations where what is at issue is what might normally be called a 'public good', such as the institutional arrangements that the delegates to the convention are imagined as deciding on. If *A* and *B* can, by agreeing to some arrangement, achieve some improvement over the status quo, then both *A* and *B* will have reason to want to implement that arrangement. But if the improvement that the arrangement provides is divisible, or the enjoyment of it is even partially 'excludable', so that A could inexpensively restrict B's enjoyment of these benefits or vice versa, then both A and B have incentives to make their endorsement of the arrangement's implementation dependent on their being given a favorable 'share' of the enjoyment of these benefits. Requiring unanimity *does* encourage such 'strategizing'; that much is obvious, at least prima facie.

Two points are relevant here.

First, less-than-unanimous voting also lends itself to strategically driven 'redistribution', even, apparently, in the case of so-called public goods such as the constitutional provisions that we are imagining that the delegates decide on. Any proposal that can pass the unanimity test is one that all delegates (and their principals) will benefit from implementing. But if only a majority of delegates need agree to such a proposal in order for it to be implemented, then coalitions of delegates can form to redefine the proposal so that they derive the entire benefit from its implementation in a revised form. For instance, while all might benefit from, and so would normally be expected to bear the costs of enforcing, certain fundamental freedoms, these freedoms can be established, and the whole cost of their enforcement can be imposed on a wealthy or a poor minority by an unscrupulous coalition of 'free riders', who will succeed in such "de facto redistribution" if only a majority is required.[94]

It may be objected that we need, in the present context, to remember the stipulation that individuals represented by the delegates are themselves 'reasonable', especially in the sense of agreeing to bear the fair burdens of achieving a cooperative surplus. From this it is then presumably meant to follow that such individuals would *not* permit their representatives to conspire, as I have imagined them doing, to form 'redistributive' coalitions to take advantage of the opportunities provided, under majority rule, to "convert purely positive-sum games of achieving allocational efficiency into games that are a combination of an allocational change and a redistribution."[95] On this account, then, delegates working in the context of a majoritarian decision rule ought to forbear to take advantage of these opportunities.

Such a response is a double-edged sword. If it works to get the majoritarian off the hook — that is, if it shows that her favored rule won't be exploited by potential 'free riders' who want to seize the 'cooperative surplus', then it will get the unanimitarian off the hook as well. As Coleman himself notes, "a unanimity rule works when individuals do not act strategically,"[96] as they won't permit their representatives to do if they are assumed to be 'reasonable' in Rawls's sense.

My first point, then, is that a majoritarian approach to the business of the convention will avoid strategizing by the delegates only when a unanimitarian approach would also avoid such behavior. Reference to the possibility of strategizing is therefore unhelpful in *distinguishing* these two approaches to constitutional decision making.

But, second, majority voting is a less adequate basis for constitutional decision making given that there are always apparently questions of distribution that will need to be addressed, if only in passing, in establishing a basis of constitutional fundamentals. It is not as if, by the mere fact that principals and delegates are 'reasonable', all prospects for attaining some distributive advantage become irrelevant. After all, we have no uncontroversial antecedent criterion for a 'fair' distribution of burdens and benefits associated with achieving a cooperative surplus. The delegates will therefore have to come to some agreement about these distributional questions. And, in this context, a majoritarian decision procedure would arguably provide a less stable basis for constitutional decision making. As Mueller observes, "[T]he redistributive characteristics of majority rule can make stable winning coalitions difficult to maintain and can lead to cycles."[97] For instance, imagine that *A* and *B* form a majority coalition against *C* to secure benefits from the imposition of some constitutional arrangement, these benefits being divided between them. The 'excluded' *C* can attempt to destabilize the coalition by offering *B*, say, a share of the total benefit larger than she now enjoys. Of course, *C* can make such an offer only by accepting a share less than the share *B* received in her original coalition with *A*. So he, *A*, can try to destabilize the *B-C* coalition by offering *C* the same size share as *B* originally had. And so on ad nauseam.

This, at least, is one advantage of a unanimity requirement. Even if it *is* subject to strategizing, and that is what is being assumed at present, the distribution of the collective surplus that does secure unanimous endorsement will not be subject to such cycles of offer and counter-offer. As Mueller says, "[O]nce attained, no other proposal could command a unanimous vote against [any unanimously endorsed proposal] . . . , and the process would come to a halt."[98]

(An obvious point of contrast between my thinking about these issues and Rawls's is this. Rawls clearly thinks that "'constitutional essentials' and questions of basic justice" are to be settled by reference to "political values alone." He says: "This means that political values alone are to settle such fundamental questions as: who has the right to vote, or what religions are to be tolerated, or who is to be assured fair equality of opportunity, or to hold property."[99] I clearly disavow any such understanding of the workings of the constitutional convention when I suggest, for instance, that bargaining cannot be precluded, or that 'neutrality' in Ackerman's sense needn't be required. Values and considerations that are not 'political' in Rawls's sense will therefore possibly be introduced.[100] Why do I reject Rawls's seemingly reasonable understanding of this matter? Because, on my account, *what counts as a 'political' value hasn't yet been settled;* indeed, the aim of constitutional theorizing by the community of interpreters is to settle this point, among others. There is, in other words, nothing both determinate and mutually reasonable that is meant when the notion of 'political values' or of a 'fair distribution' is invoked and therefore no basis on which to restrict the activities of the delegates to these kinds of considerations. Absent a determinate conception of public justification, no determinate claim is made by Rawls when he insists that "political values alone are to settle such fundamental questions.")

Notes

1. Macedo, *Liberal Virtues,* p. 273.

2. MacIntyre, *After Virtue,* p. 222. Cf. Ackerman, *We the People,* p. 34: "[T]he Constitution is more than an idea. It is an evolving historical practice, constituted by generations of Americans as they mobilized, argued, resolved their ongoing disputes over the nation's identity and destiny." Cf. also Joan Cocks, *The Oppositional Imagination,* p. 96: "The only remaining ground for social theory is some interpretation of the social world that is squarely in it — an interpretation that is at once a reading and a constituent element of social practice."

3. R. H. Newell, *Objectivity, Empiricism and Truth,* pp. 7–8. Cf. Fishkin, *The Dialogue of Justice,* p. 5: "Its distinctive prescriptions will focus, not on the substance of social justice, but on the conditions that must be satisfied by the institutions that must make the decisions."

4. *Justice and Modern Moral Philosophy,* p. 271.

5. "From Epistemology to Hermeneutics," p. 15.

6. *The Structure of Scientific Revolutions,* p. 23.

7. *Beyond Objectivism and Relativism,* p. 74.

8. *The Essential Tension,* p. 330.

9. *The Structure of Scientific Revolutions,* p. 186. In developing a broadly Kuhnian model in this setting, I implicitly reject Macedo's claimed disanalogy (*Liberal Virtues,* p. 24, n. 36): "There is too much disagreement in pluralistic societies for them to be like Kuhnian normal science writ large. . . ."

10. Cf. my paper "A 'Demographic' Approach to the Rationality of Science."

11. Obviously, I am indebted here as well to Dworkin's discussion of "Interpretive Concepts," ch. 2 of *Law's Empire.*

12. *Sources of the Self,* p. 4. Cf. Dworkin, *Law's Empire,* p. 63: "[A] social practice creates and assumes a crucial distinction between interpreting the acts and thoughts of participants one by one . . . and interpreting the practice itself, that is, interpreting what they do collectively. It assumes that distinction because the claims and arguments participants make, licensed and encouraged by the practice, are about what it means, not what they mean."

13. Cf. Rawls, *Political Liberalism,* p. 253: "Public reason further asks of us that the balance of those values we hold to be reasonable in a particular case is a balance we sincerely think can be seen to be reasonable by others." Other examples include these: (1) a community of scientists is engaged in interpreting the concept of scientific explanation and, simultaneously, in producing theoretical artifacts in the form of scientific explanations that are meant to embody this concept; (2) the community of 'lawmakers' is engaged in interpreting the concept of the law at the same time as they produce juridical artifacts in the form of laws and their applications to concrete cases. (On the latter case, cf. Dworkin, *Law's Empire,* esp. ch. 6.)

14. Thanks to Philip Pettit for helpful comments on this point.

15. Cf. Rawls, *Political Liberalism,* p. 14: "Society's main institutions, and their accepted forms of interpretation are seen as a fund of implicitly shared ideas and principles."

16. *Law's Empire,* p. 72. Cf. Ackerman, *We the People,* p. 39: "[A]t any moment of time, even the most powerful of our lawyers and judges are profoundly constrained by the patterns of argument built up by the legal community over the past two centuries of disputation."

17. Cf. Macedo, *Liberal Virtues,* p. 170: "An authentic image or icon, however, 'is what it represents; nevertheless it bids us to look at it, but through it and beyond it, to the living reality of which it is an embodiment.'"

18. *Political Liberalism,* p. 292.

19. *Political Liberalism,* p. 239.

20. *Liberal Virtues,* p. 21.

21. *Innocence and Experience,* p. 72.

22. Of course, both *A* and *B* 'prefer' a particular artifact in the sense that they believe of this artifact that it should be adopted by the community as a collectivity as an embodiment of the community's 'founding concept'.

23. Cf. Ackerman, *We the People,* p. 104: "The Old Court's defense of its comprehensive synthesis helped, not hurt, the democratic process through which the People gave new marching orders to their government in the 1930's. By dramatizing the fundamental constitutional principles raised by the New Deal, the Old Court contributed to a more focused, and democratic, transformation of constitutional identity than might otherwise have occurred."

Cf. *We the People,* p. 287: "[C]onservative countermobilization will vastly broaden and deepen the political engagement of the People on the fundamental issues at stake."

24. *The Essential Tension,* pp. 227–28, n. 2.

25. *Political Liberalism,* p. 323.

26. This is presumably an equilibrium process, a type of invisible-hand process, in Nozick's sense. Cf. *Anarchy, State, and Utopia,* p. 21, where Nozick's diction even suggests what I've called 'the wave': "We can mention here two types of invisible-hand processes by which a pattern *P* can be produced: filtering processes and equilibrium processes. Through filtering processes can pass only things fitting *P,* because processes or structures filter out all non-*P*'s; in equilibrium processes each component part responds or adjusts to 'local' conditions, with each adjustment changing the local environment of others close by, so that the sum of the ripples of the local adjustments constitutes or realizes *P.*"

27. Cf. Benjamin, *Splitting the Difference,* p. 111: "Within the parameters established by uniform, impersonal rules or criteria, different people's judgments will reflect their differing experiences. . . ."

28. I assume, in what follows, that this is an 'objective' matter, at least in the sense that the members of the community take it to be, and they aren't in dispute (except perhaps at the margins) about the value of this variable.

29. *Situating the Self,* p. 134. Cf. Brown, *Rationality,* p. 187: "[F]or a belief based on judgment to be a rational one, it must be submitted to the community of those who share the relevant expertise for evaluation against their own judgments." Cf. also Bernstein, *Beyond Objectivism and Relativism,* p. 221: "For both [Arendt and Habermas], the power of judgment rests upon a potential agreement with others. . . ."

30. Cf. Manin, "On Legitimacy and Political Deliberation," pp. 351–52: "The parties in deliberation will not be content to defend their own positions, but will try to refute the arguments of the positions of which they disapprove. New information emerges as each uncovers the potentially harmful consequences of the other parties' proposals."

31. This is a case in which the community takes advantage of what Hayek (*Law, Legislation and Liberty,* vol. 2, p. 9) calls "dispersed knowledge," which is "made possible by the fact that the opportunities for the different individuals are different."

32. *The Terms of Political Discourse,* p. 11. Cf. Lindsay, *The Essentials of Democracy,* p. 34: "The narrowness and one-sidedness of each person's point of view are corrected, and something emerges which each can recognize as embodying the truth of what he stood for. . . ."

33. *The Logic of Liberty,* p. 159.

34. *Contingency, Irony, and Solidarity,* p. 37.

35. Cf. Barber, *The Conquest of Politics,* p. 204: "For in Rousseau's conception it is only when individual interests collide and sectarian biases cancel one another out that citizens can eventually discover in the residue of their combative interaction what they share in common — that which unites them as citizens and permits them to call themselves a community. . . . Political judgment is possible only when they meet and act in common." Cf. also Ingram, "The Limits and Possibilities of Communicative Ethics for Democratic Theory," p. 300: "[T]he general will must be achieved in rational conversation, if it is to be achieved at all."

36. Rawls, *Political Liberalism,* ch. 8, secs. 10–11; the quotations are from pp. 346, 347.

37. *Public Choice II,* p. 102.

38. *Law's Empire,* pp. 87–88.

39. Cf. Judith Butler, "Contingent Foundations," p. 16: "This is not to say that there is no foundation, but rather, wherever there is one, there will also be a foundering, a contestation. That such foundations exist only to be put into question is . . . the permanent risk of the

process of democratization." Cf. Macedo, "The Politics of Justification," p. 287: "Public justification should be a never-ending commitment. It would be sheer hubris to think that we have, or ever will have, the whole political truth." Cf. Walzer, "The Virtue of Incompletion," p. 226: "[D]iverse groups of men and women shape and reshape their understandings of justice . . . by arguing over what justice means. Many arguments are always going on; there are only temporary stopping points dictated by the need to reach political decisions; there are no full stops."

40. Cf. Rorty, *Objectivity, Relativism, and Truth,* p. 90: "I think of objectivity as a matter of ability to achieve agreement on whether a particular set of desiderata has or has not been satisfied."

41. *Political Liberalism,* p. 227.

42. *Liberal Purposes,* p. 180.

43. Such a community seems to be engaged in a "quest" in MacIntyre's sense. Cf. *After Virtue,* p. 219: "Two key features of the medieval conception of a quest need to be recalled. The first is that without some at least partly determinate conception of the final telos there could not be any beginning to a quest. . . . But secondly it is clear the medieval conception of a quest is not at all that of a search for something already adequately characterized. . . . It is in the course of the quest . . . that the goal of the quest is finally to be understood."

44. Cf. Dryzek's account (*Discursive Democracy,* p. 126) of Harold Lasswell's "decision seminars": "His 'decision seminars' would be a small group of highly committed individuals in direct communication in an information-rich environment. . . . Interaction would be uncensored, as participants would be encouraged to freely disclose their ideas and freely criticize the ideas of others. Each seminar would constitute a long-term project. . . ."

45. Also of some relevance, as a supplement to formal constitution making, is Fishkin's idea (*The Dialogue of Justice,* p. 200) of "a deliberative poll . . . [that] models what the public would think if it had a more adequate chance to assess the questions at issue." Indeed, the conditions for conducting such a poll are very similar to those that are to obtain in the constitutional convention. Fishkin says (*The Dialogue of Justice,* p. 200): "Take a national random sample of the citizen voting-age population and transport them to a single site where they can interact in person, over an extended period, with the candidates for president. Prepare the delegates beforehand with briefing materials on the issues. Have the candidates respond to questions in small-group sessions broken down by issue areas. . . ."

46. *Political Liberalism,* ch. 6, sec. 6.

47. *Political Liberalism,* p. 237.

48. *We the People,* pp. 55, 57.

49. Cf. Rawls, *A Theory of Justice,* sec. 14.

50. *Situating the Self,* p. 12.

51. Cf. Walzer, "The Virtue of Incompletion," p. 226: "The aim is to fix the structure of the discourse without 'fixing,' that is, predetermining its conclusions. The justice of the structure justifies the conclusions, whatever they are."

52. *Political Liberalism,* p. 73.

53. I do not know whether this is a matter about which Rawls has changed his mind since *A Theory of Justice,* but there is certainly a prima facie disparity between Rawls's current views and those in that earlier work. Cf. *A Theory of Justice,* p. 86, where Rawls says: "A distinctive feature of pure procedural justice is that the procedure for determining the just result must actually be carried out. . . . Clearly we cannot say that a particular state of affairs is just because it could have been reached by following a fair procedure."

54. *Political Liberalism,* pp. 273–74.

55. Cf. White, *The Recent Work of Jürgen Habermas,* p. 71: "Such a universalistic claim about the shape of the good society is always unwarranted, since it tries to settle once and for

all what must be left open, if the requirement of reciprocity is to take into account voices which may not have been evident in any given discourse."

56. *Political Liberalism*, p. 54.

57. Cf. Rawls, *Political Liberalism*, p. xx: "The principles of political justice are the result of a procedure of construction in which rational persons (or their representatives), subject to reasonable conditions, adopt the principles to regulate the basic structure of society."

58. It is enough that the case be 'reasonable'; it is not required that it be incontrovertible. It would be unreasonable, in the face of a 'reasonable' case against the use of such devices for certain purposes, to insist on their use for those purposes.

59. Cf. Macedo, *Liberal Virtues*, p. 77: "We want the freedom to live our own lives, and so an intermittent release from political argument." Cf. also Baynes, *The Normative Grounds of Social Criticism*, p. 168: "Rawls claims that a life devoted to political activity is only one form of the good and, moreover, not one that is likely to be chosen by many citizens."

60. *Discursive Democracy*, p. 72.

61. *Political Liberalism*, pp. 225, 305.

62. Cf. Fishkin, *The Dialogue of Justice*, p. 130: "By 'consensus' I mean that there must be broad support across all the major cleavages in society. By a cleavage, I mean a polarization among self-identified groups. Race, class, gender, and ethnicity are dimensions that commonly define such cleavages. There may, of course, be differences that do not . . . define self-identified groups that have perceived rivalries with other self-identified groups."

63. *Discursive Democracy*, p. 99.

64. *Justice and the Politics of Difference*, pp. 184–85.

65. *The Dialogue of Justice*, p. 156.

66. *Justice and the Politics of Difference*, p. 44.

67. I owe my awareness of this problem to Jerry Gaus.

68. Anna Yeatman (*Postmodern Revisionings of the Political*, p. 82) clearly articulates the worry: "[T]he contemporary politics of voice and representation . . . contests the unity of the group . . . , the very idea that the group has a bounded, coherent identity which can be expressed as the one voice."

69. If there are differences that make a difference that is not however a 'fundamental' difference (i.e., a difference with respect to fundamentals), then these differences may well find direct expression in non-representative (and non-constitutional) acts of voting, for instance, and so are likely to be adequately catered for elsewhere in a broadly liberal system.

70. This answers Fishkin's quite telling rhetorical question (*The Dialogue of Justice*, p. 55): "What relevance does the unanimous consent of past generations have to him [of a later generation]? He is 'subject to the will of another' just as much as if he were an outvoted minority in a decision taken in the present." If changing circumstances 'de-stabilize' previously justified constitutional arrangements, then the Court may be required to act.

71. Ackerman, "What Is Neutral about Neutrality?" p. 388.

72. *Postmodern Revisionings of the Political*, p. 119.

73. *The Dialogue of Justice*, pp. 191–92.

74. "Market Contractarianism and the Unanimity Rule," p. 91.

75. Cf. Pettit, *The Common Mind*, pp. 327ff.

76. *Constructions of Reason*, p. 44.

77. I owe this point to the anonymous reader for the Press.

78. *Political Liberalism*, p. 61.

79. *We the People*, p. 280.

80. Habermas, *Moral Consciousness and Communicative Action*, p. 89.

81. See my papers "Adjudication as an Epistemological Concept" and "Teleology, Value, and the Foundations of Scientific Method."

82. *Political Liberalism,* p. 296.

83. Cf. *Social Justice in the Liberal State,* p. 11.

84. *Patterns of Moral Complexity,* p. 53.

85. Cf. Amy Gutmann and Dennis Thompson, "Moral Conflict and Political Consensus" for arguments that such 'principles of preclusion' are anyway impotent to preclude very much that really ought to be precluded without also precluding a great deal more that ought not to be.

86. *A Theory of Justice,* sec. 24, and *Political Liberalism,* p. 23.

87. Gauthier's rational utility-maximizers presumably think some such thing. Cf. sec. 11.

88. Cf. *Equality and Partiality,* p. 45: "If we find that persons . . . are still too far apart to be able to identify any arrangement that none of them could reasonably reject, . . . that is by itself a reason to reevaluate the standards of reasonableness that led to such a result."

89. Cf. Mueller, *Public Choice II,* p. 133: "Under the demand-revealing process it is possible for an outcome to emerge in which the entire private wealth of an individual is confiscated. . . . This is true of almost any voting procedure other than the unanimity rule. . . ."

90. Quoted by Mueller, *Public Choice II,* p. 43.

91. *Political Argument,* p. 249. Cf. Reiman, *Justice and Modern Moral Philosophy,* p. 236: "[R]equiring unanimity lets one person decide for all. Anything but majority rule gives some people more power than others in shaping group decisions."

92. *Public Choice II,* p. 50.

93. "Market Contractarianism and the Unanimity Rule," p. 97.

94. Cf. Mueller, *Public Choice II,* p. 106.

95. Mueller, *Public Choice II,* p. 106.

96. "Market Contractarianism and the Unanimity Rule," p. 108.

97. *Public Choice II,* p. 107.

98. *Public Choice II,* p. 80.

99. *Political Liberalism,* p. 214.

100. As Galston says (*Liberal Purposes,* p. 106): "The point of much dialogue is to invite one's interlocutor to see the world the way you do, or at least to understand what it is like to see the world the way you do. One way of doing that is the reverse of 'prescinding' from disputed issues: namely, stubbornly bearing witness to one's stance at the precise point of difference."

10

Assessing the Solution

It is not enough to overcome the suspicion that there is *no* solution to the 'problem of public justification' merely to offer a candidate-solution, as I have done in Chapter 9. It will also be necessary to defend that solution and, in particular, to show that it does not fall foul of the difficulties by which other candidate-solutions, on my account, are beset. This is my project in this chapter, where I will try to show the following: delegates do adequately 'represent' the interests of their principals (sec. 36); the prospects for convergence on some substantive set of constitutional principles are no worse on my account than they are likely to be on others (sec. 37); and my conception of public justification, embodied in the 'wave model', does in adequate measure satisfy the desiderata on such conceptions that jointly constitute the ideal of public justification (sec. 38).

36.   Delegates and Their Principals

Two residual problems remain to be addressed before we can be satisfied about the propriety of my argument in section 35. First, we need to consider whether all the delegates to the convention must be 'reasonable', and, second, we need to consider the basis on which delegates are 'commissioned' by individual citizens or groups of citizens.

We are entitled to wonder about the propriety of my restriction of 'pre-constitutional theorizing' to the model case of the 'reasonable' individual. First, a point of clarification. I believe that 'unreasonable' individuals ought to be represented in the convention—by 'reasonable' delegates whose sole concern is, within the limits of *their* 'reasonableness', the adequate representation of all the interests (and not just the 'reasonable' interests) of the individuals who commission them. Delegates of this kind thus will argue, though reasonably, for whatever is required to support and protect even the unreasonable activities and attitudes of their 'principals'. And they may well succeed. Indeed, they may do better for their 'principals' than those individuals would have done for themselves; the 'unreasonable' are often ineffectual in argumentation. Nevertheless, some 'unreasonable' individuals may still find it very hard to 'identify with' the delegates who represent them in the constitutional convention. In particular, individuals who have not renounced the use of violence in settling disagreements will be represented in the convention by delegates who have. Individuals who do not or cannot accept that they labor under the 'burdens of judgment' will be represented in the convention by delegates who can and do accept this.

Does this matter? It might. Because unreasonable individuals are represented in the convention by delegates who are themselves reasonable, the regime endorsed by the delegates may not be to the liking of unreasonable individuals, and so they may not be properly motivated to conform to the demands of this regime. Four observations are pertinent.

First, even a moral theory that *is* concerned with the realism of its assumptions cannot be held responsible for securing the salience of its outcome for *these* kinds of individuals. These individuals, and alas they are all too numerous, cannot properly be the concern of moral theory, even of a political approach to moral theorizing; they mark the moral limits on public justification. (See sec. 7.) If you cannot reason with the unreasonable, then nothing can be justified publicly, except *per accidens,* so long as they themselves are included in the body of people that constitutes the justificatory community. At least in these cases, Nagel's concern is entirely appropriate — namely, "It is not clear how one can allow supposed psychological facts about human resistance to impartiality to determine the conditions of moral justification, without being guilty of simple human *badness.*"[1] It would indeed be "simple human badness" to contrive to conciliate the 'unreasonable' in Rawls's semitechnical sense, that is, the fanatics who will not acknowledge the 'burdens of reason' and the 'free riders' who will not bear their fair share of the burdens necessarily borne if a 'cooperative surplus' is to be realized.

Second, it is not clear a priori that unreasonable individuals would be so poorly served by the reasonable delegates who represent them that they would in fact find conformity difficult with the demands of a 'dominant' regime. As I have already suggested, there may be reasonable arguments that can be provided for the protection and support of those not themselves willing to provide these arguments. Even fanatics who are not willing to acknowledge the burdens of judgment can be beneficiaries of institutional guarantees of religious freedom that they themselves would not have wanted to argue for. Indeed, such individuals may do better by being represented by reasonable delegates than they would if they had represented themselves.[2] Were they to remain intransigent, and thus block the adoption of constitutional fundamentals that a wholly reasonable body of delegates would have been able to agree on unanimously, they may block the adoption of precisely the fundamentals whose implementation they would have derived great benefit from.

Third, it could even be argued that so-called unreasonable individuals are quasi-committed to the principles of 'reasonable' social interaction and so are quite properly represented by delegates who are explicitly and straightforwardly committed to these principles. The idea of 'quasi-commitment' is, crudely, already implicit in the 'anthropological' approach to philosophical ethics that Benn and Gaus employ. They argue that moral ideas like that of 'reasonableness' are so thoroughly, centrally, and strategically embedded in our ideas of moral personality, in general, and of friendship, resentment, responsibility, and so on, in particular, that anyone who claims to reject these ideas subjects herself to a kind of 'cultural death', in the sense that she deprives herself of the (coherent) use of a great body of concepts that she characteristically *does* use or presuppose in her everyday interactions with other individuals.[3] (This is not, of course, the 'transcendental' strategy of Habermas and others. Benn and Gaus do not claim that these ideas are presuppositions of all possible discourse, merely that they are presupposed or employed in 'our' discourse.)

Fourth, and finally, the representation of 'the unreasonable' by 'reasonable' delegates may be a 'mutual second-best'. Second-best for reasonable individuals, who might prefer that 'the unreasonable' be unrepresented in the convention, and second-best for 'the unreasonable', who might prefer to represent themselves. This proposal thus has the virtues of a compromise.

For all these reasons, I do not think that there is any cause for concern in the way I have understood the relation between historically situated individuals and the delegates who represent them in the constitutional convention whose results will bind them. Of course, this claim would be a great deal more compelling if we had a better understanding of the ways in which delegates and their principals interact with one another, and, especially, if we had a more or less concrete model of the way in which delegates are selected by individuals or groups of individuals. In this regard, some ideas of Fishkin are very helpful. Adapting a suggestion of Philippe Schmitter, Fishkin asks us to imagine that each citizen is issued with a voucher that she can redeem by commissioning the services of a particular 'political action committee' that is pledged to work to secure the kinds of outcomes that that individual herself favors.[4]

These ideas can be adapted still further to the constitutional context. To see how, assume that membership of the convention is to be limited; there are realistic considerations that suggest it must be. In this case, my proposal is that those individuals are legitimately 'commissioned' as delegates to the convention who attract some minimum number of vouchers. If there are to be n delegates, then, if there are m citizens, it will be enough to gain election as a delegate for an individual to secure m/n vouchers. Notice that the system proposed does *not* involve the 'proportional' representation of citizens by delegates in accordance with the numbers of citizens who support the 'platforms' of the various candidates. (A 'party' that secures $2 \cdot m/n$ vouchers still secures only one 'seat' in the convention.) Ordinary democratic modes of representation are not embraced in this context because they are an incitement to the 'homogenization' of platforms[5] and are therefore likely to 'disenfranchise' almost all individuals, whose own views are likely to vary in ways that no merely homiletic platform could do justice to, however effective it might be in securing vouchers from a wide cross section of groups and interests.

If we want all the main views to be represented, and clearly we do, then we must ensure that there are no such incentives to collapse views or to elide the differences between them, and my proposal does, I think, answer this need.[6] If any given candidate knows that it will be enough to gain election as a delegate to secure m/n vouchers and that there is no advantage in securing even one more voucher than m/n, then she has no incentive to form coalitions with other individuals, at least at this stage of proceedings, and therefore no need to compromise with them about platform commitments. She can therefore engage in 'niche marketing', identifying that group or family of groups whose views she thinks she could effectively (and coherently) espouse who are just numerous enough to give her the m/n vouchers that she needs to secure her election. As Fishkin says, "Vouchers would give organizations incentives to take seriously the interests of those who are now left out of the dialogue."[7]

This is the relation between individuals and the delegates whom they commission. Each delegate represents no fewer than, and ideally no more than, m/n of the individuals and is commissioned by them to espouse the interests and concerns that they consider important and, especially, to do so distinctively, championing these interests rather than others that might be only marginally different from them.[8] This is an effective method of selecting delegates and therefore an effective form of representation by delegates.

37. The Prospects for Convergence

Even at this level of abstraction, we are entitled to wonder whether there would indeed be convergence, via the 'wave model', on even a partial public conception of public justification. As Rawls warns, in another but related context, "it may turn out that, for us, there exists no reasonable and workable conception of justice at all."[9] There can, I think, be no guarantee that any given community will succeed in interpreting its founding concept in the way portrayed. There are two cases: where we interpret the procedure 'representationally' and where we interpret it 'constitutively'.[10]

In cases where the concept is a concept that *represents* its domain, whether the concept can be attached to its objects will depend, a great deal, on how adequate the concept is to those objects.[11] If it is not very adequate, then the prospects for successful sustained convergence on even a partial public conception of that concept are not good. In science, for instance, we often witness the "degeneration of the research programme"[12] when multiple competing conceptions are developed and no resolution is achieved. Suppose that the founding concept is itself inadequate, for example, in relying on a false ontology (as in the case of phlogiston chemistry) or on a misconceived methodology (as in the case of behavioristic linguistics). The difficulties of attaching that concept to the objects of study will then prove very serious. When different theorists, struggling to do so, articulate different conceptions and produce different artifacts as embodiments of this concept, since each inevitably only partially succeeds by the standards that underlie the concept, the proliferation of articulations that develops is never entirely superseded by some dominant interpretation. Eventually, suspecting that the concept itself is the source of these difficulties in achieving agreement, people abandon the concept in favor of some other. (This is what Kuhn's 'revolutionary science' amounts to, on my account.)

In cases where the concept is a concept that *constitutes* its domain, whether a public conception can be developed will depend, a great deal, on prior agreement within the community of interpreters/artisans.[13] In law, for instance, there may be too little by way of shared background culture and morality to permit the consistent interpretation, within a given 'community', of the concepts of justice and welfare. Because of this, theorists articulating these concepts to concrete social phenomena may implicitly articulate different conceptions, none of which is very likely, in view of these deeper and unresolved disagreements, to attract widespread support within the 'community'. As in the case of a scientific project that is inadequately 'grounded', any legal project that is inadequately grounded in basic cultural agreement is unlikely to succeed in achieving convergence on even a partial public conception of its founding concepts. (In this case, an attitude, in Dworkin's language, of "internal scepticism" about 'the law' might be warranted.[14])

Ethical 'realists' may think of the ethico-political project of interpretation representationally, on the model of science. Constructivists such as Rawls may think of it constitutively.[15] In either case, there can be no guarantee that the project of articulation will in fact succeed. The success of a representationalist project depends on the 'fit' between the founding concept and the social world that it is trying to model. The success of a constitutive project depends on reservoirs of prior cultural agreement.

All this would be cause for grave concern except for two crucial points. If a public conception cannot be articulated by some such means as I have identified, then (1) it is not clear that it can be articulated in any other way either, so the failure of the 'wave model' does not differentially tell against that model, and (2) it is not clear that any other means of articulating a public conception ought to succeed. Let us consider these points.

In the representational case, the 'wave model' for articulating a concept to its domain fails because the concept inadequately represents the domain. But in this case, there can be no adequate articulation of the concept to its domain. Since it misrepresents the domain, it cannot be articulated to it, and, precisely because of its representational inadequacy, it *should not* be articulated to it, even if, by some contrivance, we could seem to succeed in doing so.

In the constitutive case, the 'wave model' fails to articulate the concept, that is, it fails to identify a public conception of that concept, because there is an inadequate basis of prior agreement for any conception to attract the uncoerced and well-informed assent of relevant members of the community. But in this case, only some method that relied on coercion or fraud *could* succeed in identifying a public conception of this concept. Of course, in such a situation, this may be exactly what is necessary if civil war or worse is to be prevented, so I will not say, in this case, that no such 'method' should *ever* be employed. But it cannot be held to count against a method employing the 'wave model' that it fails in cases where only fraud or force could succeed. This is not a criticism that tells differentially against the 'wave model' when it is compared with other ethical-theoretical methods.

There is another way of putting these points. The very expectation that a mode of public justification *should* infallibly provide a basis of convergence presupposes a fundamentally monistic ontology, an "ontology of concord," as Connolly puts it; an ontology, in other words, that "assumes that when properly constituted and situated the individual or collective subject achieves harmony with itself and with the other elements of social life."[16] And this kind of assumption is one we have no reason to make in the pluralistic environment that I have postulated. (See sec. 5.) Indeed, the failure of a project of public justification, or even indeed its limited success, may be salutary. Young says:

> If the alternative to stalled decisionmaking is a unified public that makes decisions
> ostensibly embodying the general interest which systematically ignore, suppress, or
> conflict with the interests of particular groups, then stalled decisionmaking may
> sometimes be just.[17]

Of course, there are no prospects for convergence unless there are some prospects for the formation of an interpretive 'wave' with respect to disputed issues. We must therefore consider the propriety of the claim, implicit in much of the argumentation of Chapter 9, that 'reasonable' individuals do indeed constitute the convention in such a way as to facilitate the mechanism identified by the 'wave model'. I will now try to show that this claim can be sustained and therefore doesn't need simply to be assumed. Let us see what is required if 'the wave' is to have any chance of getting started among the delegates to the constitutional convention.

First, diversity of conceptions of public justification must be represented, and it clearly is. Each of the delegates represents a type of individual found in the community in question. Since members of the community have diverse conceptions of public justification, the delegates too will have diverse conceptions.

Second, the delegates must be committed to articulating a conception of public justification that is to serve as the public conception; they are not to be oriented merely to the articulation of their own subjectively favored conceptions. This condition will be satisfied on account of the requirement of unanimity and the prohibition on the use of force. Persons who know that they must obtain the unanimous uncoerced consent of the body of delegates will naturally try to develop a conception of public justification that could serve as a basis of public argumentation; typically, unanimity can't be achieved, especially among persons who disagree with respect to a range of issues, merely by appealing to one's own subjectively preferred conceptions and opinions. (It is not that this is 'improper'; it is that it is ineffectual. If A's delegate α wants A's conception to prevail, he will have to show B's delegate β that it is reasonably taken as B's conception as well. As Miller says, "[T]he need to reach an agreement forces each participant to put forward proposals under the rubric of general principles or policy considerations that others could accept."[18])

Finally, if 'the wave' is to get started, delegates must share some views about devices that are paradigmatic in relation to the founding concept—devices, in other words, that concretely embody this concept. That this condition will be satisfied is ensured by assumptions that 'reasonable' individuals are forced to make, by the nature of the problem they hope the delegates will help them solve, about the knowledge with which the delegates ought to be endowed. 'Reasonable' individuals know that the delegates need to know about these paradigms if they are to solve the problem the constitutional convention is organized to solve. The parties therefore commission as delegates only individuals who have this kind of knowledge.

If 'the wave' is to get started, delegates must conduct themselves in accordance with 'reasonable' rules of order. I have already mentioned Coleman's requirement: these rules must be 'self-enforcing'. (See sec. 35.) Are they? Here, Pettit's idea of "the intangible hand" promises to be helpful. Crudely, this idea is simple enough. We try to arrange matters so that any individual who violates or is seriously tempted to violate the rules of discursive interaction will suffer a loss of social esteem.[19] This will be easy enough to do, as Pettit's own example of the jury system makes very evident. We simply arrange for delegates to be socialized to value the meta-justificatory discourse that they are engaged in and to derive esteem from their (rule-conforming) successful participation in it. In this case, if violations of the rules are met with a withdrawal or diminution of honor, they are likely to be infrequent and ineffectual.

Notice, furthermore, that each of the 'principals' has reason to accept this kind of socialization regime for the delegate who represents her. Remember that justification is undertaken *modulo* the assumption of reasonableness. But discursive rules à la Alexy are certainly the sort of rules that would be appropriate given the various factors that lie behind an individual's acceptance of this assumption—namely, her awareness of her (and her delegate's) finitude and fallibility. Any individual who *is* aware of her limited powers of cognition and of impartiality will see in these rules a reasonable basis for a collective discussion.

Diversity of conceptions, a 'public' orientation, some agreed exemplars, and 'reasonable' rules of order: these are necessary conditions for an idealized community of interpreters. They are also criteria for judging the adequacy of the public discourse of concrete communities. If we want to know how closely public debate in our society approximates to the demanding requirements of public justification, the first (though not the only) question is how completely these criteria are satisfied. Are a range of views adequately presented? Does advocacy rise above thinly disguised promotion of self-interest? Is the discussion disciplined by the examination of concrete cases? If so, the conclusion reached (if any) has a fair claim to being justified, publicly.

I have not yet said what the 'dominant' regime amounts to, which is identified by such a 'community of interpreters', how it balances the competing demands of 'realistic' and 'moralistic' desiderata, and so on. *Nor can I do so.* For this is a matter not for the theorist but, instead, for the delegates to the constitutional convention that I have described, or, rather, for all the various conventions that would be needed to represent various communities of concrete and historically situated individuals. As Bruce Brower says, concrete "principles will result from rational dialogue, and [since] we cannot know the outcome of future discussion," we cannot say in advance what these principles will turn out to be.[20] My kind of pure proceduralism is, as I've said, participative, not substitutive. Like Walzer and Habermas, I too see "the attempt of the political theorist to provide citizens with a normative yardstick as a preemption of their right to democratic politics."[21] Like Foucault, I am "openly suspicious of attempts to formulate a positive, theoretical basis for critique . . . [since] such efforts are implicitly totalitarian because totalizing . . . normalizing because normative. . . ."[22] And so I make no apology, indeed celebrate, the substantive 'emptiness' of my solution to the problem of legitimacy. Indeed, since, as Rawls says, "[t]he struggle for reflective equilibrium continues indefinitely,"[23] any substantive conclusion that is given by the actual application of the procedure is always necessarily tentative.

38. Satisfaction of the Desiderata?

A very intricate chore now confronts us. To establish the adequacy, let alone the superiority, of the 'wave model', I must now consider how this approach is likely to fare with respect to the various desiderata associated with the ideal of public justification.[24]

Universality (Moralistic and Realistic)

It will be instructive to treat these two desiderata together, as they offer slightly different interpretations of and rationales for what is, in effect, one and the same requirement. This requirement is embodied in the claim that no regime is legitimate for a given community *unless it is reasonable for every member of that community.*

From a moralistic point of view, the rationale for this requirement is the need to honor the free and equal moral personality of each individual human being. From this point of view, a constitutional convention established on the terms outlined rates very highly. All the main types of reasonable *and* unreasonable individuals are represented by delegates who aim to do as well for these individuals as they can. The moral personality of no individual is slighted by the arrangements made for her representation in the kind of constitutional convention I have described. Although some individuals are represented by delegates who are more articulate and better informed than they are themselves, and although other individuals are represented by 'reasonable' delegates when they are themselves unreasonable, no concrete individual is (otherwise) represented by a delegate whose fundamental understanding of the social and natural world is so much at variance with her own that that person could not, in any sense, be said to be properly represented by that delegate. We have, in particular, none of the problems that many feminist theorists detect in Rawls's characterization of the parties to the original position, whose 'character' is very different from that of many ordinary individuals, male and female, though perhaps especially the latter, and whose representation of such parties seems, really, to *dis*honor their moral personalities.

From a realistic point of view, the rationale for this requirement is the need to minimize the costs of ensuring compliance with the requirements of any regime deemed to be publicly justified. From this point of view, a constitutional convention established on the terms outlined rates reasonably highly. All the main types of reasonable *and* unreasonable individuals are represented by delegates who aim to do as well for these individuals as they can. Of course, some individuals are represented by delegates who are more articulate and better informed than they are themselves, but that should be no impediment to the compliance of these individuals with the requirements approved by their delegates. After all, these individuals have benefited from the superior representation they have received from those delegates, who have, in all likelihood, gotten them a 'better deal' and, hence, one easier to comply with, than they could have gotten for themselves. Similarly, other individuals are represented by 'reasonable' delegates when they are themselves unreasonable. It cannot be guaranteed, in this case, that compliance costs can be avoided. However, these individuals represent the *moral* limit on public justification, and so we must be prepared to bear these costs, so long as they are not so great that the viability of 'morality' is itself thrown into doubt. Notice, furthermore, that some 'unreasonable' individuals may even benefit so much from citizenship that their own compliance with the regime's demands can in fact be obtained without any special or excessive expenditures.

Independence

According to this requirement, a regime's principles must be independent of individuals' possibly biased and ideologically self-serving or self-enslaving attitudes, and of the contingencies of their situations that might give some of them inappropriately greater power than others. It is hard to be sure how well the 'wave model' rates in regard to this desideratum.

On the one hand, constitutional fundamentals are decided on by delegates who, aside from being reasonable whereas some of the individuals are not, differ from concrete, historically situated individuals only in being more effective representatives of the interests of those individuals and in being better informed than they are about the problem of public justification, the ideal of public justification, and such paradigms of publicly justified social arrangements as may have been enacted or discussed historically. It stretches credulity, I think, to imagine that these differences are enough to secure full and 'instant' independence in the sense that is relevant. If it is not unreasonable that certain individuals have certain attitudes (beliefs, desires, and so on), then their delegates will argue and otherwise 'carry on' in the constitutional convention in the terms suggested by these attitudes, even if those attitudes are, in fact, ideologically corrupted. This suggests that the 'wave model' is going to rate rather poorly in relation to the requirement of independence.

On the other hand, individual members of a given community may themselves claim some understanding of ideological processes, and the delegates who represent these individuals will certainly press for recognition of these processes. Since individuals who do not themselves recognize them may nevertheless benefit if they are recognized, even those individuals' delegates will have reason, acting as 'trustees', to recognize at least some such claims about ideological processes (especially the ones that can be argued for 'reasonably'). The delegates as a body may therefore be able to attain some independence of ideologically corrupted attitudes. When we add that the enactments of the convention are to be reviewed periodically and as necessary by a Supreme or a High Court, the 'wave model' may provide as much 'Archimedean leverage' as can in fact be obtained by any purely 'secular' mechanism.[25] (Any mechanism that gave us what Hilary Putnam calls a 'God's-eye view' of the social world would, of course, provide more such 'leverage'.[26] But, absent divine intervention that is universally recognized as such, no such mechanism can in fact give us such a perspective.[27])

Transparency

According to this requirement, the considerations that are held to tell in favor of a regime must be accessible to all individuals. Of course, some concrete individuals assign greater importance than others do to the 'transparency' of their social arrangements. Some such individuals are content to know relatively little of these matters and to concentrate their attention on the kinds of lives they find they can and want to lead in the regime they are citizens of. Other individuals take a great interest in, and indeed devote themselves, to the continuing articulation of the community's standards of public justification. Both of these postures are arguably 'reasonable' ones. It would therefore be unreasonable to require all individuals to care about the transparency of their regime. On the other hand, only full and universal transparency adequately reflects the desire lying behind this requirement "[t]o show [people] that they all have sufficient reason to accept [such a system and make] . . . this involuntary condition voluntary."[28]

In the face of these apparently conflicting considerations, the 'wave model' rates rather highly in relation to transparency. On the one hand, every delegate to the convention who endorses a particular regime knows all the grounds favoring the identification of that regime as the 'dominant' regime for the community she and other such delegates collectively represent. This satisfies the demand for full and universal transparency. On the other hand, those many concrete individuals who do not themselves care very much about the transparency of their regimes are not compelled to take an *interest* in this matter; their *interests* in it, now in a different sense, are adequately represented by the delegates they commission. We get, through the employment of delegates, the benefits without the burdens of full and universal transparency.

Reflexivity

If a regime is to be justified for a community, then, at least potentially, not only the regime itself but also the apparatus used in its public justification must be publicly justifiable. The apparatus associated with the 'wave model' satisfies this requirement to a very high degree. To ensure that it did was, after all, the point of the so-called pre-constitutional theorizing outlined in section 35. I tried to show that any 'reasonable' individual would agree to be represented by a certain kind of delegate to a convention structured in a certain kind of way and so, given her reasonable endorsement of this apparatus, could be expected to find reasonable the regime her delegate identified as the 'dominant' one for her community.

Determinacy (Moralistic and Realistic)

Again, it will be instructive to treat these desiderata together. We want the regulative principles and practices of a legitimate regime to be determinate in their implications for the conduct of individual members of the community. Here we encounter a difficulty in assessing the 'wave model' that is a direct consequence of the nature of that approach. I have admitted, indeed insisted, that I cannot say what the 'dominant' regime for a given community amounts to; this is a matter not for the theorist but, instead, for the delegates to the constitutional convention that I have described. And I have, accordingly, provided no characterization of any such regime and, a fortiori, no basis for 'calculating' how determinate that regime is. Of course, the delegates to the convention that identifies a 'dominant' regime are committed to the realization, as far as possible, of the ideal of public justification and so at least *ceteris paribus,* to satisfying the demand for determinacy. However, we already know, and the delegates may be imagined to know, that it may not be possible to satisfy this demand to any great extent if other demands are also to be satisfied, such as universality, salience, and stability. (See Table 6.1.) The delegates may therefore

reasonably prefer to identify as the 'dominant' regime for their community a regime
that *is* determinate in its implications (a) for, but only for, those forms of conduct
touching on constitutional fundamentals that are actually in dispute and (b) for that
machinery needed to settle questions that might come to be disputed, leaving the
substantive resolution of these issues indeterminate in the meantime. This is the presumption of common-law adjudication. Issues are not to be addressed with a view
to their settlement until they are actually, and not merely hypothetically, disputed.
Indeed, to satisfy the demand for determinacy within the boundaries implied by this
presumption may be all that can be required of *any* procedure. Since the 'wave
model' seems to succeed at least to this extent, it may be considered fully satisfactory with respect to this desideratum.

We thus come to the remaining realistic desiderata.

Salience

Individuals must be motivated, by considerations that figure in the justificatory
argument, actually to behave in accordance with the various requirements that are
publicly justified. This demand is more than adequately acknowledged by the 'wave
model'. Indeed, I have already suggested that both 'reasonable' and even indeed at
least some 'unreasonable' individuals will have adequate motives to comply with
the demands of any regime identified as the 'dominant' one for their community.

In the case of 'reasonable' individuals, it is reasonable that they commission delegates to represent them rather than acting for themselves, and, given that delegates
act as 'trustees' for the interests of the individuals they represent, it would be unreasonable for these individuals to balk at the demands of any regime agreed to on their
behalf by their representatives. This regime represents, in the opinion of each delegate, the best she can do for the individual(s) she represents, and only an unreasonable disinclination to play a role in securing cooperative benefits could stand in the
way of willing compliance.

The case is harder to make for unreasonable individuals, but it is not utterly
implausible; salience will be achieved where it can reasonably be expected to be
achieved. We need to distinguish at least the following cases. (a) The fanatic who
refuses to or simply cannot acknowledge the 'burdens of judgment' but who in fact
benefits from protections, for example, of freedom of thought and religion, that perhaps couldn't have been agreed on had she represented herself. Her compliance may
be grudging, but she would be 'irrational' not to comply, also in Rawls's semitechnical sense,[29] for she certainly benefits from these kinds of arrangements. (b) The
fanatic who doesn't in fact benefit from the overall organization of the regime that
the delegates identify as the 'dominant' one for the community. Her compliance
cannot be guaranteed, for the regime is not salient for her, even purely instrumentally as in case (a). Finally, (c) the 'free rider' who isn't willing to bear her share of
the burdens associated with the terms of fair cooperation. Here too compliance cannot be guaranteed even on a purely instrumental basis; the kinds of considerations
that tell with 'reasonable' individuals do not tell with the 'free rider'.

Given these failures of salience, how does the 'wave model' rate? Not badly.
After all, it is only individuals like those considered at (b) and (c) for whom a 'dom-

inant' regime will not be salient, at least in some purely instrumental sense. And the only ways in which salience might be attained in these cases is by 'bribery' in the form of 'side payments' that do indeed represent what Barry calls a ransom.

The case of the potential 'free rider' is the more obvious one. She is disposed to comply if and only if she must, on account of effective supervision, do so in order to benefit. She might therefore demand, as the cost of her promise to comply *without* supervision, a side payment nearly equal to the costs of the effective supervision of her activities. But this is plainly a bribe, and Nagel's proviso about "simple human *badness*" certainly applies.

The case of the fanatic whose compliance cannot be secured even purely instrumentally is a bit more controversial, but fundamentally it is the same as that of the potential free rider. The fanatic will not recognize the 'burdens of judgment' in relation at least to certain kinds of issues and so is not willing to endorse any regime in which her preferred comprehensive religious and/or philosophical doctrine is not politically enforced. If we take it that no regime is adequate unless it is salient for all, including the fanatic, then, in view of the fact that other individuals, reasonable and unreasonable, could not submit to the demands of such a regime without compromising *their* comprehensive religious and/or philosophical doctrines, we will have to conclude that there is no adequate regime for any community in which there are fanatics of this kind. But, in this case, Nagel's other proviso surely seems relevant — namely, "[i]f we find that persons . . . are still too far apart to be able to identify any arrangement that none of them could reasonably reject, . . . that is by itself a reason to reevaluate the standards of reasonableness that led to such a result."[30] If salience for all cannot be achieved so long as salience for the fanatic is required, then perhaps we ought to re-assess the notion that salience for all is indeed always required. In view of the 'unreasonableness' of such individuals, it would in fact be unreasonable not to re-assess our notions of salience in this case. In any event, since this is an implication for *any* approach to the problem of public justification, it cannot differentially *dis*favor the 'wave model'.

Intelligibility

"Since no one could rationally support a practice for which he could not see sufficient reason, . . . the arguments for any proposal must be simple enough to be understood by any moral agent. . . ."[31] Again, it is hard to assess the 'wave model' in relation to this requirement. On the one hand, much rather abstruse argumentation must surely occur in the convention, argumentation of a kind that many ordinary individuals could not fully understand. Furthermore, much of what transpires in the convention, particularly in relation to 'the wave', will not admit of ready verbalization or even intuitive apprehension anyway, involving as it does delicate judgments where "our capacity to resolve conflicts in particular cases may extend beyond our capacity to enunciate general principles that explain those resolutions."[32] Nevertheless, I think that, here too, we get benefits without burdens on account, precisely, of the device of representation.

Adapting an argument already employed, we might say, on the one hand, that the delegates have been chosen for their superior aptitudes and so can be expected to understand as fully as anyone can the grounds favoring the identification of a regime as the 'dominant' regime for the community they collectively represent. This, it seems to me, partially satisfies the demand for intelligibility.

On the other hand, the delegates are commissioned by individuals who may not have their intellectual powers and so might not be able to understand the deliberations of the delegates in precisely the terms that were salient for the delegates themselves. Still, two points soften this difficulty. First, there are some limits on how 'esoteric' even the delegates' deliberations can be. After all, I have already argued (sec. 18) that we cannot sensibly permit, even in the constitutional convention, the use of techniques for decision making that are *too* time-consuming or *too* far beyond the cognitive powers of the ordinary moral agent. Second, we have imagined the delegates representing concrete individuals as 'trustees' for their interests. It is part of the role of effective 'trustee' to explain, in terms the 'principal' can herself understand, why one has acted on her behalf as one in fact has done. In 'translating' from the language of the convention to the language of the community at large, some simplification may be required, but there is no reason to believe that out-and-out falsification or mystification would be necessary. A great deal of inspired political rhetoric, like that of the late Martin Luther King, achieved precisely this kind of simplification-without-falsification.

Stability

The basis of a regimes's justification for a community should not be too sensitive to such changes in the attitudes and attributes of its members as can ordinarily be expected to occur within (historically) short periods of time. The 'wave model' rates very highly in relation to this requirement. The key point is that 'reasonable' individuals have no motive for withdrawing their support from some system of social arrangements that their representatives have agreed to in the constitutional convention or judicially (at the level of the Supreme or High Court) simply in view of the fact that they could now, on account of their larger numbers, effectively sabotage this system. *Ex hypothesi,* such individuals *are* 'reasonable' and, as such, "desire for its own sake a social world in which they, as free and equal, can cooperate with others *on terms all can accept*"[33] — not just in the sense that others can acquiesce, in Gauthier's sense,[34] but, more 'reasonably', that others can comply in virtue of the 'reasonableness' of the terms of agreement. As Scanlon puts it, "[M]oral argument concerns the possibility of agreement among persons who are all moved by this desire" — namely, "to find and agree on principles which no one who had this desire could reasonably reject."[35] But since individuals held to 'ransom' by their now more numerous fellows could 'reasonably' reject new terms that extracted a 'side payment' for continued cooperation, 'reasonable' individuals couldn't demand it in the first place. Stability is assured relative to the assumption of reasonableness.

My approach to the problem of public justification does meet the requirements implicit in the ideal of public justification. In many cases, this is guaranteed by the division of labor between concrete, historically situated individuals and the delegates they commission to identify a 'dominant' regime for them. I invoke the distinction between the delegates and their 'principals' to secure many of the benefits that other theorists secure by much greater degrees of abstraction and/or idealization — for example, independence, transparency, intelligibility, and so on. But I invoke it, and the quite mild abstractions and idealizations that it embodies compared to other approaches (e.g., no 'thick' veil of ignorance, no assumption of perfect information or perfect sympathy, etc.), in order to allay the suspicion that what I have bought with one hand I have given away with the other. To be sure, there is a price, even for this delicate balancing of competing demands. My approach is an example of participative pure proceduralism and thus remains silent on substantive issues until it is actually implemented. My approach therefore implicitly repudiates, and *a fortiori* altogether fails to satisfy, a hankering, long felt by political theorists, to substitute the judgment of the theorist for the collective judgment of the community. But this is a price that I, anyway, am perfectly happy to pay. Macedo says: "Public justification should be a never-ending commitment. It would be sheer hubris to think that we have, or ever will have, the whole political truth. We are always learning and confronting new circumstances; we will always have progress to make."[36] Or, in Judith Butler's even more vivid formulation: "This is not to say that there is no foundation, but rather, wherever there is one, there will also be a foundering, a contestation. That such foundations exist only to be put into question is . . . the permanent risk of the process of democratization."[37]

Notes

1. *Equality and Partiality,* p. 26.

2. Cf. Ackerman, *Social Justice in the Liberal State,* p. 373: "Even a subcommunity devoted to the silent obedience of its spiritual leader must assign some of its members the task of responding to the question of legitimacy. . . ."

3. Cf. Benn, *A Theory of Freedom,* ch. 6 and Gaus, *Value and Justification,* sec. 17.

4. Cf. *The Dialogue of Justice,* sec. 3.6.

5. According to the 'spatial theory of voting', in certain conditions (roughly, when individuals' views are normally distributed on issue dimensions), whenever candidates are better off the more votes they attract, all candidates have incentives to adopt platforms that are as close as possible to the 'median' along the various policy dimensions and thus to formulate platforms that are, as near as makes no difference, identical to those formulated by all the others. Cf. Mueller, *Public Choice II,* ch. 10. In this case, very few relevant policy differences will actually be at issue in the election, and very few distinct and specific positions will actually be effectively represented at subsequent meetings of the legislature — or, in my case, of the constitutional convention.

6. This proposal seems to be a variant of a recommendation by Mueller, who proposes (*Public Choice II,* p. 219 and n. 2) setting a minimum number of votes (or vouchers) required to proceed to the second stage of candidacy and then, to secure election of genuinely 'representative' agents, having a runoff election in which, to determine how many votes each second-stage candidate will be able to cast in the convention, each principal votes for the second-stage candidate whose views are closest to her own. As Mueller notes, "[I]f alienation leads voters to abstain when no candidates come close to their ideal points, a spreading out of candidates can be expected."

7. *The Dialogue of Justice,* p. 198.

8. This method thus satisfies the demand (Mueller, *Public Choice II,* p. 218) for "an

assembly in which each citizen is represented by someone whose interests are identical to" her own.

9. "Kantian Constructivism in Moral Theory," pp. 569–70. On the other hand, I suspect that Rawls now sees this kind of project as threatened only by unreasonableness and not by any reasonable pluralism, however extensive it might be. He says (*Political Liberalism*, p. 126): "An overlapping consensus of reasonable doctrines may not be possible under many historical conditions, as the efforts to achieve it may be overwhelmed by unreasonable and even irrational (and sometimes mad) comprehensive doctrines." Since Rawls doesn't mention here other factors that might prevent the formation of an effective overlapping consensus, and since the idea of "reasonable pluralism" seems to do much of the work in justifying the two principles of justice, I think that he would probably reject the idea that my community of interpreters might fail to come up with some substantive proposals for the constitution they are charged with framing. (That the notion of "reasonable pluralism" seems to do much of the work in justifying the two principles of justice, is shown at *Political Liberalism*, pp. 164, 175: "simple pluralism moves toward reasonable pluralism and constitutional consensus is achieved"; "the political conception . . . is not formulated in terms of any comprehensive doctrine but in terms of certain fundamental ideas viewed as latent in the public political culture of a democratic society.")

10. Cf. Rawls, *Political Liberalism*, p. 93: "[P]ractical reason is concerned with the production of objects according to a conception of those objects . . . while theoretical reason is concerned with the knowledge of given objects."

11. In using this language, I do not want to be seen as buying into the debate about how well fitted the idea of representation is to the various projects, especially science, with which it has been associated. Rorty has recently criticized any project grounded in strong, epistemological notions of representational transparency. Cf. *Philosophy and the Mirror of Nature*, passim. What I do want to provide for is a distinction, recognized by many, between, on the one hand, projects that aim at the description of objects or phenomena whose causal relations with other objects or phenomena are (in crucial respects) independent of our conceptualizations of those relations, and, on the other hand, projects that aim at constituting their objects and phenomena precisely as objects and phenomena whose relations are dependent on our conceptualizations of those relations.

12. Cf. Imre Lakatos, "Falsification and the Methodology of Scientific Research Programmes."

13. This 'constructivist' interpretation of the project is arguably the preferred interpretation for political purposes of the kind I have in mind. As Rawls says (*Political Liberalism*, p. 97), "[I]t is only by affirming a constructivist conception . . . that citizens generally can expect to find principles that all can accept."

14. Cf. *Law's Empire*, pp. 78ff.

15. Cf. *Political Liberalism*, pp. 90ff.

16. *Politics and Ambiguity*, p. 10.

17. *Justice and the Politics of Difference*, p. 189.

18. "Deliberative Democracy and Social Choice," p. 55.

19. Cf. Pettit, *The Common Mind*, p. 226.

20. "The Limits of Public Reason," p. 25.

21. Benhabib, *Situating the Self,* p. 81. Cf. Albrecht Wellmer, "Reason, Utopia and the *Dialectics of Enlightenment*," p. 58: "[I]t is not the task of the theoretician to determine what the content of a future social consensus will be."

22. Fraser, *Unruly Practices,* p. 56.

23. *Political Liberalism*, p. 97.

24. In sec. 39 I consider the standing of my particular approach in relation to the identi-

fied weaknesses and alleged strengths of substitutionist approaches such as Hurley's, Ackerman's, and Gauthier's.

25. Indeed, Ackerman notes (*We the People,* p. 19) that, as a matter of fact, "Americans have, time and again, successfully repudiated large chunks of their past and transformed their higher law to express deep changes in their political identities." This, surely, is a valid form of 'secular' independence, relying on roughly the mechanisms posited here.

26. Cf. Putnam, *Reason, Truth and History,* p. 50.

27. Cf. my paper "Transcendence and Conversation."

28. Nagel, *Equality and Partiality,* p. 36.

29. Cf. "Kantian Constructivism in Moral Theory," p. 528: "Given a specification of the parties' highest-order interests, they are rational in their deliberations to the extent that sensible principles of rational choice guide their deliberations."

30. *Equality and Partiality,* p. 45.

31. Michael Davis, "The Moral Legislature," p. 308.

32. Nagel, *Mortal Questions,* p. 135.

33. Rawls, *Political Liberalism,* p. 50.

34. Cf. *Morals by Agreement,* p. 230: "We should distinguish between compliance, as the disposition to accept fair and optimal co-operative arrangements, and acquiescence, the disposition to accept co-operative arrangements that are less than fair, in order to ensure mutual benefit."

35. "Contractualism and Utilitarianism," p. 111.

36. "The Politics of Justification," p. 287.

37. "Contingent Foundations," p. 16.

11

Conclusion

Postmodernity . . . is *modernity without illusions*. The illusions in question boil down to the belief that the 'messiness' of the human condition is but a temporary state, sooner or later to be replaced by the orderly and systematic rule of reason. The truth in question is that the 'messiness' will stay whatever we do or know, that the little orders and 'systems' we carve out in the world are brittle, until-further-notice, and as arbitrary and in the end contingent as their alternatives.

ZYGMUNT BAUMAN, Postmodern Ethics

I think it is clear, as promised, that the 'wave model' approach to public justification is political, rather than substitutionist. (See secs. 31 and 32.) It will be helpful, and will complement the arguments of Chapter 10, to consider how this approach fares with respect to the strengths and weaknesses of the competing, substitutionist approach. This is my project in section 39. I then consider, in section 40, a number of purely descriptive issues that couldn't elsewhere easily be integrated into the stream of argumentation. In the final section (sec. 41), I propose a slightly modified understanding, or perhaps just re-emphasize a neglected interpretation of Gallie's essential contestability thesis, and I show what this interpretation implies about our understanding of philosophical activity.

39. The Superiority of a Political Approach

First of all, how does the 'wave model' fare with respect to the identified strengths and weaknesses of such substitutionist approaches as those of Ackerman, Gauthier, Gaus, Hurley, and others? (See sec. 31.)

Let us consider first the alleged strengths of substitutionism.

Remember that the substitutionist approach is designed to honor important moralistic desiderata like transparency and reflexivity. How does the 'wave model' rate on these criteria? Arguably, pretty well. As already indicated, we secure transparency via the device of representation (of individuals by delegates); reflexivity via pre-constitutional theorizing from the points of view of 'reasonable' individuals; and independence via the community's own resources and, especially, its own theories about the ideological corruption of attitudes and practices. (See sec. 38.)

Substitutionist techniques are heralded as explicitly challenging "the idea that 'might makes right'. . . . Access to such schemes is especially necessary when unequal power relations exist . . . [it being] in the interest of the weak to contest on the ground of truth rather than with force."[1] As I have said before, some care is needed here, for we must not claim, in defense of substitutionism, that it altogether eliminates the effects of power in all its various guises. For instance, majoritarian voting techniques will typically reward political groups that are powerful, if in no other sense, then at least in the sense of having many members. Still, the use of such techniques *is* a substitute for what might be called blatant displays of naked power, typically in the form of force (i.e., violence) or the threat to employ it. And this, surely, is a *valid* substitution in the circumstances of politics.

How does the 'wave model' fare in this regard? Rather well. Certainly, there is even less opportunity for differential power to distort moral argumentation on my account than, for example, on Ackerman's. Ackerman (and Gaus) would presumably favor that regime as the 'dominant' regime which a majority of individuals thought of as such, *prior* to argumentation (or, at least, prior to the 'conclusion' of argumentation) about the relative merits of various alternatives. (See sec. 24.) The question of 'dominance' is to be settled in accordance with 'the numbers'. This is only a very imperfect abstraction from empirical distributions of (in this case, political) power. Using the 'wave model', we find that the (morally) disturbing influences of differential power are not entirely excluded. Bargaining might be permitted in the convention; see section 34. These influences are nevertheless very much attenuated by two factors that I emphasize. First of all, there is discursive involvement in the identification of a dominant regime. Individuals or at least their delegates actually need to consider one another's *arguments about* rather than merely mechanically amalgamating their pre-discursive *preferences for* the various competing regimes. Second, the requirement of unanimity effectively secures an optimal compromise among the various possibly opposed interests and thus avoids majority tyranny.

Also relevant in this regard is Reiman's 'subjugation condition', as I will call it. According to Reiman, "Overcoming suspicion of subjugation is the natural test of moral requirements."[2] Any allegedly moral requirement might in fact function as a means of domination ("assertions of moral authority evoke the suspicion of subjugation"). We therefore must show, of each such requirement, that "it would be reasonable for people willingly to accept" it.[3] And the test, according to Reiman, is this: "The social contract works as a test of subjugation, then, if, because a principle would be agreed to under its imaginary conditions, we can infer that it would be reasonable for all the people who actually end up in any of the positions that principle yields to accept those positions."[4] This condition is satisfied by the 'wave model'. The delegates are trustees for the individuals they represent. Any agreement that they might reach therefore ought to be reasonable for these individuals. After all, the principles agreed to were agreed to on their behalf by delegates charged with securing their interests and equipped to do so effectively (within the limits of 'the reasonable'). Each individual therefore has reason to accept these principles — that they are 'reasonable' for her is a condition of her representative's acceptance of them. (She may not herself be reasonable and so may not *actually accept* these principles, but securing actual acceptance is not required by the 'subjugation condition'.)

Remember too that, in its yearning for some "abstract and computational" basis for "explicit and univocal decision-procedures," a substitutionist approach is responsive to exactly the difficulties in which the problem of public justification is grounded — namely, the absence of antecedent agreement about what to do, indeed about how to decide what to do. Given a 'moral algorithm' of the kind sought by substitutionists, "rational individuals need not debate over what criteria should be applied" in the case of political disputes any more than they need to in the case of disputed claims about some mathematical problem.[5]

This, surely, *is* a considerable benefit. But the 'wave model' also does a good job in this regard. Although a political approach denies the need for and eschews providing any 'moral algorithm', it does indeed tackle 'head on' the problem of public justification. It does so institutionally, rather than 'geometrically'. Most importantly, a political approach demands that we establish a constitutional convention specifically devoted to the solution of this problem. The delegates to the convention are chosen for their knowledge about the problem and for their commitment, on behalf of their 'principals', to its solution.

It has to be admitted that the 'wave model' does not actually provide or identify a determinate substantive solution to the problem of public justification, in the way that some substitutionist approaches would claim to be able to. But any such claim is itself of doubtful validity. This is not a point that tells differentially against the 'wave model'. Indeed, majoritarian and concessional approaches are no more determinately substantive in their results than the 'wave model', even though they 'give away' much of the sensitivity to nuances and circumstances that that approach retains, indeed jealously guards. When we are told to amalgamate individuals' preferences for regimes using these kinds of techniques, we know no better what the socially legitimate regime will be like than when we are told to embody a constitutional convention in order to make this determination.

How does a political approach fare with respect to the supposed weaknesses of substitutionist alternatives?

Because of its Procrustean tendencies, any substitutionist approach of course "will require a degree of idealization and abstraction that limits its usefulness for many of the practical concerns that give morality its point."[6] A political approach is much less restrictive in this regard and so is superior on this point. To be sure, there is some idealization and abstraction associated with the 'wave model'. After all, public morality is the province of delegates to a constitutional convention who may differ, in two respects, from the individuals they represent: (1) all delegates are 'reasonable', whereas some principals are not; and (2) all delegates are well informed about and have the talents necessary for addressing the problem of public justification, whereas many of their principals will lack these characteristics. Still, the delegates are not otherwise 'abnormal' in their psychology. They know their own identities and those of the individuals they represent. They try to secure the interests, even the 'unreasonable' interests, of their 'principals', rather than concerning themselves with some allegedly determinable quantum of total or average 'utility'. And so on. Altogether, the delegates are much freer than the parties to Rawls's original position or those to Harsanyi's, for instance, to treat the matters before them largely 'in their own terms', rather than in the terms established by some allegedly canonical framework.[7]

As I have reported, a substitutionist approach is widely considered suspect on account of "the abstract and disembodied distorting and nostalgic ideal of the autonomous male ego which the universalist tradition privileges."[8] But this is a problem that the 'wave model' altogether avoids—again, precisely because delegates do differ from such other 'surrogates' as the Rawlsian parties. Of course, I do impose the following requirements on delegates: (a) The delegates must be reasonable and must participate in the activities of the convention in accordance with the requirements of 'the reasonable'. (b) The delegates must be well informed about and committed to solving the problem of public justification in a way that satisfies the various desiderata associated with the ideal of public justification. (c) The delegates must be articulate and effective 'trustees' of the (reasonable and unreasonable) interests of the individual(s) they represent and must represent their 'principals' as those individuals would want to be represented (subject to requirement (a)), so that, for example, those individuals who want to stress emotive and expressive elements in the advocacy of regimes will be represented by delegates equipped to honor this desire. These requirements do implicitly demand a 'mild' idealization of empirical realities, but they do not 'privilege' some dominant male (or 'western' or 'imperialistic' or 'entrepreneurial') perspective, whatever that might mean.

Furthermore, consider qualms about the style of theorizing that is implied in substitutionist approaches—for example, that the very idea of substituting 'model-conceptions' for concrete individuals is itself the kind of 'move', in theorizing, that men are more likely to make than women. Clearly, a political approach again nullifies these objections, precisely because there is no attempt to substitute 'model-conceptions' for concrete, historically situated individuals, but only, of course, an insistence on their adequate and effective representation in the forum in which their life-prospects will largely be determined. (Of course, 'unreasonable' individuals will not think that their interests are adequately represented by the delegates who are commissioned for them. But this is not what feminist critics of liberalism have had in mind.)

Obviously, the hostility to plurality, diversity, and otherness that many commentators detect in the substitutionist approach—the possibility that its techniques "are implicitly totalitarian because totalizing . . . normalizing because normative"[9]—is absent in the 'wave model'. Whereas the substitutionist seeks to prescribe for all individuals, despite their concrete differences, those who advocate a political approach renounce precisely such a substitution of 'theory' for the democratic self-definition of a community of citizens. Again, there are some constraints implicit even in the political approach. For instance, we do not honor the demand of 'unreasonable' individuals to be represented by delegates who argue unreasonably for their unreasonable interests and attitudes. But we do recognize, at least within the limits of 'reasonable' argumentation, even these unreasonable interests and attitudes. More than this is not possible unless delegates representing 'reasonable' individuals are asked to sacrifice the interests of *their* principals in order to satisfy the unreasonable demands of 'free riders'. At least with respect to these individuals, some 'normalization' seems unavoidable. (It is important to remember that normalization is indeed unavoidable within this kind of framework. There is no alternative to it. But we can still ask who is to be 'normalized', given that someone has to be. It does not seem unreasonable to normalize the 'unreasonable' — or, at least, to demand that their representatives behave 'reasonably'.)

Notice, furthermore, that a political approach does not depend on the contrary-to-fact assumption that it is possible to identify fixed and determinate inputs to processes of calculation. I make no assumption, as Manin puts it, ". . . that individuals in society possess an already formed will, already know exactly what they want" and that theorists therefore need only to calculate on the basis of such information about what people want.[10] Indeed, this is perhaps the most marked difference between political and substitutionist approaches. Insofar as a substitutionist approach maintains *any* contact with empirical realities, it must 'freeze' them at some point and in some 'canonical' format if they are to provide 'inputs' to the calculative devices that it relies on. On the other hand, it is precisely the notion of a 'canonical' format or a privileged 'freezing' of states of play that is rejected in a political approach. Indeed, this approach facilitates the presentation — in the terms she thinks pertinent — of each individual's potentially unique contribution to the process of constructing a collectively acceptable interpretation of the demands of communal living.

Finally, the 'wave model' clearly answers the demand for salience in a way that more abstractive, distanced, and idealizing substitutionist approaches may not be able to. The 'problem of recognition' poses no difficulty, as it may with substitutionist approaches such as Hurley's. There are no reasons why a 'reasonable' individual, however concrete and historically situated, should balk at the demands she might be required to meet in some regime identified as 'dominant' in a properly constituted convention. The situation is 'transparent' to her, at least in the sense that she recognizes (1) that she has commissioned a delegate to act as trustee for her interests, (2) that her delegate had to agree, on her behalf, before any proposal could be ratified, and (3) that some particular proposal was indeed ratified. If all this is transparent, then the particular individual will indeed recognize her obligation to acknowledge the proposal that has been ratified. However obscure the argumentation in the convention, points (1)–(3) suffice to secure 'recognition'.

All in all, then, a political approach is demonstrably superior to its substitutionist rival. It has all of the alleged strengths, indeed perhaps in even greater measure, and none of the well-known weaknesses of that approach. The political alternative meets the minimal condition for acceptability that is implicit in the congeries of requirements that together make up the ideal of public justification (sec. 38). This approach is thus not only more worthy of acceptance than any substitutionist alternative, it is worthy *simpliciter.*

40. Further Remarks about Constitution Making

One reason why a political approach is demonstrably superior to substitutionist approaches is that the former acknowledges, indeed insists on, the fundamentally *collective* nature of human judgment, decision making, and problem solving. Indeed, this is built into the Kuhnian model of science from which I have so heavily borrowed. On my account, it is not that my, or some other individual's, privileged access to some (possibly transcendent) perspective enables us, as individuals, to identify a 'dominant' regime for a given community. It is, rather, that the confrontation of the different perspectives of the various delegates enables them, collectively, to identify such a regime. As Barber puts it:

> Political judgment is thus "we-judgment" or public judgment of common-willing (in Rousseau's phrase, general willing). I cannot judge politically, only we can judge politically; in assuming the mantle of citizenship, the I becomes a We. . . . Political judgment is the multitude deliberating, the multitude in action.[11]

This kind of 'justificatory collectivism' raises a point that was slighted in my earlier analysis of the workings of the convention. This is the importance of *parties* and other coalitions. In fact, the organization of the delegates into groups of relatively like-minded individuals prepared to work together and, together, 'against' other such groups (and their individual members) can be expected to play a number of important roles in the workings of the convention.

First, considerable effort is required by *A* to formulate and 'pre-test' arguments intended to persuade *B*, who currently disparages his favored regime, to join him in promoting its prospects in the larger community of which they are members. There is no reason to think that *A* alone will be able to think of all that might be thought of, or even indeed of very much that might be thought of that might have this kind of persuasive effect on *B*. He will thus benefit from the collaboration of others in trying to formulate and present such arguments and so from membership in a party of individuals devoted, at least pro tem, to the advancement of their favored regime.

Second, I have already noted the possibility, as Nagel puts it, that "our capacity to resolve conflicts in particular cases may extend beyond our capacity to enunciate general principles that explain those resolutions."[12] This kind of 'ineffability' may facilitate the collective identification of a 'dominant' regime via the contemplation of paradigmatic instances. But such ineffability also poses a threat to objectivity. If we cannot explain why some particular case should be treated in one way rather than another, how can we be sure that our conviction that it should be is not purely idiosyncratic, or possibly delusory? The embeddedness of individuals in parties at least ameliorates this difficulty, even if it does not altogether eliminate it. Where ineffable judgments are collectively established and monitored, there is at least some pressure against purely idiosyncratic and privately delusory judgments being accepted as veridical.

Third, parties within the convention help facilitate a division of labor that may permit the satisfaction of realistic desiderata like intelligibility that might otherwise have to be slighted. Within a party different individuals can be assigned different subtasks in the articulation of their collectively preferred regime and the grounds for it. This enables each individual delegate to face a problem her cognitive powers are adequate for dealing with, at the same time as the group as a whole tackles a problem that is probably beyond the powers of any one of them. By maintaining a plurality of such parties, delegates can develop a plurality of different approaches, involving different divisions of labor and different arguments, and then, on 'the floor' of the convention, compare and contrast them for the mutual benefit of all.

Without an organization of individuals, there can be no effective problem solving, and without parties, that is, a multiplicity of such organizations, there are no hedges against the possibility that some particular approach is misguided, incomplete, or otherwise inadequate. Parties are a natural response to such limitations on individual cognitive powers as are implicit in Cherniak's "finitary predicament."

Indeed, fourth and finally, the organized diversity represented by parties arguably plays a crucial role in relation to the idea, associated with 'pure proceduralism', that whatever the outcome of the deliberations of the delegates, that regime is the 'dominant' one precisely in being identified by them as such. Stanley Kleinberg makes an important point in a related context:

> The readier people are to respond to calls for change, the more confidently we can view the endurance of a practice or institution as an indication of merit. Conversely the greater the number who are conservatively disposed, the weaker the grounds for supposing that the mere survival of the institution or practice is an indication of merit.[13]

I take this to mean that, in pure proceduralism, there has to be an arduous contest if a result is to be considered the right result by the very fact of its being the result of that contest. One way of ensuring that the contest in the convention is sufficiently arduous between competing ground plans for regimes is, of course, by encouraging the formation of 'conservative' and 'radical' parties in the convention.

Of course, it is not enough, though it may be very important, that parties contest the disputed concept of public justification. This is not enough because a solution to the problem of public justification requires eventual agreement in the face of antecedent disagreement. The members of parties will therefore have to have a disposition, associated with their 'reasonableness' in Rawls's sense, that many of the concrete individuals whom they represent probably will not have in very great measure. The delegates will have to be persuasible, and, for that to occur, they will have to find accessible appeals even to those desiderata, implicated in the ideal of public justification, that they do not themselves weight very heavily. The delegate β representing the moralistic B will have to 'feel the tug' of those considerations that persuade the delegate α representing the realistic A to prefer X to Z even though she does not herself rate these considerations very highly. If A prefers X to Z on account of X's superiority with respect to realistic desiderata, β can acknowledge that this is a reason for preferring X even though, given the current disposition of considerations, X's superiority on this score is not enough to warrant a judgment of *overall* superiority for her 'principal' B. Without such 'sympathy', neither α nor β will ever be able to persuade the other of the superiority of her favored regime — or, perhaps, of some other that represents an 'optimal compromise' of both of their initially favored regimes. And, in this case, the wave will never get started, antecedent disagreement will never be composed, and the problem of public justification will never be solved.

There is every reason, within a pluralist perspective, for supposing that this kind of 'sympathy' is indeed available. In section 5, I suggested, in particular, that it is integral to this perspective that individuals who reach different conclusions about the overall relative merits of alternatives may nevertheless recognize the reasonableness of each other's decisions. Donna Haraway puts the point well:

> Subjectivity is multidimensional; so, therefore, is vision. The knowing self is par-
> tial in all its guises; it is always constructed and stitched together imperfectly, and
> *therefore* able to join with another, to see together without claiming to be another.[14]

While O'Neill is certainly right to say that "[a]t any stage previous assumptions can be queried, and at no stage are definitive answers established,"[15] there is nevertheless no particular reason to worry that a party-based convention will never, however temporarily, be able to settle on some collectively acceptable judgment about the nature of a 'dominant' regime.

Indeed, we can even hazard a guess about the nature of the artifacts that are likely to be approved, in a 'wave'-like fashion, within a community of interpreters. If some particular institutional arrangement is to be approved by a number of quite different individuals, that arrangement will have to be multifaceted, at least in the sense that it can 'fit' with one individual's psychology at the same time that it can also 'fit' with quite different elements in the psychology of another individual. Such an institutional arrangement needs, in other words, to 'look good' from a variety of different perspectives. And yet, at the same time, it also needs to be coherent, at least 'pragmatically', that is, at least in the sense that its various component elements can really be implemented in some concrete and non-contradictory fashion. It needs to possess at least some of the features of what Robert Nozick calls an "organic unity."[16] And it therefore needs to be thought of, not so much as a discovery of something pre-existent or, indeed, even as the embodiment, concretely, of some pre-existing 'blueprint' (perhaps in the manner of a Platonic 'idea'), but, instead, as the *creation* of something novel and yet appropriate to its circumstances, in the sense of answering a (perhaps strongly felt) need that arises within them. Any such artifact is, in other words, a product of true human creativity in no lesser, and perhaps in an immeasurably greater, sense than the work of the world's 'artists'.

On the 'wave model', the problem of public justification is addressed within a community of delegates organized at two levels, reflecting Rorty's two attitudes toward difference, the cosmopolitan and the ethnocentric. The convention itself is certainly a cosmopolitan gathering much like Rorty's bazaar, where "many of the people" are pictured "as preferring to die rather than share the beliefs of many of those with whom they are haggling. . . ."[17] And the organized parties that constitute the effective units of the convention are, within the limits of 'the reasonable', mildly ethnocentric clubs of like-minded individuals who can, as Rorty puts it, "rationally change their beliefs and desires only by holding most of those beliefs and desires constant."[18] The convention, as Rorty says, is "a bazaar surrounded by [I would prefer, 'incorporating'] lots and lots of exclusive private clubs."[19] Such a setting is, I think, one, indeed perhaps the only one, that "preserves the conditions in which the search for right answers can continue. . . ."[20]

One final point. There is a definite, if perhaps purely metaphorical, sense in which the constitutional convention embodies a quasi-Darwinian mechanism of choice. Several features are salient in this regard.[21]

First, it is vital to the workings of the convention that there be considerable initial variation among the delegates in their conceptions of public justification. Without someone's efforts in improving it, made because she has a lower 'acceptance-threshold' than others, no proposed conception is likely, except purely fortuitously, to be accepted by *all* delegates, and the convention is therefore likely to take a random walk through the space of possible conceptions, rather than, as would undoubtedly be more efficient, investing some of its energies in developing at least the more promising proposals. Variation is crucial to the workings of the community of interpreters — as it is, of course, in the Darwinian model of natural selection (of well-adapted variants from a pool of variously adapted competitors).

Second, it is also vital to the workings of the convention that there be competition among the proponents of the various conceptions of the founding concept. The improvement of variants that are not initially satisfactory results only because their proponents are offering them not simply as *their* favored alternatives but, rather, as alternatives that the community as a whole ought to accept. And this brings the proponents of different conceptions into competition with one another. If *A* says that J_A is the best conception of public justification, and *B* says that J_B is the best conception, then, if $J_A \neq J_B$, they cannot both be right and will be forced, by the logic of their commitments, to try to establish grounds, telling with the delegates, for endorsing their favored conceptions. They will have to compete, in short.

Third, the process of communal interpretation, like that of organic evolution, cannot be said to optimize once and for all the objects that it throws up.[22] In the case of organic evolution, the environment can only differentiate among the variants that are actually thrown up (by the 'genetic lottery') — and the one that is, 'objectively', the very best may never *be* thrown up. Furthermore, the variant selected is that which is better than available alternatives against a given ecological background and so might not have prevailed over even these alternatives had conditions been slightly different. The situation is much the same in the convention. Only those institutional arrangements that are actually proposed will be compared by the delegates, and which proposal is formally ratified will depend on the argumentative background. There is no reason to believe that this process is 'optimizing'. Perhaps the 'best' set of arrangements is never proposed; perhaps a poor set is well defended by its proponents, whereas a better set is poorly defended.

The 'wave model' is therefore arguably a quasi-Darwinian model. It shares two of the most distinctive features of the Darwinian model of organic change. It is non-teleological, and it has a populationist, not an individualistic ontology. The fundamental site of activity is the population, the group, the *community* of interpreters; the work of the individual is significant only in this context.

41. Perpetual Instability and the Nature of Philosophical Thinking

I said earlier (sec. 6) that the concept of public justification is arguably an essentially contestable concept in Gallie's sense so that its "proper use . . . inevitably involves endless disputes" that are "not resolvable by argument of any kind."[23] I now want to repudiate this view and, indeed, Gallie's notion of 'essential contestability'. While there may be essentially contestable concepts in *his* sense, concepts whose proper uses are unsettleable by rational argumentation, I do not believe that the concept of public justification is such a concept, nor do I believe that other concepts often taken to be essentially contestable are so in Gallie's particular sense.

What is the point of disagreement between us? It is this. I believe that there are concepts whose uses are likely to be disputed, for all the reasons Gallie himself identified (and which are summarized in secs. 5 and 6). But I believe that disputes about some of these concepts *can* be resolved, if only transiently, by rational argumentation. Indeed, I believe that there are social arrangements that can be instituted in order to facilitate the resolution of disputes about such concepts. I believe that communities of scientists are institutional means for resolving disputes about scientific explanation. I believe that communities of jurists are institutional means for resolving disputes about 'the concept of law'. And, obviously, I believe that a community of delegates is an institutional means for resolving disputes about the idea of public justification. While these ideas might *seem* to be essentially contestable in Gallie's sense, disputes about them may, at least from time to time, actually be settled by collective argumentation.

When I say that disputes about these concepts can actually be settled, I do not mean that they can be settled *once and for all*. (Here perhaps I am reconciled to Gallie.) Circumstances change and changed circumstances alter cases, so what *was* settled can become *un*settled. For instance, we might decide that a particular regime is 'dominant' for us. We might decide this on the basis of such considerations as the delegates we commissioned were able to think of and effectively present during their deliberations. But perhaps there were arguments, unconsidered by the delegates because unthought of at the time, whose relevance to our decision later becomes obvious, for example, because one of us comes, belatedly, to think of them. The consensus is then destabilized, and further reflection on our circumstances may be required. (This is what the Supreme or the High Court is for, in part: to consider those arguments unconsidered by the constitutional conventioneers.[24])

Or perhaps the arrangements made for implementing the dominant regime have 'unanticipated consequences' that, when discovered, persuade us that a regime of this kind cannot be the 'dominant' one for us, since, once encountered, these consequences are unacceptable. (This is another function of the Supreme or High Court: to consider previously unconsidered consequences of the implementation of the allegedly 'dominant' regime.)

In arriving at a collective judgment about the 'dominant' regime, perhaps we slight some of the desiderata that constitute our ideal for such regimes and, when the regime is indeed implemented, its relatively unsatisfactory character in relation to these slighted desiderata creates pressure toward a regime that is strong where this one is weak. Fishkin gives something like this account for the 'cycling' between substantively 'conservative' and substantively 'liberal' regimes that we see in many of the western democracies:

> Each element of moral conflict, if taken seriously, would lead public policy in a quite different direction. This may force an intuitionistic balancing of particular cases to take policy, over time, in a cycle. Because progress in one direction may force us to retrace our steps along another valued dimension, patterns of moral conflict can eventually take us back to where we started.[25]

For all these reasons I accept the perpetual instability of our concepts even as I deny the significance of essential contestability claims. There are concepts we are bound perpetually to argue about because of the central role they play in our collective lives, because of their sensitivity to circumstances that are bound to change, even in the medium-term historically, and, finally, because of the sensitivity of our arguments about them to our own finitude and its many manifestations in argumentative contexts.

For me, the last of these three points is especially important. It points to a general lesson for philosophy as a discipline. As Hayek points out, it is a delusion (he calls it the "synoptic delusion") that "all the relevant facts are known to some one mind, and that it is possible to construct from this knowledge of the particulars a desirable social order."[26] Indeed, I would go further and deny that "all the relevant facts" are or can be known even to 'all the relevant minds' considered collectively if we mean by this that there is some one instant, or even epoch, when all that might be said, thought, or felt that is of relevance to some disputed issue is available for saying, thinking, or feeling. This denies both the historicity and the creativity of individuals and the groups they constitute. People think what was hitherto unthought, and their doing so destabilizes what had previously been justified for their community. This fact is a condition for progress in philosophy and, simultaneously, marks the limits on the possibility of once-and-for-all philosophizing. (See sec. 7.) And it is, *inter alia,* the reason why I cannot say what the 'dominant' regime might look like for our community. The answer to that question depends on what we would actually say, and its stability depends on how much of what might have been said we do actually manage to say — and both of these factors are variables whose values I could not even begin to estimate.

I said, in the Preface, that I had learned much about the value of collective democratic decision making from my experience as an academic administrator. But I also learned much about the fragility of reason during my tenure, about the perpetual instability of even our most labored and conscientious argumentation. My job involved settling 'hard cases' in relation to the regulations governing the awards of the university — for example, did Jones satisfy the requirements for the award of the B.A.? might Smith be excused from satisfying some normal requirement of her course? and so on. Within the limits of time and energy available for these chores, I addressed myself conscientiously to them, mugging up the relevant regulations, consulting with my administrative colleagues, from time to time even considering matters, with advocates pro and con, in meetings of the Faculty Board. And many (indeed too many) times, I would wake in the middle of the night to realize that a point could have been made that hadn't been and that, had it been, the case might have been decided in an entirely different way. (In some cases, I was able to re-open matters with these hitherto unconsidered arguments now given a fair hearing.) More gauche autobiography? I hope not. The lesson is one for philosophers, and it is, indeed, the lesson of this work.

All of our reasoning is unstable in this sense. It always depends on what we are clever enough and clearheaded enough to think of at the time, and so it can be overturned, if we are honest with ourselves, as soon as the incompleteness or inadequacy of what we did manage to think of is exposed by someone who has had the wit to think something hitherto unthought or, at least, to express something hitherto unexpressed. *Any* final and decisive closure of debate is therefore *always* premature. As White says, "[A] universalistic claim about the shape of the good society is always unwarranted, since it tries to settle once and for all what must be left open, if the requirement of reciprocity is to take into account voices which may not have been evident in any given discourse."[27] And it is for this reason that democratic institutions like those embodied in the constitutional convention are so valuable. The diversity and the freedom of intercourse that they embody maximize the prospects that the unthought will be thought, that the unexpressed will be expressed. Like democracy, philosophy is an unstable collective project, contrary to an image now recently criticized, however fairly, by many 'postmodernists' — canonically that of Descartes shut up alone in an overheated room in search of permanently stabilized foundations for knowledge.[28] That this is an image that ought to be rejected is, I hope, an implication of much of the argumentation here, especially that of Chapter 7, where a variety of substitutes for communal judgment were found wanting. I conclude, with Rorty, that "[s]olidarity is not discovered by reflection but created. . . ."[29] And, with him, I reject the idea — and the ideal of *theory* that it presupposes (see sec. 1) — that "philosophers . . . should do their best to attain knowledge of something less dubious than the values of the democratic freedoms" on which to 'ground' those freedoms.[29] On this account, it is *conversation,* not *theory,* that settles matters of public concern, and those matters remain unsettled until proposals are formulated that are reasonable from every point of view.

Yeatman articulates a lingering worry:

> In this context, the response of master subjects who recognize the crisis of authority, and who recommend the development of non-foundationalist, intellectual "conversation" is a familiar liberal's attempt to get the raucous and dangerous mobs off the streets by tempting some of their leaders into safely cloistered polite conversation in civilized comfort with the decision-making elite.[30]

To be sure. Nevertheless, I have here tried to show how to free public reason from Yeatman's "master subjects" (i.e. apologetic 'theorists'), in order to realign it with Lincoln's great project — that of sketching the lineaments of a government that is genuinely (constructed) of, by, and for 'the people.'

Notes

1. Flax, "The End of Innocence," p. 456.
2. *Justice and Modern Moral Philosophy,* p. 67.
3. *Justice and Modern Moral Philosophy,* pp. 65, 36.
4. *Justice and Modern Moral Philosophy,* p. 291.
5. Brown, *Rationality,* pp. 12–13.
6. Benjamin, *Splitting the Difference,* pp. 75–76.
7. Recall in this regard the spate of complaints about Rawls's use of social primary goods as the basis for the decision making of the parties to the original position.
8. Benhabib, *Situating the Self,* p. 3.
9. Fraser, *Unruly Practices,* p. 56, reporting the views of Foucault.
10. "On Legitimacy and Political Deliberation," p. 351.
11. *The Conquest of Politics,* pp. 200–201, 209–10.
12. *Mortal Questions,* p. 135.
13. *Politics and Philosophy,* p. 116.

14. "Situated Knowledges," p. 586.

15. *Constructions of Reason*, p. 21.

16. Cf. *Philosophical Explanations*, pp. 415ff.

17. *Objectivity, Relativism, and Truth*, p. 209. The convention is not exactly like Rorty's bazaar since, by stipulation, all the delegates are 'reasonable' and so would not prefer to die rather than share the beliefs of their argumentative opponents.

18. *Objectivity, Relativism, and Truth*, p. 212.

19. *Objectivity, Relativism, and Truth*, p. 209. Cf. Fuller, *Social Epistemology*, pp. 208ff.

20. Hurley, *Natural Reasons*, p. 326. Cf. Vattimo, *The Transparent Society*, p. 94.

21. I do not resile from my earlier critique (sec. 30) of the 'authoritarian' appeal to evolutionary ideas. Methodological conservatives such as Hayek need to claim, to defend extant institutions, that these institutions survived an open competition with alternative institutions and that they did so, not fortuitously or as a result of 'external' factors, but because of their better 'adaptation' to local circumstances. But I make no appeal in what follows and indeed explicitly deny that the 'community of interpreters' settles on some optimally adapted set of institutions for their circumstances. Furthermore, I don't stipulate competition, I build it into the convention.

22. Cf. Simon, *Reason in Human Affairs*, p. 41.

23. Gallie, "Essentially Contested Concepts," p. 169.

24. I argued in sec. 35 that emotive or expressive presentation of issues was appropriate and perhaps even desirable in the constitutional convention. But surely it is out of place in the deliberations of a High or Supreme Court. Is it? On Dworkin's account, judges are charged with interpreting the law in a way that reveals it in the best possible light relative to its fundamental constitutive values. Since emotive and expressive presentations are effective in tapping into systems of values, they may help clarify, rather than distort, the reflections of the justices.

25. *The Dialogue of Justice*, p. 29.

26. *Law, Legislation, and Liberty*, vol. 1, p. 14.

27. *The Recent Work of Jürgen Habermas*, p. 71.

28. Cf. Gellner, *Reason and Culture*, p. 3: "Descartes's rationalism is also profoundly individualistic. . . . The rational is the private, and perhaps the private is also the rational."

29. *Contingency, Irony, and Solidarity*, p. xvi.

30. *Postmodern Revisionings of the Political*, p. 31.

Bibliography

Ackerman, Bruce, *Social Justice in the Liberal State* (New Haven, 1980: Yale University Press).

———, "What is Neutral about Neutrality?" *Ethics,* vol. 93 (1983), pp. 372–90.

———, "Why Dialogue?" *The Journal of Philosophy,* vol. 86 (1989), pp. 5–23.

———, *We the People, 1: Foundations* (Cambridge, 1991: Belknap Press of Harvard University Press).

———, "Political Liberalisms," *The Journal of Philosophy,* vol. 91 (1994), pp. 364–86.

Anscombe, G. E. M., *Intention* (Oxford, 1958: Basil Blackwell).

Baier, Kurt, "Justice and the Aims of Political Philosophy," *Ethics,* vol. 99 (1989), pp. 771–90.

Barber, Benjamin, *The Conquest of Politics* (Princeton, 1988: Princeton University Press).

Barry, Brian, *Theories of Justice* (London, 1989: Harvester-Wheatsheaf).

———, *Political Argument,* 2nd ed. (Berkeley and Los Angeles, 1990: University of California Press).

Bartley, William W. III, "Rationality versus the Theory of Rationality" in Mario Bunge, ed., *The Critical Approach to Science and Philosophy* (New York, 1964: The Free Press of Glencoe).

Bauman, Zygmunt, *Legislators and Interpreters* (Cambridge, 1987: Polity Press).

———, *Postmodern Ethics* (Oxford, 1993: Blackwell).

Baynes, Kenneth, *The Normative Grounds of Social Criticism: Kant, Rawls, and Habermas* (Albany, 1992: State University of New York Press).

Beiner, Ronald, *Political Judgment* (London, 1983: Methuen).

Benhabib, Seyla, *Situating the Self: Gender, Community and Postmodernism in Contemporary Ethics* (Cambridge, 1992: Polity Press).

Benjamin, Martin, *Splitting the Difference: Compromise and Integrity in Ethics and Politics* (Lawrence, 1990: University Press of Kansas).

Benn, Stanley I., *A Theory of Freedom* (Cambridge, 1988: Cambridge University Press).

——— and Gaus, Gerald F., "Practical Rationality and Commitment," *American Philosophical Quarterly,* vol. 23 (1986), pp. 255–66.

Berlin, Isaiah, *Four Essays on Liberty* (London, 1969: Oxford University Press).

Bernstein, Richard J., *Beyond Objectivism and Relativism* (Oxford, 1983: Basil Blackwell).

———, *The New Constellation: The Ethico-Political Horizons of Modernity/Postmodernity* (Cambridge, 1991: Polity Press).

Blau, Peter M. and Meyer, Marshall W., *Bureaucracy in Modern Society,* 3rd ed. (New York, 1987: McGraw-Hill Publishing Company).

Bronowski, Jacob, *Science and Human Values* (London, 1961: Hutchinson).

Brower, Bruce, "The Limits of Public Reason," *The Journal of Philosophy,* vol. 91 (1994), pp. 5–26.

Brown, Harold I., *Rationality* (London, 1988: Routledge).

Buchanan, James and Tullock, Gordon, *The Calculus of Consent* (Ann Arbor, 1965: University of Michigan Press).

Butler, Judith, "Contingent Foundations: Feminism and the Question of 'Postmodernism'" in

Judith Butler and Joan W. Scott, eds., *Feminists Theorize the Political* (New York & London, 1992: Routledge).

Campbell, Tom D., *Justice* (London, 1988: Macmillan).

Cherniak, Christopher, *Minimal Rationality* (Cambridge, 1986: The MIT Press).

Cocks, Joan, *The Oppositional Imagination* (London & New York, 1989: Routledge).

Cohen, Joshua, "The Economic Basis of Deliberative Democracy," *Social Philosophy and Policy,* vol. 6 (1989), pp. 25–50.

_____, "Moral Pluralism and Political Consensus" in David Copp and Jean Hampton, eds., *The Idea of Democracy* (Cambridge, 1993: Cambridge University Press).

Coleman, Jules L., "Market Contractarianism and the Unanimity Rule" in Ellen Frankel Paul, Fred D. Miller, Jr., and Jeffrey Paul, eds., *Ethics and Economics* (Oxford, 1985: Basil Blackwell).

Connolly, William, *The Terms of Political Discourse,* 2nd ed. (Oxford, 1983: Martin Robertson).

_____, *Politics and Ambiguity* (Madison, 1987: University of Wisconsin Press).

Crick, Bernard, *In Defense of Politics* (Harmondsworth, 1962: Penguin Books).

Crowder, George, "Pluralism and Liberalism," *Political Studies,* vol. 42 (1994), pp. 293–305.

D'Agostino, Fred, "Adjudication as an Epistemological Concept," *Synthese,* vol. 79 (1989), pp. 231–56.

_____, "The Aimless Rationality of Science," *International Studies in the Philosophy of Science,* vol. 4 (1990), pp. 33–50.

_____, "Teleology, Value, and the Foundations of Scientific Method," *Methodology and Science,* vol. 24 (1991), pp. 119–34.

_____, "A 'Demographic' Approach to the Rationality of Science: The Wave Model," *Methodology and Science,* vol. 26 (1992), pp. 244–56.

_____, "Transcendence and Conversation: Two Conceptions of Objectivity," *American Philosophical Quarterly,* vol. 30 (1993), pp. 87–108.

Davis, Michael, "The Moral Legislature: Contractualism without an Archimedean Point," *Ethics,* vol. 102 (1992), pp. 303–18.

Dryzek, John S., *Discursive Democracy: Politics, Policy, and Political Science* (Cambridge, 1990: Cambridge University Press).

Dworkin, Ronald, *Taking Rights Seriously* (London, 1977: Duckworth).

_____, *Law's Empire* (London, 1986: Fontana Press).

Elshtain, Jean Bethke, *Public Man, Private Woman* (Oxford, 1981: Martin Robertson).

Elster, Jon, *Sour Grapes* (Cambridge, 1983: Cambridge University Press).

_____, "The Market and the Forum: Three Varieties of Political Theory" in Jon Elster and Aanund Hylland, eds., *Foundations of Social Choice Theory* (Cambridge, 1986: Cambridge University Press).

Feyerabend, Paul, *Science in a Free Society* (London, 1978: Verso).

Fine, Arthur, "Unnatural Attitudes: Realist and Instrumentalist Attachments to Science," *Mind,* vol. 95 (1986), pp. 149–79.

Fishkin, James S., *The Dialogue of Justice: Toward a Self-Reflective Society* (New Haven & London, 1992: Yale Univesity Press).

Flax, Jane, "The End of Innocence" in Judith Butler and Joan W. Scott, eds., *Feminists Theorize the Political* (New York & London, 1992: Routledge).

Foucault, Michel, "Human Nature: Justice versus Power" (an interview with Noam Chomsky) in Fons Elders, ed., *Reflexive Water: The Basic Concerns of Mankind* (London, 1974: Souvenir Press).

_____, *The Foucault Reader,* ed. Paul Rabinow (Harmondsworth, 1991: Penguin Books).

Fraser, Nancy, *Unruly Practices* (Cambridge, 1989: Polity Press).

Friedman, Marilyn, "The Impracticality of Impartiality," *The Journal of Philosophy,* vol. 86 (1989), pp. 645–56.

Fuller, Steve, *Social Epistemology* (Bloomington & Indianapolis, 1988: Indiana University Press).

Gallie, W. B., "Essentially Contested Concepts," *Proceedings of the Aristotelian Society, 1955–6,* pp. 167–98.

Galston, William A., "Pluralism and Social Unity," *Ethics,* vol. 99 (1989), pp. 711–26.

————, *Liberal Purposes: Goods, Virtues, and Diversity in the Liberal State* (Cambridge, 1991: Cambridge University Press).

Gaus, Gerald F., *Value and Justification: The Foundations of Liberal Theory* (Cambridge, 1990: Cambridge University Press).

————, "Public Justification and Democratic Adjudication," *Constitutional Political Economy,* vol. 2 (1991), pp. 251–81.

————, *Justificatory Liberalism* (Oxford, forthcoming: Oxford University Press).

Gaut, Berys, "Moral Pluralism," *Philosophical Papers,* vol. 22 (1993), pp. 17–40.

Gauthier, David, *Morals by Agreement* (Oxford, 1986: Clarendon Press).

Gellner, Ernest, *Reason and Culture: The Historic Role of Rationality and Rationalism* (Oxford, 1992: Blackwell).

Gould, Stephen Jay, *The Panda's Thumb* (Harmondsworth, 1983: Penguin Books).

————, *An Urchin in the Storm* (London, 1988: Collins Harvill).

Graham, Gordon, "Liberalism: Metaphysical, Political, Historical," *Philosophical Papers,* vol. 22 (1993), pp. 97–122.

Gray, John N., "On the Contestability of Social and Political Concepts," *Political Theory,* vol. 5 (1977), pp. 331–48.

Grice, G. R., "Moral Theories and Received Opinion," *Aristotelian Society Supplementary Volume,* vol. 52 (1978), pp. 1–12.

Grosz, Elizabeth, "Philosophy" in Sneja Gunew, ed., *Feminist Knowledge: Critique and Construct* (London & New York, 1990: Routledge).

Gutmann, Amy and Thompson, Dennis, "Moral Conflict and Political Consensus," *Ethics,* vol. 101 (1990), pp. 64–88.

Habermas, Jürgen, *Legitimation Crisis,* trans. Thomas McCarthy (Boston, 1975: Beacon Press).

————, *Moral Consciousness and Communicative Action,* trans. Christian Lenhardt and Shierry Weber Nicolsen (Cambridge, 1990: Polity Press).

Hampshire, Stuart, *Morality and Conflict* (Oxford, 1983: Basil Blackwell).

————, *Innocence and Experience* (Harmondsworth, 1992: Penguin Books).

Haraway, Donna, "Situated Knowledges: The Science Question in Feminism and the Privilege of Partial Perspective," *Feminist Studies,* vol. 14 (1988), pp. 575–99.

Hare, R. M., *Moral Thinking* (Oxford, 1981: Clarendon Press).

Harsanyi, John C., "Cardinal Welfare, Individualistic Ethics, and Interpersonal Comparisons of Utility" in *Essays on Ethics, Social Behaviour and Scientific Explanation* (Dordrecht, 1977: Reidel).

Hart, H. L. A., *The Concept of Law* (Oxford, 1962: Clarendon Press).

Hayek, F. A. von, *Law, Legislation and Liberty,* 3 vols. (Chicago, 1973–79: University of Chicago Press).

Hearn, Frank, *Reason and Freedom in Sociological Thought* (Boston, 1983: Allen & Unwin).

Hekman, Susan J., *Gender and Knowledge* (Boston, 1990: New England Universities Press).

Held, David, *Models of Democracy* (Cambridge, 1987: Polity Press).

Herzog, Don, *Without Foundations* (Ithaca, 1985: Cornell University Press).

Hill, Thomas E., Jr., "Kantian Pluralism," *Ethics,* vol. 102 (1992), pp. 743–62.

Hollis, Martin, *The Cunning of Reason* (Cambridge, 1987: Cambridge University Press).

Hurley, S. L., *Natural Reasons: Personality and Polity* (New York & Oxford, 1989: Oxford University Press).

Ingram, David, "The Limits and Possibilities of Communicative Ethics for Democratic Theory," *Political Theory,* vol. 21 (1993), pp. 294–321.

Kekes, John, *A Justification of Rationality* (Albany, 1976: State University of New York Press).

———, *Moral Tradition and Individuality* (Princeton, 1989: Princeton University Press).

———, "The Incompatibility of Liberalism and Pluralism," *American Philosophical Quarterly,* vol. 29 (1992), pp. 141–51.

Kleinberg, Stanley S., *Politics and Philosophy: The Necessity and Limitations of Rational Argument* (Oxford, 1991: Blackwell).

Krieger, Leonard, "Authority" in P. P. Wiener, ed., *Dictionary of the History of Ideas,* vol. 1 (New York, 1973: Charles Scribner's Sons).

Kuhn, Thomas S., *The Structure of Scientific Revolutions,* 2nd ed. (Chicago, 1970: University of Chicago Press).

———, *The Essential Tension* (Chicago, 1977: University of Chicago Press).

Kukathas, Chandran and Pettit, Philip, *Rawls: A Theory of Justice and Its Critics* (Cambridge, 1990: Polity Press).

Kymlicka, Will, "Liberalism and Communitarianism," *Philosophy and Public Affairs,* vol. 18 (1988), pp. 181–204.

Lakatos, Imre, "Falsification and the Methodology of Scientific Research Programmes" in Imre Lakatos and Alan Musgrave, eds., *Criticism and the Growth of Knowledge* (Cambridge, 1970: Cambridge University Press).

Larmore, Charles, *Patterns of Moral Complexity* (Cambridge, 1987: Cambridge University Press).

Lawson, Hilary, "Stories about Stories" in Hilary Lawson and Lisa Appignanesi, eds., *Dismantling Truth* (London, 1989: Weidenfeld and Nicolson).

Lessnoff, Michael, *Social Contract* (London, 1986: Macmillan).

Lindsay, A. D., *The Essentials of Democracy,* 2nd ed. (London, 1935: Oxford University Press).

Lomasky, Loren E., *Persons, Rights, and the Moral Community* (New York, 1987: Oxford University Press).

Lukes, Steven, *Power: A Radical View* (London, 1974: Macmillan).

———, *Moral Conflict and Politics* (Oxford, 1991: Clarendon Press).

Lyotard, Jean-François, *The Postmodern Condition: A Report on Knowledge,* trans. Geoff Bennington and Brian Massumi (Manchester, 1984: Manchester University Press).

MacCallum, Gerald C., *Political Philosophy* (Englewood Cliffs, 1987: Prentice-Hall).

Macedo, Stephen, "The Politics of Justification," *Political Theory,* vol. 18 (1990), pp. 280–304.

———, *Liberal Virtues: Citizenship, Virtue, and Community in Liberal Constitutionalism* (Oxford, 1991: Clarendon Press).

MacIntyre, Alasdair, *After Virtue: A Study in Moral Theory,* 2nd ed. (Notre Dame, 1984: University of Notre Dame Press).

———, *Three Rival Versions of Moral Enquiry: Encyclopaedia, Genealogy, and Tradition* (Notre Dame, 1990: University of Notre Dame Press).

Manin, Bernard, "On Legitimacy and Political Deliberation," *Political Theory,* vol. 15 (1987), pp. 338–68.

March, James G., "Bounded Rationality, Ambiguity, and the Engineering of Choice" in Jon Elster, ed., *Rational Choice* (Oxford, 1986: Basil Blackwell).

Mason, Andrew, "On Explaining Political Disagreement: The Notion of an Essentially Contested Concept," *Inquiry,* vol. 33 (1982), pp. 81–98.

Mayo, H. B., *An Introduction to Democratic Theory* (New York, 1960: Oxford University Press).

McLain, Iain, *Public Choice: An Introduction* (Oxford, 1987: Basil Blackwell).

McNaughton, David, *Moral Vision* (Oxford, 1987: Basil Blackwell).

McNay, Lois, *Foucault and Feminism: Power, Gender and the Self* (Cambridge, 1992: Polity Press).

Mendus, Susan, *Toleration and the Limits of Liberalism* (London, 1989: Macmillan).

Merton, Robert, "Science and Democratic Social Structure" in *Social Theory and Social Structure,* rev. ed. (New York, 1957: The Free Press).

Miller, David, "Anarchism" in David Miller, ed., *The Blackwell Encyclopaedia of Political Thought* (Oxford, 1987: Basil Blackwell).

_____, "Deliberative Democracy and Social Choice," *Political Studies,* special issue 1992, pp. 54–67.

Mouffe, Chantal, *The Return of the Political* (London & New York, 1993: Verso).

Mueller, Dennis C., *Public Choice* (Cambridge, 1979: Cambridge University Press).

_____, *Public Choice II: A Revised Edition of Public Choice* (Cambridge, 1989: Cambridge University Press).

Nagel, Thomas, *Mortal Questions* (Cambridge, 1979: Cambridge University Press).

_____, *The View from Nowhere* (New York, 1986: Oxford University Press).

_____, "Moral Conflict and Political Legitimacy," *Philosophy and Public Affairs,* vol. 16 (1987), pp. 215–40.

_____, *Equality and Partiality* (New York & Oxford, 1991: Oxford University Press).

Nelson, William N., *On Justifying Democracy* (London, 1980: Routledge and Kegan Paul).

Newell, R. H., *Objectivity, Empiricism and Truth* (London & New York, 1986: Routledge and Kegan Paul).

Nozick, Robert, *Anarchy, State, and Utopia* (Oxford, 1974: Basil Blackwell).

_____, *Philosophical Explanations* (Oxford, 1981: Clarendon Press).

Oakeshott, Michael, *Rationalism in Politics and Other Essays* (London, 1962: Methuen).

Okin, Susan Moller, *Justice, Gender and the Family* (New York, 1989: Basic Books).

O'Neill, Onora, "Ethical Reasoning and Ideological Pluralism," *Ethics,* vol. 98 (1988), pp. 705–22.

_____, *Constructions of Reason: Explorations of Kant's Practical Philosophy* (Cambridge, 1989: Cambridge University Press).

Pettit, Philip, "Habermas on Truth and Justice" in G. H. R. Parkinson, ed., *Marx and Marxisms* (Cambridge, 1982: Cambridge University Press).

_____, *The Common Mind: An Essay on Psychology, Society, and Politics* (New York & Oxford, 1993: Oxford University Press)

Phillips, Anne, *Engendering Democracy* (Cambridge, 1991: Polity Press).

Platts, Mark, *Ways of Meaning* (London, 1982: Routledge and Kegan Paul).

Pogge, Thomas, *Realizing Rawls* (Ithaca & London, 1989: Cornell University Press).

Polanyi, Michael, *The Logic of Liberty* (Chicago, 1951: University of Chicago Press).

_____, "The Republic of Science" in Edward Shils, ed., *Criteria for Scientific Development* (Cambridge, 1962: The MIT Press).

Popper, Karl, *The Open Society and Its Enemies,* 3rd ed. (London, 1957: Routledge and Kegan Paul).

_____, "Public Opinion and Liberal Principles" in *Conjectures and Refutations* (London, 1963: Routledge and Kegan Paul).

Putnam, Hilary, *Reason, Truth and History* (Cambridge, 1981: Cambridge University Press).

Rawls, John, *A Theory of Justice* (Oxford, 1973: Oxford University Press).

_____, "Kantian Constructivism in Moral Theory," *The Journal of Philosophy*, vol. 77 (1980), pp. 515–72.

_____, "Justice as Fairness: Political not Metaphysical," *Philosophy and Public Affairs*, vol. 14 (1985), pp. 223–51.

_____, "The Idea of an Overlapping Consensus," *Oxford Journal of Legal Studies*, vol. 7 (1987), pp. 1–25.

_____, "The Domain of the Political and Overlapping Consensus," *New York University Law Review*, vol. 64 (1989), pp. 233–55.

_____, *Political Liberalism* (New York, 1993: Columbia University Press).

Raz, Joseph, *The Morality of Freedom* (Oxford, 1986: Clarendon Press).

_____, "Facing Diversity: The Case of Epistemic Abstinence," *Philosophy and Public Affairs*, vol. 19 (1990), pp. 3–46.

Reiman, Jeffrey, *Justice and Modern Moral Philosophy* (New Haven & London, 1990: Yale University Press).

Rescher, Nicholas, *Pluralism: Against the Demand for Consensus* (Oxford, 1993: Clarendon Press).

Riker, William H., *Liberalism Against Populism: A Confrontation between the Theory of Democracy and the Theory of Social Choice* (Prospect Heights, Ill., 1982: Waveland Press).

Rorty, Richard, "From Epistemology to Hermeneutics," *Acta Philosophica Fennica*, vol. 30 (1978), pp. 11–30.

_____, *Philosophy and the Mirror of Nature* (Princeton, 1979: Princeton University Press).

_____, *Contingency, Irony, and Solidarity* (Cambridge, 1989: Cambridge University Press).

_____, *Objectivity, Relativism, and Truth* (Cambridge, 1991: Cambridge University Press).

Said, Edward, *The World, the Text, and the Critic* (London & Boston, 1984: Faber and Faber).

Sandel, Michael J., *Liberalism and the Limits of Justice* (Cambridge, 1982: Cambridge University Press).

Scanlon, T. M., "Contractualism and Utilitarianism" in Amartya Sen and Bernard Williams, eds., *Utilitarianism and Beyond* (Cambridge, 1982: Cambridge University Press).

Scruton, Roger, *The Meaning of Conservatism* (Harmondsworth, 1980: Penguin Books).

Simon, Herbert A., "From Substantive to Procedural Rationality" in Frank Hahn and Martin Hollis, eds., *Philosophy and Economic Theory* (Oxford, 1979: Oxford University Press).

_____, *Reason in Human Affairs* (Oxford, 1983: Basil Blackwell).

Slote, Michael, *Beyond Optimizing: A Study of Rational Choice* (Cambridge, 1989: Harvard University Press).

Smith, Michael, "The Humean Theory of Motivation," *Mind*, vol. 96 (1987), pp. 36–61.

Steiner, Hillel, *An Essay on Rights* (Oxford, 1994: Blackwell).

Taylor, Charles, *Sources of the Self: The Making of the Modern Identity* (Cambridge, 1989: Cambridge University Press).

Toulmin, Stephen, *Cosmopolis: The Hidden Agenda of Modernity* (Chicago, 1990: University of Chicago Press).

Trigg, Roger, *Reason and Commitment* (Cambridge, 1973: Cambridge University Press).

Vattimo, Gianni, *The Transparent Society*, trans. David Webb (Cambridge, 1992: Polity Press).

Waldron, Jeremy, "Theoretical Foundations of Liberalism," *The Philosophical Quarterly*, vol. 37 (1987), pp. 127–50.

Walzer, Michael, *Spheres of Justice: A Defence of Pluralism and Equality* (Oxford, 1983: Basil Blackwell).

_____, *Interpretation and Social Criticism* (Cambridge, 1987: Harvard University Press).

_____, "The Virtue of Incompletion," *Theory and Society,* vol. 19 (1990), pp. 225–29.

Wellmer, Albrecht, "Reason, Utopia, and the *Dialectics of Enlightenment*" in Richard J. Bernstein, ed., *Habermas and Modernity* (Cambridge, 1985: Polity Press).

White, Stephen K., *The Recent Work of Jürgen Habermas: Reason, Justice and Modernity* (Cambridge, 1988: Cambridge University Press).

_____, *Political Theory and Postmodernism* (Cambridge, 1991: Cambridge University Press).

Williams, Bernard, "Conflicts of Values" in Alan Ryan, ed., *The Idea of Freedom* (Oxford, 1979: Oxford University Press).

_____, *Ethics and the Limits of Philosophy* (London, 1985: Fontana Press/Collins).

Wolf, Susan, "Two Levels of Pluralism," *Ethics,* vol. 92 (1992), pp. 785–98.

Wong, David B., "Coping with Moral Conflict and Ambiguity," *Ethics,* vol. 102 (1992), pp. 763–84.

Yeatman, Anna, *Postmodern Revisionings of the Political* (New York & London, 1994: Routledge).

Young, Iris Marion, "Impartiality and the Civic Public" in Seyla Benhabib and Drucilla Cornell, eds., *Feminism as Critique* (Cambridge, 1987: Polity Press).

_____, *Justice and the Politics of Difference* (Princeton, 1990: Princeton University Press).

Ziman, John, *Reliable Knowledge* (Cambridge, 1978: Cambridge University Press).

Zolo, Danilo, *Democracy and Complexity,* trans. David McKie (University Park, 1992: The Pennsylvania State University Press).

Index